Portraits
of Jewish Learning

PORTRAITS OF JEWISH LEARNING

Viewing Contemporary Jewish Education Close-In

Edited by
DIANE TICKTON SCHUSTER

Foreword by David Bryfman

WIPF & STOCK · Eugene, Oregon

PORTRAITS OF JEWISH LEARNING
Viewing Contemporary Jewish Education Close-In

Wipf & Stock
An Imprint of Wipf and Stock Publishers
199 W. 8th Ave., Suite 3
Eugene, OR 97401

www.wipfandstock.com

PAPERBACK ISBN: 978-1-5326-5907-2
HARDCOVER ISBN: 978-1-5326-5908-9
EBOOK ISBN: 978-1-5326-5909-6

Manufactured in the U.S.A.   01/23/19

For Jack H. Schuster:
In celebration of all we have learned and created together.

For our grandsons Gershom, Rachmael, and Toby:
In joyous anticipation of all the learning that is yet to come.

A century ago a group of educators led an effort to transform American Jewish education to enable it to operate successfully in the 20th century. Today, with American Jews living under very different conditions, a similar effort is needed to reinvent Jewish education for the 21st century. Changes and new initiatives already taking place on the educational landscape point the way toward a set of paradigm shifts that will make Jewish education more learner-centered, relationship-infused, and life-relevant.

JONATHAN WOOCHER
REINVENTING JEWISH EDUCATION FOR THE 21ST CENTURY

CONTENTS

FOREWORD

David Bryfman

IN RECENT MONTHS I have gravitated towards spin classes as a way of both keeping fit and mindfulness practice. There are two instructors in particular to whom I and many others are devoted. Jodie and Joe[1] exemplify the very best in spin class instructors. As they dim the lights and begin to blast their playlists, these teachers create a welcoming environment for their students. Interspersed with brief snippets from their personal lives, they give instructions, teach by demonstration, and offer just enough personal motivation to inspire and challenge the class of cyclists for the ensuing hour. Despite my commitment to these classes, it is apparent to me that these instructors are not for everyone, and what's more, although many people proclaim to want to exercise, spinning just isn't what some people want to learn.

Portraits of Jewish Learning, just like my spin class, is a reminder of the inexact science—or is it art?—that is education. Educators understand that quality learning experiences involve a mix of Joseph Schwab's commonplaces: the teacher, the learner, the curriculum, and the milieu.[2] But as readers of this volume will be reminded, there exists no formula, recipe, or even a guidebook that can categorically state what makes for the ideal educational experience.

Complicating matters further is that we are all an amalgam of our educational histories, and it is often precisely because of our own biographies that understanding education is so difficult. At some point, we have all been both learners and teachers, with the likely result that we have

1. The educators I reference from my own life in this foreword have *not* had their names altered. I name them here so they may get some of the recognition they truly deserve.

2. Schwab, Joseph. "The Practical 3: Translation into Curriculum." *School Review* 83 (1973) 501–22.

developed personal theories of what constitutes good and bad education. However, given the visceral reactions that our memories elicit, we are not in a position to objectively deconstruct how the teaching and learning actually occurred.

Portraits of Jewish Learning goes beyond the typologies and characteristics that typically are offered to advance our understanding of good education. Readers will find themselves drawn rapidly into familiar and unfamiliar educational settings, introduced to educators to whom they can often relate, and intrigued by a deep sense of connection to what is unfolding in each chapter. The book provides captivating descriptions of nine different and wonderfully engaging Jewish learning environments. Each author writes with refreshing honesty and integrity. Each chapter depicts in vivid detail that which is frequently left unexplained: the beauty and majesty of the learning process. For someone whose current day-to-day work involves considerable time theorizing and intellectualizing about education, *Portraits of Jewish Learning* is a welcome reminder of why I became a Jewish educator.

As I read this volume, I could not help but be reminded of some of the times in my life when I have most enjoyed learning. Studying Jewish history with Danny in a fourth grade classroom, conducting experiments with Shirley in a science lab, hiking with Jonnie at Habonim summer camp, walking with Steve around the streets of Jerusalem, sitting in a coffee shop with Barry, studying with Niobe at university . . . and so many more memories came back to me, evoked by these accounts of Jewish learning. Each experience was so distinct and so powerful. I hope and anticipate that readers of this book will also be drawn to reflect on the learning they have experienced in their own lives.

Readers will confront the reality that Jewish education is the imprecise, if not messy, compilation of the sum of its parts. For Jewish educators, rabbis, cantors, funders, parents, and any others who care about Jewish education, this anthology will serve as a compendium of case studies to be analyzed and dissected for many years to come.

There was a moment while reading this volume that I became self-conscious, as I wondered what an onlooker might have thought as they saw me smiling. Perhaps they would think I was reading a fantasy novel or a good piece of fiction. It might have been difficult to explain to this onlooker that what I was reading was neither fiction nor fantasy; it was a way into encountering the reality of what transpires in good Jewish educational settings. In a field that is often maligned, it was a joy to be taken into these classrooms and behind the scenes, and I could not help but smile as I read. I was left imagining a better world in which the Jewish educational experience and Jewish educators are central in the lives of thousands of learners. After reading this book, spin classes are never quite the same. Even while absorbed in the class I can't help but deconstruct the core components that at first glance appear to make the learning just happen. As you embark on the journey of reading this book, may you be inspired, as I was, to reflect on the learning experiences that have brought you to where you are today.

ACKNOWLEDGMENTS

Rabbi Chanina taught: "I have learned much from my teachers. I have learned more from my colleagues than my teachers. But I have learned more from my students than from all of them." (Babylonian Talmud, Taanit 7a)

WITH THE COMPLETION OF *Portraits of Jewish Learning* (PoJL), I am once again affirmed in my long-held view that exciting intellectual discourse thrives when one has the good fortune to find the teachers, colleagues, and students who "live inside the same questions" as we do. Indeed, when Jon Levisohn, director of the Jack, Joseph and Morton Mandel Center for Studies in Jewish Education at Brandeis University, shared some of his questions about the experiences of Jewish learners with me in 2016, I realized that a new and meaningful conversation with a much-admired colleague was about to unfold.

Jon told me that he had recently commissioned two gifted research-ers to develop narrative portraits of the students they had observed while collecting data for their doctoral dissertations about Jewish education. Now, Jon was wondering whether it might be possible to recruit others in the field to do similar work. He noted that, while many of our colleagues had been reporting on the practices of Jewish *educators*, few had nar-ratively described the experiences of *students*. I responded that I not only thought that would it would be beneficial to search out those who could write such portraits, but that I also believed the time was ripe to bring these stories of Jewish learning beyond the pages of academic journals— to share emerging research with a more general audience. The responses to my earlier work on adult Jewish learning had showed me that there are many people in the Jewish community and beyond who "live inside" questions about Jewish education, both within and outside the walls of the academy.

As I discovered through gathering the case examples presented in my book *Jewish Lives, Jewish Learning*: When we engage with stories about learners—their educational aspirations and challenges, the teachers and content that inspire them, the settings that afford opportunities for connection and community—we find ourselves reflecting about the core purposes of Jewish education, and about our own and others' goals and visions for what this learning can be. In addition, when we actively get inside stories about "Jewish learners learning," we develop frameworks for thinking critically about the learning process and the short- and long-term impacts of Jewish education on Jewish personal and communal life overall. Perhaps, I speculated, new stories about learners in new, twenty-first-century settings could prompt compelling conversation about both our learners and their teachers and, to use Jonathan Woocher's terminology, about how contemporary Jewish education should be reinventing itself.

At Jon Levisohn's invitation, I announced the availability of modest stipends (through a block grant the Mandel Center had received from CASJE, the Consortium for Applied Studies in Jewish Education) for researchers and practitioners to become part of a project dedicated to both gathering data about Jewish learning *and* creating portraits of that learning, written for a broad readership. To my delight, within two weeks of my announcement, I received more than thirty proposals from around the world. Although I could select only a third of these for an initial cohort, the range and scope of the applications persuaded me that the response to this project might be signaling a new era of Jewish educational research in which the rich diversity of Jewish learners and learning experiences could be chronicled and explored. In that sense, the work of the PoJL project is only beginning, and I hope that, following the publication of this collection, other portraitists will soon enrich the field with additional contributions.

The production of this volume could not have been achieved without the help of a nurturing community of colleagues. In addition to gratefully acknowledging Jon Levisohn's outstanding guidance and support, my thanks go to:

Susanne Shavelson, the Mandel Center's wise and generous Associate Director, whose patience and dedication to excellence enabled me to efficiently manage a team of authors and to produce a cohesive collection of their work.

The Mandel Center's staff, including Elizabeth DiNolfo, Pamela Endo, Sarah Flatley, and Amanda Votta, who graciously provided administrative and editorial assistance.

Carol Ingall, who offered insightful consultation about how portraiture can help us to understand and strengthen the field of Jewish education. Carol's careful feedback on earlier drafts, combined with her rigorous commitment to artful scholarship, contributed significantly to the refinement of each chapter.

David Bryfman and Sharon Feiman-Nemser, who stepped up with opening and closing statements, each adding to the longer view of what we mean by Jewish learning and of what can be learned from our learners.

The Consortium for Applied Studies in Jewish Education (CASJE), a forward-facing organization that not only strengthens the activity of the Mandel Center but strives to "improve the quality of knowledge used to guide Jewish education."

Judy Irwin and Laura Zuckerman, whose critical feedback on the book proposal paved the way to immediate interest from the first publishers I approached, and Sheryl Kujawa-Holbrook, Vice President for Academic Affairs at the Claremont School of Theology, who recommended that I reach out to Wipf and Stock, a well-recognized publisher in religious education but less widely known in the Jewish community.

Matthew Wimer, Assistant Managing Editor at Wipf and Stock, who promptly said that, yes, this was the kind of work he and his colleagues were looking for, and who then provided clear and encouraging support throughout the publication process. Particular thanks to Stephanie Hough whose meticulous editorial oversight enhanced the final product. I am honored to have this volume join the Wipf and Stock list and look forward to reaching readers across religious traditions.

Los Angeles County Museum of Art docent Rosalyn Firemark, who offered me a private tutorial about artist David Hockney's "20-hour exposure" approach. Her insights helped clarify how the stories in *Portraits of Jewish Learning* fit into a larger aesthetic of how we look at and portray human experience.

I am blessed with an extraordinary group of colleagues and friends who have nourished and sustained me throughout this endeavor. My heartfelt gratitude goes to my "partners in spirit": Leslie Adams, Lauren Applebaum, Isa Aron, Rose Ash, Elizabeth Brenenstal, Karen Dalton,

Madelyn Gordon, Lisa Grant, Judy Irwin, Patricia Karlin-Neumann, Marshall Jung, Deborah Klein, Judy Rose, Phyllis Sonnenschein, Jill Rosenberg, Ethel Steinberger, Miriam Heller Stern, Sara Truitt, Laura Zuckerman, and the Battis and Kudlats families. Each has contributed to my equanimity and enthusiasm as I have brought this project to fruition. I am also particularly mindful of the enduring legacy in my work of my colleagues Andrew J. Berner, z"l, and Rami Wernik, z"l, and, always, my parents Reva and Sidney Tickton, z"l. Unending appreciation goes as well to my husband, Jack H. Schuster, who for more than fifty years of marriage has championed my growth and welcomed the "mind sharpening" of our dialogue.

Finally, it is to the full cohort of PoJL Fellows—chapter writers Allison, Jon, Jordi, Matt, Nachama, Nicki, Orit, Rachel, Rafi, Stefani, and Ziva, as well as Nettie Aharon, Mijal Bitton, and Matt Williams—that I am the most grateful. Working closely with these writers as they crafted their portraits has taught me so much about the value of the co-creation of knowledge. There is a true joy in getting to challenge smart and thoughtful people who are ready to drill down to the through line and then to help them drill down even further to say things in the clearest, most meaningful way. My thanks go to each of you, not only for your excitement about this collective endeavor, but for embracing me as we lived inside our shared questions together.

List of Contributors

Rabbi Jordana Schuster Battis is Associate Rabbi at Temple Shir Tikva, Wayland, MA.

David Bryfman is Chief Innovation Officer at The Jewish Education Project, New York, NY.

Stefani E. Carlson is Director of Congregational Learning at Congregation Emanu El, Houston, TX.

Rafael M. Cashman is Head of School at Netivot HaTorah Day School, Toronto, Canada.

Allison Cook is Director of the Pedagogy of Partnership, as well as founding Coordinator of the Instructional Leadership for Congregational Education Program at Hebrew College, Newton, MA.

Sharon Feiman-Nemser is Professor and Jack, Joseph and Morton Mandel Chair in Jewish Education at Brandeis University, Waltham, MA.

Rabbi Nicole M. Greninger is Director of Education at Temple Isaiah, Lafayette, CA.

Rachel C. Happel is Director of K-12 Learning at Temple Beth Shalom, Needham, MA.

Ziva R. Hassenfeld is Post-Doctoral Fellow at the Jack, Joseph and Morton Mandel Center for Studies in Jewish Education, Brandeis University, Waltham, MA, and Post-Doctoral Fellow at DevTech Research Group, Tufts University, Medford, MA.

Orit Kent is Director of the Pedagogy of Partnership, as well as Senior Researcher at Helix Learning Partners, Boston, MA.

Jon A. Levisohn is Associate Professor and Jack, Joseph and Morton Mandel Chair in Jewish Educational Thought at Brandeis University, Waltham, MA.

Nachama Skolnik Moskowitz is Director of Curriculum Resources and Senior Director at the Jewish Education Center, Cleveland, OH.

Matt Reingold is a member of the Jewish Studies faculty at TanenbaumCHAT, Toronto, Canada.

Diane Tickton Schuster is Director of the Portraits of Jewish Learning project at the Jack, Joseph and Morton Mandel Center for Studies in Jewish Education at Brandeis University, Waltham, MA.

INTRODUCTION

Diane Tickton Schuster

ON A RECENT SUNDAY afternoon, I ventured to the Los Angeles County Museum of Art to attend a tour of an exhibit of David Hockney's work, *82 Portraits and 1 Still-Life*.[1] A few minutes into the docent's introduction, I had a startling realization: Hockney's decision to capture the likenesses of his friends, helpers, and colleagues—people in his inner circle whom he painted while they each sat for three days, in their own natural poses, wearing their own self-selected clothing—was strikingly parallel to the work in which I had been engaged as director of Portraits of Jewish Learning (PoJL), a project sponsored by the Jack, Joseph, and Morton Mandel Center for Studies in Jewish Education at Brandeis University. For months I had been working with a dozen researchers and practitioners who were grappling with fundamental questions in Jewish education, questions like "What *is* Jewish learning?" and "What does Jewish learning look like?" and "What can we learn from the experience of Jewish learners today?" Each of these colleagues had been developing a portrait of learners learning over an extended period of time. Rather than producing snapshot images of Jewish education (as might be shown, say, through students' test scores, teachers' curricular plans, or innovative classroom architecture), the PoJL authors were engaged in a process of getting inside Jewish learning as it occurs over time. Through their focused inquiries, they were discerning the nuances and subtle dynamics of what transpires in Jewish education, benefitting from extended contact with their subjects—what David Hockney characterized as "20-hour exposure" rather than brief-moment photos. There was another similarity between the PoJL process and the Hockney exhibit that occurred to

---

1. Shown online at: http://www.davidhockney.co/index.php/works/paintings/82-portraits

me. Like Hockney, the PoJL authors avoided creating idealized images of elegantly adorned personages, the stuff of larger-than-life Renaissance-era portraits. Instead, they were zeroing in on the unfolding process of Jewish learning as it really happens, taking notice of the complex (and sometimes messy) details of how students think, how teachers work to engage learners, how the content may or may not be understood, and how the setting impacts the learning experience.

At the exhibit, as I looked across the 82 portraits that the artist had created—all similar (each of his subjects sat in the same chair) and each distinctive due to the individuality that Hockney so brilliantly portrayed—I understood why this celebrated collection has sparked so much enthusiastic conversation in the art world. Taken together, the portraits invite us as viewers to look at a collective in a new way. Seeing the pictures side by side, we begin by taking in the individual images; then, moving around the gallery display, looking across the unified collection of portraits, we are stimulated to think more holistically, ultimately considering the range of personalities, relationships, attitudes, and choices that characterize the particular community under our gaze.

Portraits of Jewish Learning in Context

Just as Hockney's collection of portraits showcases images of a range of individuals who were part of the artist's larger story, the nine portraits in this book feature close-in images of a diverse group of people—both students and teachers—who are part of a larger context and whose experiences should be considered in relation to their lives in today's world. For present purposes, the context for the portraits is the changing landscape of North American Jewish education in the early twenty-first century, a context described in a detailed commentary by visionary educator Jonathan Woocher z"l[2] in 2012. Woocher wrote that over the past 100 years, as American Jews have become more and more successfully assimilated into the larger society, the paradigm for meeting their educational needs has shifted. Whereas Jewish communal leaders in the early-to-mid-twentieth century were concerned about how to "keep Jews Jewish," many of today's Jews are living under societal and cultural conditions that prompt them to search for relevance and purpose in their Jewish lives. They seek a Judaism they consider meaningful, one that is reinforced by

2. Woocher, "Reinventing Jewish Education," 182–226.

high-quality interpersonal experiences and opportunities for developing self-efficacy.[3] In Woocher's view, this shift requires the contemporary Jewish community to ask: *"How can we help Jews find in their Jewishness resources that will help them live more meaningful, purposeful, and fulfilling human lives?"*[4] The subtext of this new question, Woocher asserted, is not how to help people *stay* Jewish, but how to *be* Jewish. And the answer, he argued, rests in how Jewish education responds—how it "reinvents" itself to offer learning experiences that intentionally help to "make our Jewishness something of value, something that Jews will not only acknowledge (which the vast majority do), but actively embrace as one of their many salient identities, perhaps even as the core 'operating system' for their lives."[5]

Emblematic of the kind of reinvention Woocher called for are programs that are "learner-centered" rather than "provider-centered." Educational initiatives that begin with the learner are built on three core ideas:

1. Learners (and their families) should have an active role in shaping their own learning.

2. Learning should be relevant to learners' lives, reflecting their life circumstances, the society we live in, and responding to their authentic needs, questions, and aspirations.

3. Learning should be designed to be readily accessible to learners and to encourage learners to move along personal trajectories of growth.[6]

These framing principles put the *experience of learning* at the center of educational endeavors that strive to impact more learners in more lasting and more meaningful ways. The values that underlie these principles align philosophically with the values of the PoJL project. Just as Woocher advocated for Jewish educational environments that are learner-centered, the PoJL authors prize inquiry that zeroes in on learners and learning. The objective of their portraits is not to try to remake learning environments directly or to prescribe best practices. Instead, by taking seriously

---

3. Woocher defines this as "a sense that we are competent and able to accomplish the purposes that matter to us."

4. Woocher, "Reinventing Jewish Education," 189.

5. Woocher, "Reinventing Jewish Education," 190.

6. Woocher, "Reinventing Jewish Education," 195.

the intellectual task of describing and portraying the learning experience, their work is meant to complement Woocher's bold call to the Jewish community to reimagine the priorities of Jewish education today.

Nine Portraits of Jewish Learning

In the pages that follow are nine portraits that challenge us to think anew about what we mean by Jewish learning. Rather than presented as refined models or as exemplars of excellence, these accounts depict Jewish education in process—including several programs and classrooms that have a particularly experimental nature. Overall, they show interactions among learners, teachers, curricular materials, and settings (commonly referred to as "the commonplaces" of education[7]) that may well disrupt old assumptions about what Jewish learning looks like. As such, they cause us to stop and look, to suspend expectations, and to bring fresh eyes as we *watch learning* unfold.

The authors bring both the "art and science" of portraiture[8] to their work; they offer colorful, multi-dimensional descriptions while adhering to the rigors of social science research. As they note, they are not neutral observers detached from the people or programs under their gaze; they are part of the stories they describe and they care deeply about showing how learning is occurring—sometimes in unexpected ways.

At the same time, the authors bring to their work an analytic mindset, offering the reader theoretical constructs and empirical data that support their inquiries. From these more academic frameworks, they show us how the field of Jewish education is enriched by scholarship from various disciplines, including human development, cognitive psychology, gender studies, literary interpretation, language acquisition, mentoring, and group behavior. Rather than being linked by a single intellectual tradition, the authors come at the question of "What is Jewish learning?" from multiple perspectives grounded in diverse fields.

In addition to their analyses, at the end of their chapters each author steps back and responds to a question: "What have I learned about Jewish learning as a result of this research?" Their responses to this question provides a foundation for a larger conversation about Jewish learning to be held among lay leaders, clergy, policymakers, philanthropists,

---

7. Schwab, "The Practical 3," 508–12.

8. Lawrence-Lightfoot, "Reflections on Portraiture," 3–15.

and parents, as well as educators and those aspiring to work in Jewish education.

The book proceeds along a basic developmental trajectory. It begins with portraits of young school-age children and then moves on to accounts of students in middle school, high school, and college. As we progress through these sequential phases, we encounter teachers in varying roles who are engaging students with a wide array of curricular content. The learning occurs variously in day schools, synagogues, and college classrooms—environments across the religious spectrum[9] that welcomed this research about the learning going on within their walls.[10]

In chapter one, Ziva Hassenfeld describes the text-learning experiences of seven-year-old students in a Jewish day school. She showcases how a gifted teacher engages these very young learners in the process of studying texts and introduces them to essential interpretive skills: noticing symbolism, recognizing dramatic irony, identifying seemingly superfluous words and repeated words, and naming ambiguities. Through a series of vignettes Hassenfeld explains how, over time, these children become fully engaged as interpreters of text and actively probe issues that are meaningful to them.

In chapter two, Jordana Schuster Battis and Rachel Happel present a portrait of a synagogue's daily afterschool program in which primary-grade students participate in a family-like educational environment. They document the experiences of two children who, through daily attendance, learn Hebrew, practice ritual, observe holiday customs, and internalize Jewish values. Interviews with teachers and parents illuminate how a shift in the amount of time learners spend in a holistic Jewish education setting can potentially shape Jewish identity, family life, and connection to community.

In the first of three chapters about middle school learners, Nachama Skolnik Moskowitz (chapter three) draws on extensive video data as the basis for her portrait of sixth-graders who engage in a novel discovery

9. For more about this spectrum, see: https://www.myjewishlearning.com/article/the-jewish-denominations/

10. This is not to imply that other Jewish education settings are averse to similar inquiry. Indeed, as discussed elsewhere in this volume, the time is ripe for the development of portraits of the Jewish learning experiences of other groups: preschoolers, campers, students with learning challenges, adults, participants in experiential learning programs, Jews by choice, immigrants, online learners, etc. Hopefully the present collection will motivate the crafting of additional portraits to enrich this burgeoning subfield of Jewish education research.

learning program in a synagogue school. How these tweens respond to the "mystery room" elements of the program suggests the many ways that such activities can tap into students' Jewish learning resources and challenge them to think about big ideas. This portrait highlights the ways that young adolescents begin to apply logic and use stored information as they learn about Jewish values.

In chapter four, Orit Kent and Allison Cook build on their extensive experience with helping students of all ages to engage in havruta learning (in which two students sit together as partners to study a sacred text, independent from the direct mediation of a teacher). They describe how two seventh-grade boys learn to develop a meaningful partnership with one another and with the texts they are studying. As the boys systematically acquire and apply partnership skills, they focus on the cause of particular events in a textual narrative and develop a "wondering stance" for exploring alternative interpretations. Over time they become increasingly able to co-construct knowledge and move toward more sophisticated theological discussions that are grounded in the textual details. Interviews with the students reveal how they perceive their learning.

Then Nicole Greninger (chapter five) describes a revamped Hebrew education program in a Reform synagogue in which students become motivated to learn Hebrew. Drawing on interviews with two b'nai mitzvah tutors, she shows how the program's innovations have helped to support middle schoolers' sense of mastery and purpose in their b'nai mitzvah preparations. Greninger's findings exemplify recent theory about student motivation and the impact of language on group identity.

In chapters six through eight, we encounter the experiences of high school learners. First, Rafael Cashman (chapter six) offers a portrait of young, modern Orthodox high school girls learning Torah texts. He describes how, despite their strong sense of individual autonomy and attachment to modern values and culture, the students adopt and accept traditional religious authorities, finding a way to "own" the tradition as their own—a process called "personalizing." Cashman shows how texts become the basis for decisions that are both autonomous (internally determined) and heteronomous (subject to external authority). As the girls move fluidly back and forth between self-determination about moral issues and acceptance of *halakhic* positions, they develop ways simultaneously to express their own opinions and to use textual narratives to make sense of moral dilemmas.

Then, Stefani Carlson (chapter seven) recounts the experiences of two male high school students in a synagogue program for *madrichim* (classroom aides). The portrait shows how the boys' learning is enriched by their engagement in a "Relational Learning Community," a systematic learning experience in which there is an intentional commitment to "the construction and nurturing of relationships between and among the participants, facilitators, texts/content, and context." The RLC provides a setting for these students to engage as peers with faculty mentors and to reflect on their development as novice teachers. Carlson shows how the *madrichim* program supports the teens' developmental needs as they transition toward adult modes of thinking and look ahead to their futures as Jewish adults.

In chapter eight, Matt Reingold's portrait of Jewish day school seniors learning counter-narratives about the State of Israel's complex history provides insight into the challenges of teaching disruptive ideas to adolescent learners. Drawing on student journals, written assignments, and interviews collected during the year he taught about the Arab-Israeli conflict and events involving Israeli military brutality, and Reingold explores how North American Jewish teens come to terms with issues of moral complexity and negotiate mixed emotions about their attachment to Israel.

Finally, in chapter nine Jon Levisohn describes the learning experiences of two undergraduate women in a course called "Studying Sacred Texts." He explores "what happens when Jewish college students encounter ideas that disrupt their previously held notions about Judaism and Jewish texts." In addition to reviewing the students' oral and written comments during the course, Levisohn reports on these young adults' reflections at two later times: two years after the class and ten years after college. He argues that for one student the encounter with the texts ultimately led her to look at texts and her Jewish identity with critical awareness and a greater sense of personal ownership; for the other woman, the learning experience ultimately helped her to overcome her distrust of textual criticism and acquire greater equanimity in her stance toward the study of biblical texts.

The volume concludes with a commentary about the nine portraits by Sharon Feiman-Nemser (chapter ten). Drawing on her decades of leadership in teacher education in both secular and Jewish university settings, Feiman-Nemser offers a contemporary framework for understanding the concept of learning. Looking across the portraits, she discusses what these accounts have to say about "learning as a process" and "learning as an outcome." Then, she explores the question of what's Jewish about the learning depicted by the PoJL authors and highlights "the indispensable role educators play in enabling ambitious learning." Finally, she asserts that learning *about* Jewish learning can help communal leaders, researchers, practitioners, and policy-makers to open up a broad and inclusive conversation about how to support the development of meaningful Jewish education across the community.

Bibliography

Lawrence-Lightfoot, Sara. "Reflections on Portraiture: A Dialogue Between Art and Science." *Qualitative Inquiry* 11 (2005) 3–15.

Schwab, Joseph. "The Practical 3: Translation into Curriculum." *School Review* 83 (1973) 501–22.

Woocher, Jonathan. "Reinventing Jewish Education for the 21st Century." *Journal of Jewish Education* 78 (2012) 182–226.

1

THE MISTAKEN ASSUMPTION
Text Study Has to Wait

Ziva R. Hassenfeld

I FIRST MET KOBI[1] at a Shabbat meal. He was a Jewish studies teacher at a day school near the university where I was just beginning my graduate studies in Jewish education. My prior life as a *Tanakh* (Bible) teacher still loomed large in my sense of self. Nonetheless, I didn't imagine Kobi and I had much to talk about. I had taught high school. He taught second grade. I had spent my time in the classroom working to develop sophisticated, skilled and confident readers of the biblical text. I imagined Kobi spent his time singing songs and reading picture books, between chaperoned trips to the bathroom. After all, he taught seven-year-olds. Kobi picked up on my dismissive attitude towards his students and challenged me in no uncertain terms. "Come see my class," he offered, leaning across the table. "Just come see. I, too, started as a high school teacher thinking only high school students could really engage in text study. But these children, believe me, they are engaging in text study."

Kobi is one of those overwhelmingly engaging personalities. His interest and enthusiasm during a conversation, whether he agrees or disagrees, are palpable and infectious. He's the type of conversation partner who makes you want to keep talking, arguing, moving towards consensus

---

1. Kobi is a pseudonym, as are all the names in this piece. Though the teacher discussed in this piece deserves accolades for his work, the terms of this research require anonymity for the privacy of the school, the students, and their families.

1

or even deepening the rift of disagreement. As I would learn in the coming months, his innate excitement for life was magnified in the classroom. He absolutely loved biblical texts. Questions from students, even ones he had heard year after year, made him break out in huge smiles. Novel questions and interpretations practically caused him to break out in dance. Kobi not only taught in a day school but throughout the community: the JCC, various congregations, Hebrew schools, and adult education programs. And he was beloved everywhere.

He was also an avid student. He made it a point to attend text classes whenever he could. And he was always the first person to raise his hand, waving excitedly, eager to ask his question. It didn't matter whether he was sitting in a *shiur* (Talmudic study session) at the local *kollel* (center for adult education) or a bat mitzvah speech at the Reform temple—he wanted to talk Torah. Tall, slender, and usually dressed in a sweater vest and white button-down shirt, Kobi would happily regale anyone who would listen with ideas his students had come up with about biblical texts.

But none of that factored into my response. At that particular dinner I was still new to the area and had no intention of antagonizing anyone, so I politely accepted his invitation, sure that he and I were, at the very least, using the term "text study" to refer to two very different activities.

What I saw during my first visit will be sketched in my mind forever. Yes, the children were as tiny as I imagined they would be (this was before I had my own children and seven-year-olds became huge), but they were not singing songs and reading picture books. All of the students had a copy of the biblical text[2] they were studying out in front of them on their desks. One student would read a verse and then multiple hands would shoot up. Students asked questions rooted in a close reading[3] of the text. To my amazement, the students then began offering answers to their classmates' questions. One student, for example, asked a question about a repeated phrase in a verse and a few minutes later another student raised her hand and offered an explanation for the repetition. Kobi orchestrated the conversation, calling on students and repeating their

---

2. The students had a version of the biblical text with Hebrew on one side and the Jewish Publication Society translation on the other side.

3. Literacy expert Beth Burke defines close reading as a "thoughtful, critical analysis of a text that focuses on significant details or patterns in order to develop a deep, precise understanding of the text's form, craft, meanings, etc." (Burke, "A Close Look," 2).

ideas to the class, but he did not, even once, tell the students what the text meant. I left humbled and fascinated.

Learning is Located in the Activity of Learning

There is no question that the biblical text poses many challenges to a second-grader. It is elliptical and cryptic, it speaks to events outside their experience, and it uses archaic language. For that reason, I and many others have assumed that "real" text study, the kind of stuff we hope Jewish day school graduates engage in, is not possible at early ages. We believe that those early years need to be spent focusing on learning *how* to read: focusing on fluency, vocabulary, comprehension, and reading strategies. We conclude that once students are more comfortable with the biblical text, they can then engage in the activity of text study. But Kobi challenged these assumptions. He showed me that it is possible to help young students engage in the activity of text study even in the earliest grades. He showed me how a skilled teacher can facilitate all of the building blocks of text study *through engagement in* text study. From Kobi I learned that even when working with children who are only seven, we need not stop at simply familiarizing them with the biblical stories outside of the text or preparing them *for* text study. We can engage these young students in the most authentic of Jewish activities, text study, and they can learn *how* as they *do*.

After my first observation of Kobi's classroom, I knew I had to go back and spend significant time in his classroom. I needed to understand how Kobi's students were engaging in such high-level textual interpretation and discussion at such a young age. What had I missed? When did Kobi teach these students how to engage in close reading and ask text-intensive questions? When had he modeled that for them?

So I returned. I spent the next two years observing Kobi's class, bringing a camera along with me to capture the students' learning. What I learned was that there was no moment of direct instruction in Kobi's class. The students learned how to engage in sophisticated textual interpretation through the activity of engaging in textual interpretation.

What I observed was consistent with the findings of Jean Lave, an educational anthropologist who studied people's knowledge of arithmetic. In her groundbreaking book, *Cognition in Practice: Mind, Mathematics and Culture in Everyday Life*, Lave reported that the same people who did not "know" arithmetic when doing arithmetic problems in classrooms and on tests were able to perform arithmetic computations and calculations correctly when faced with them in real-life situations such as grocery shopping and cooking.[4] Her foundational work helped give rise to the social constructivist theory of learning. Perhaps the most significant implication of this theory is that knowledge does not have an independent existence. Rather, it is always located within real-life activity. Like Lave's study participants who knew math in the context of shopping and cooking, elementary school-age students come to possess knowledge in the context of an activity. This activity can be test-taking or it can be model building, but whatever it is, the knowledge is always located in, and accessible through, the activity.

Gordon Wells, another influential social constructivist learning theorist, also demonstrated how, at the earliest ages, the acquisition of knowledge happens through activity. Wells illustrated this point by presenting a dialogue between a toddler and his mother:

> Mark (age 2) is standing by a central heating radiator and can feel the heat coming from it. He initiates the following conversation with his mother.
>
> Mark: 'Ot, Mummy?
>
> Mother: Hot? (checking) Yes, that's the radiator.
>
> Mark: Been-burn?
>
> Mother: Burn? (checking)
>
> Mark: Yeh
>
> Mother: Yes, you know it'll burn don't you?

A few minutes later Mark is looking out of the window, where he can see a man who is burning garden waste.

> Mark: A man's fire, Mummy
>
> Mother: Man's fire? (checking)
>
> Mark: Yeh
>
> Mother: (coming to look) Oh, yes, the bonfire
>
> Mark: Bonfire . . . Oh, hot, Mummy. Oh hot. it hot. it hot.
>
> Mother: Mm. It will burn, won't it?
>
> Mark: Yes. burn. it burn.[5]

---

4. Lave, *Cognition in Practice*, 45–72.

5. Wells, *Dialogic Inquiry*, 12–13.

Unpacking the learning that took place, Wells explained:

> When—as here—the adult is able to follow the child's lead and
> make contributions that are relevant to the child's focus of inter-
> est and attention, meanings that are initially co-constructed can
> be taken over by the child and brought to bear in new situa-
> tions in which they apply. This can clearly be seen happening
> in Mark's observation that, like the radiator, the bonfire is "hot"
> and may "burn."[6]

Wells added a dimension to Lave's theoretical framework that is
particularly relevant to children. He posited that when young children
learn through activity (in his example, the activity of inquiry and discussion) they rely on the help of adults. By engaging with young children in
activity and contributing to it, parents and teachers offer them knowledge resources with which to make sense of their world. When offered
knowledge resources that are relevant, young children organically absorb
them into their own understanding.

Unpacking Kobi's Approach

Kobi, a very experienced teacher, engaged his students in a similar process to the one Wells described. As in the example above, Kobi involved
his students in the activity of inquiry and discussion—but instead of
radiators, the source of inquiry was the biblical text. Instead of rudi-
mentary concept and language acquisition, the knowledge resources he
introduced were those related to textual interpretation. In other words,
Kobi taught his students some of the most essential interpretive skills—
noticing symbolism, recognizing dramatic irony, identifying seemingly
superfluous words and repeated words, and naming ambiguities—but he
did this through the activity of text study itself.

My understanding of the dynamics in Kobi's classroom was deep-
ened by my two years of observations, as well as by a series of interviews
in which I asked him to reflect on his pedagogy and priorities. In these
conversations, Kobi repeatedly referenced his desire to let his students
"play in the text." He told me that he wanted students to "notice patterns,
perspective, symbols, and ambiguities." But, he explained, his approach
was to introduce these text interpretation skills as they became relevant
to whatever the students were focusing on—what got their interest and

6. Wells, *Dialogic Inquiry*, 13.

attention. He also said that, when offering interpretations, sometimes a student would say things that were not entirely clear or would pose interpretations or questions rooted in a misreading of the biblical content (responses that might be expected of a seven-year-old). Kobi's deliberate response was "to fill in and clarify" and thus, through a process of co-construction, to become the student's partner in text interpretation.

The portrait of student learning that follows is taken from my observations in Kobi's classroom, presented through exemplary vignettes. They reveal how, by allowing second graders to explore their own understandings of the text, Kobi helped his students to become more sensitive and skilled readers. The portrait concludes with a vignette from one of the last classes I observed, in which the students took the interpretive skills that had been introduced in earlier classes and brought them to bear on new biblical texts and their textual interpretation thereof.

Vignette 1: Acquiring Interpretive Skills Through Close Reading

In one of the first classes I observed, the students were reading Genesis 39, in which Joseph goes to work for Potiphar in Egypt. The class had already read aloud and discussed the first three verses:

> When Joseph was taken down to Egypt, a certain Egyptian, Potiphar, a courtier of Pharaoh and his chief steward, bought him from the Ishmaelites who had brought him there. The Lord was with Joseph and he was a successful man; and he stayed in the house of his Egyptian master. And when his master saw that the Lord was with him and that the Lord lent success to everything he undertook, he took a liking to Joseph.

The class moved on to a discussion of the next two verses that described the benefits for Joseph and consequently for Potiphar that came with God's presence:

> He made him his personal attendant and put him in charge of his household and of all that he owned. The Lord blessed the house for Joseph's sake, so that the blessing of the Lord was on everything that he owned, in the house and outside.

Perhaps provoked by the colorful picture of a life filled with such fortune that everything you touch metaphorically turns to gold, a student named Danielle raised her hand to ask a question:

Danielle: Did Joseph know that God was with him?

Kobi responded:

Kobi: Wow! It says Potiphar knew that God was with him, but does Joseph know?

In a subtle re-phrasing of Danielle's question, Kobi reinforced two important interpretive skills: (1) the ability to notice what the text *doesn't* say and (2) more generally, the ability to read the text closely in order to find meaning. Kobi's comment implied that the text's silences can be as important and full of meaning as the text's words. His message to Danielle was that the imagery of God's favor on Joseph is so evocative that it made sense that Danielle had wondered whether Joseph knew that.

Building on Danielle's question about what Joseph "knew," Kobi seized the opportunity. First he referenced the point that the biblical text states that Potiphar understood what was going on ("When his master saw that the Lord was with him and that the Lord lent success to everything he undertook, he took a liking to Joseph"), but then he presented a challenge to the student about how the biblical text is noticeably silent about Joseph: Potiphar understood, but did Joseph?

By re-articulating Danielle's question, but also referencing the biblical text and its own words, Kobi modeled and reinforced the interpretive skill of close reading and specifically the skill of noticing the text's silences. Rather than "teach" these skills, he waited until the student's interest in the text afforded the right moment to encourage a more thoughtful analysis of details and a more nuanced awareness of the content overall.

Vignette 2: Learning How the Biblical Text Uses Symbolism

In the next class I observed, students were reading Genesis 40, in which Joseph is in jail and the butler and the baker bring their dreams to him to interpret. The students took an interest in some of the stranger features of the baker's dream. The baker dreamed that there were three baskets on his head and in the highest basket were delicacies for Pharaoh that he had baked. But birds kept coming and eating the baked delicacies. One student, Jon, asked a question.

Jon: Why on top of his head?

Jon was curious about a strange detail from the dream. The baskets that the baker carried were described as resting on the top of his head. Kobi invited Jon to flesh out his question.

> Kobi: Why would he dream that the baskets were on top of his head? What would make more sense, Jon?
>
> Jon: If the baskets were in his hands.

By pointing out that baskets on the head is strange, Kobi moved the question toward the interpretive skill of recognizing how in the text some objects, persons, or situations might be *symbolic*, that is, that they might represent ideas beyond the literal. In this case, perhaps the biblical text purposefully placed the baskets on top of the baker's head *because* it was strange (or, as Kobi's comment indicated, this dream image didn't make complete sense). Perhaps, Kobi speculated, the placement of the baskets on top of the baker's head represented something more complex. Implicit in Kobi's response was an invitation to Jon and his classmates to textually hypothesize about what the baskets on the top of the baker's head might symbolize. A second student, Sarah, weighed in:

> Sarah: Because at bar mitzvahs there's usually someone who has a bottle on top of their head and they walk around with it.

Sarah offered a "text-to-self" connection, connecting the text to her own lived experience. Resisting the idea that the baskets on the head might represent anything, Sarah made the case that they are logical and literal. She argued that this behavior has something to do with a contemporary custom she is familiar with from bar mitzvah celebrations or from a scene from *Fiddler on the Roof*: just as things are carried on one's head by dancers at a party, so too are they carried on one's head in the Torah.

Without missing a beat and ignoring the potential anachronism, Kobi reacted to Sarah's comment as plausible, but not altogether logical:

> Kobi: Then it should be the *maskeh* [butler]. The butler would have something on his head but why the baker?

Following Sarah's reasoning, Kobi wondered why, if this behavior is connected to the tradition of dancing with a bottle on one's head at Jewish celebrations, would it not make more sense for the butler to have dreamed about carrying something on his head? Kobi gently pushed forward the idea that the placement of the baskets on top of the butler's head might hold symbolic meaning.

A third student, Jacob, picked up on the ideas both Jon and Kobi were advancing:

> Jacob: Well, why he had it on top of his head is because he was the chief baker! The baskets were on top.
> Kobi: "*Ha-Elyon*," the highest. That is to show he is the chief?
> Jacob: Yes.

Using his emerging understanding of symbolism, Jacob offered an interpretation that the placement of the baskets on the top of the baker's head represented the baker's position in the hierarchy of Pharaoh's workforce. Kobi repeated back Jacob's interpretation concerning the symbolism behind the baskets on the head and Jacob confirmed his teacher's observation.

In sum, in this classroom interaction, one student, Jon, noticed something strange in the text. The teacher, Kobi, validated the strangeness and invited Jon and his classmates to make meaning of it. When another student, Sarah, pushed back against the premise that the biblical text might be employing symbolism, Kobi engaged her sincerely. And when a third student, Jacob, offered an interpretation of what the placement of the baskets might be signifying, Kobi reinforced the occurrence of symbolic thinking by restating Jacob's point. This dialogue, rooted in student inquiry, provided dynamic evidence of these second-graders' increasing capacity to first notice and then interpret symbols in the text they were studying.

Vignette 3: Developing an Appreciation for Dramatic Irony

Another literary device that was particularly important to Kobi was dramatic irony, that is, the text's capacity to tell readers something that the characters themselves don't know. When relevant, Kobi made sure to cultivate in his students the ability to notice dramatic irony. In another example from the class session discussed above, the students had just read Genesis 41:34–35:

> Let Pharaoh find a man of discernment and wisdom and set him over the land of Egypt. And let Pharaoh take steps to appoint overseers over the land and organize the land of Egypt in the

seven years of plenty. Let all the food of those good years be gathered and let the grain be collected under Pharaoh's authority as food to be stored in the cities.

After they finished reading these verses out loud together a student, Susie, raised her hand.

> Susie: If he [Pharaoh] wanted to let him [Joseph] out, he needs to remember that God is in his [Joseph's] hands.

The meaning of Susie's comment was not entirely clear. She seemed to be interested in what it would mean to bring God and Pharaoh into such close contact vis-à-vis Joseph, given Pharaoh's own self-understanding of himself as a god. She likely was thinking of an earlier verse, Genesis 39:34, that explains "God was with him [Joseph]" and that "God caused all that he did to prosper in his hand." Perhaps Susie was suggesting that Pharaoh would have to treat Joseph well because God was with him. To zero in on Susie's point, Kobi asked her some clarifying questions:

> Kobi: Who needs to remember that?
> Susie: Pharaoh.
> Kobi: How does Pharaoh know that?
> Susie: It says in the Torah.
> Kobi: But did Pharaoh read the Torah? How does Pharaoh know that?

While at once honoring Susie's interpretive interest and focus, Kobi simultaneously introduced the interpretive skill of recognizing dramatic irony. Through his questions he reinforced the point that while we, the readers, have been told that "God is with Joseph," it is not clear whether Pharaoh knows or even if Joseph knows (as discussed in Vignette 1). In creating room for Susie's question and focus of inquiry, Kobi reminded her and the class that just because they, the readers, know something, that should not be confused with the characters' knowing. At the same time, just because the text doesn't tell the reader something explicitly doesn't mean it can't be possible. In sum, Kobi conveyed the message that if Susie was interested in what Pharaoh knew about Joseph's divine protection, she might look for hints in the text—hints that could lead her, the reader, to a more nuanced understanding of the Joseph story.

Vignette 4: Becoming Fully Engaged as Interpreters of Texts

My research did not utilize explicit metrics for measuring learning or for assessing students' attitudes toward text study.[7] Nonetheless, by sitting in on this classroom over many months, I found abundant evidence that through the process of engaging in the *activity* of textual discussion and interpretation, these second-graders were indeed learning and embracing the *skills* of text interpretation. Even though these skills and reading strategies were not written out on a poster in the classroom or re-stated by the students as part of a test, they were the interpretive norms that guided their activity. Over time, I observed how, through discussing and interpreting the biblical text with Kobi and their classmates, the students were increasingly able to apply these skills to new texts.

In one of the last classes I attended, the students were up to the point in the Joseph story in which Joseph is finally rewarded by Pharaoh for interpreting his dream.[8] In the discussion, a student asked why Pharaoh would so lavishly reward a prisoner. As they talked, the students referenced other parts of the Joseph narrative that they had studied (Genesis 37–41) and set their new interpretive skills to work as they made sense of the biblical text. Opening the discussion, a girl named Shayna posed a question to the class about why Pharaoh would give a prisoner authority:

> Shayna: Why is he putting a prisoner in charge?! You can't trust a prisoner. They did something bad enough to be put into prison, so how can you trust them with your whole entire house?

A boy named Jon responded:

> Jon (calling out): Joseph didn't do anything bad. He didn't do anything bad.

Rising to the occasion, Shayna defended her initial premise and question against Jon's critique:

> Shayna: But he was in jail and Pharaoh didn't know what he did.

---

7. For more about this, see: Hassenfeld, "Putting Students Front and Center;" Hassenfeld, "Teaching Sacred Texts;" and Hassenfeld, "Reading Sacred Texts."

8. Though chronologically this is not too far past the biblical texts discussed in earlier vignettes, because this class progressed through *Tanakh* very slowly and paused between Genesis units to study other texts, this example occurred three months after the earlier classes presented above.

Shayna's response showed that she understood that even though the reader knows that Joseph is innocent, Pharaoh didn't. All Pharaoh knew was that Joseph was in jail. Here, Shayna was applying her knowledge of dramatic irony, an interpretive skill we saw Kobi contribute earlier in his exchange with Susie. Now Shayna used this interpretive skill in defending her textual question. A third student, Amy, jumped in.

> Amy: Pharaoh doesn't know he was in prison! Potiphar does!
>
> Jon (jumping out of his seat and pointing to the biblical text on his desk): It says, "There is a guy in prison named Joseph and he can interpret dreams really well!"
>
> Amy: Well how do you know Pharaoh doesn't forget stuff?!
>
> Jon: No!
>
> Shayna: It was the same day!

Amy initially argued that Pharaoh was not aware that Joseph was in jail and that only Potiphar, the highest-ranking official in Pharaoh's court, knew. She reasoned that if Pharaoh didn't know that Joseph was a prisoner, then the textual problem of his appointing a prisoner to a leadership role disappeared. Jon immediately came in with textual evidence refuting this hypothesis. Jon recognized that the biblical text contradicted Amy's argument. He cited textual evidence: that the butler, when speaking to Pharaoh, referred to Joseph as a prisoner. Jon here applied the interpretive skill of citing textual evidence. Amy then attempted to defend her reading, arguing that Pharaoh may have forgotten this exchange with the butler. Jon was not convinced. Nor was Shayna. Shayna brought additional textual evidence that suggested that Pharaoh did indeed know that Joseph was in jail.

In this student-driven textual discussion lies a portrait of Jewish learning that we rarely witness among novice learners of any age. Note that in this dialogue the teacher didn't make any comments; confident in their abilities, Kobi gave his students a wide berth to engage the text and to apply the interpretive skills they had been developing. As with many other group discussions that I witnessed during my two years in Kobi's classroom, the evidence of these children's learning was manifest in the increasingly spontaneous behavior that unfolded before my eyes.

Conclusion

It might surprise us to see second-graders reading Torah texts with the degree of textual awareness that these children displayed. It certainly surprised me. Our surprise should lead us to ask: What was their teacher doing that allowed them to develop such a sophisticated capacity for textual discussion and interpretation at such a young age? The answer is revealing. Kobi was engaging his students in text study. He was not preparing them for text study and he was not making them wait until they had more skills. Already, at age seven, Kobi's students were participating fully in the activity of textual discussion and interpretation.

As an educator, Kobi has been guided by two convictions that allow him, and might allow others, to teach this way. First, he believes that even misunderstandings of the text are fruitful. Kobi is able to be non-directive in text discussion because he believes that whatever ideas his students throw out, right or wrong, they are valuable and necessary steps in the process of interpretation. He isn't concerned that students will walk away with "wrong" ideas. In the process of discussion and debate, Kobi's students help each other move towards new understanding of what they are reading.

Second, Kobi trusts that opportunities will present themselves for skill building. He believes that if he is clear about what he wants to teach his students, he can get there inductively through the process of student-directed discussion. He knows he does not need to front-load text study with teacher-centered lectures.

Ultimately Kobi fosters two learning outcomes that many educators and parents experience as being in tension: meaning-making and skill-building. This teacher allows his students to follow their own interpretive priorities, asking the questions that speak to them and offering interpretations that feel compelling to them, even questions and interpretations that might not seem important or compelling to the adult reader. In the process, he creates a student-centered classroom that fully encourages his students to dive into text study and probe the text on their own terms.

But this is only half of Kobi's agenda. In the midst of facilitating his students' textual interpretation, he is continually building their skills as interpreters. He knows what interpretive skills and knowledge he wants his students to have. He does not pause the activity of text study to teach these skills. Rather, he introduces these skills as they become relevant to the students' experience.

Kobi's pedagogical brilliance and educational innovation—his *hiddush*—is in allowing students to engage in the activity of text study without losing the elements of formal instruction. His distinctive contribution to Jewish education is his faith in seven-year-olds, his conviction that young students are able to engage in text study and learn as they do so. As Gordon Wells and others in the field of education have shown, activity is at the heart of learning. If students are not engaging in the activity for which their studies are intended, then they are engaging in some other, unintended, activity. If we want to properly prepare students for Jewish text study then we must allow them to *engage* in Jewish text study, even at the early age of seven.

Further Reflections About Jewish Learning

This portrait of Jewish learning presents two big ideas. The first is the idea that even very young children are able to study Torah. I am suggesting that children can participate in the *activity* of text study with some capacity at every stage of development. Of course, there are discrete skills and knowledge that they are missing, but many of these skills can be acquired as they participate in the activity itself. This is so important because we don't want students turned off to text study before they even begin. We also don't want what was once a very natural activity—making meaning—to become unlearned in the classroom. Further, I hope that reading about Kobi inspires us to think about how all the adults in children's lives can support them in text study. Each one of us can alter our orientation towards a child from one of "deficit" to that of "capacity." Every adult can shift from telling young children what a sign, book, story or picture means, to instead listening to the children's own sensemaking. Every adult can forgive missing context and focus on promising process. In other words, when a young child looks at a squirrel and says "woof," we can train ourselves to first hear the connection she is making between fur and animals before focusing on her mistake. Likewise, we can train ourselves, as math educators now do, that when a child says, "6 - 4 = 10," to first hear the mathematical thinking behind the statement before focusing on the mistaken calculation.

The second big, if not novel, idea is the importance of the teacher. In this chapter, readers come to know Kobi as a gifted, experienced, and thoughtful teacher—someone who embodies a stance of inquiry towards his practice and models such a stance for his students. Nothing he does in the classroom is without intention and reflection, and the sophisticated nature of the students' responses show the powerful impact of such careful pedagogy. As we think about Jewish learning, we dare not ignore or diminish the many benefits that come from supporting teachers like Kobi and helping them grow in their practice. Surely such educators are exemplars of teaching *and* learning at their best.

Bibliography

Burke, Beth. "A Close Look at Close Reading: Scaffolding Students with Complete Texts." https://nieonline.com/tbtimes/downloads/CCSS_reading.pdf.

Hassenfeld, Ziva R. "Putting Students Front and Center in the Hebrew Bible Classroom: Inquiry-Oriented Pedagogy in the Orthodox and Liberal Classroom." *Journal of Jewish Education* 84 (2018) 4–31.

———. "Reading Sacred Texts in the Classroom: The Alignment Between Students and Their Teacher's Interpretive Stances When Reading the Hebrew Bible." *Journal of Jewish Education* 82 (2016) 81–107.

———. "Teaching Sacred Texts in the Classroom: The Pedagogy of Transmission and the Pedagogy of Interpretive Facilitation." *Journal of Jewish Education* 83 (2017) 339–66.

Lave, Jean. *Cognition in Practice: Mind, Mathematics and Culture in Everyday Life.* Cambridge, UK: Cambridge University Press, 1988.

Wells, Gordon. *Dialogic Inquiry: Towards a Socio-Cultural Practice and Theory of Education.* Cambridge, UK: Cambridge University Press, 1999.

2

Weaving Judaism into Children's Daily Lives

The Mayim Tamid Experience

Jordana Schuster Battis and Rachel C. Happel

Mayim Tamid (Mayim Always[1]) *is an everyday after-school program at Temple Beth Shalom (TBS) in Needham, Massachusetts. Connected with TBS's larger elementary supplementary school program, which is called Mayim, Mayim Tamid offers a Jewish alternative to other local after-school programs. Parents register their children for the school year, committing to which days of the week each child will attend for the year. Parents are offered the range of two to five days a week. Children come by bus from the five public elementary schools in Needham and spend the remainder of the afternoon together. This portrait illustrates our experience in the pilot year of this multi-day-a-week program (2016–2017), in which nine children took part. Since that time, our numbers have continued to grow, so far doubling in size each year.*

---

1. For the Hebrew speakers and grammarians among us: "Tamid" here modifies the program name "Mayim," rather than the word "waters." So, even though it may sound awkward on a first read, the singular "Tamid" with the plural "Mayim" is intentional!

A Day in the Life of Mayim Tamid

Walk up past the student-designed Genesis mural in the stairwell and turn down the hall, past the windowed classrooms where small groups of fourth- and fifth-graders are learning Hebrew. Pass the bathrooms toward the end of the hall, turn right, and make your way to the back corner of the building and into the Mayim Tamid room. It is dark, but ready. On your right is a bank of natural wood cubbies, each labeled with a child's name. On top sit small plastic weaving looms with half-finished potholders. On your left, next to a cluttered kitchen counter and sink, are two child-height wooden tables surrounded by wooden chairs. A basket of whole apples, individually wrapped cheese sticks, cups of pretzels, and napkins await. Look up. In one corner of the room are orange couches around a gray shag area rug. A bookshelf nearby displays picture books about Passover and other books with stereotypically Jewish-named protagonists. In another corner, a sensory table holds water beads, next to a wooden play kitchen, a doll area, and a basket of Magnatiles. Across the room is a writing center and an easel displaying a half-completed game with dots to connect into squares. On the walls are printed Hebrew letters and children's artwork. On the window sills are photos of first- and second- graders with their families, interspersed with child-constructed Lego scenes of the story of the Exodus. An art-drying rack against one wall holds a number of half-sewn Passover pillows.

At 3:45 p.m., there is a clamor of footsteps in the hallway. Though the room may at first glance have seemed to have qualities of a preschool classroom with its dramatic play area and Legos, these children are older: ages six to eight. Four girls and two boys, all sweaty from their time downstairs on the playground and their run up the stairs, come into the room. One of the boys, blond, giggles with a slight girl with straight light brown hair. The other boy, stocky with wavy brown hair, speaks in an ongoing monologue to whomever is nearby.

As they run to the room and drop their jackets and backpacks into their cubbies, we hear the children ask, "Liron, Liron! What's for snack today? I'm starving!" Liron calmly replies, "Everyone will have enough to eat. OK, Mayim Tamid—line up to wash your hands before we start our *kibud* [snack]." After taking off their shoes and changing into slippers, half of the children rush to the sink in the classroom while the other half head to the nearby bathroom to wash hands.

The children come to the tables and take a seat. One exclaims, "Yay! Apples!" Another child sees the cheese sticks and says, "Ooh, we have cheese sticks today! Did you go shopping?" Another whines, "Pretzels again? Liron, can I have something else?" Liron answers, "Yes, we had a *kibud* delivery today, so we have cheese sticks," then bends down and says, "Spencer,[2] I'll see what else we have besides pretzels. What would you like today?" Meanwhile, Nisso, the Israeli *shin-shin*,[3] starts handing out apples, saying, "*Mi rotzeh tapuach?*" The children raise their hands and respond, "*Ani!*" Liron reaches into the cabinets above the sink and finds crackers. She shows them to Spencer, who nods. Then she offers a choice of crackers or pretzels to each of the children. Bringing out a pitcher of water, Liron asks, "*Mi rotzeh mayim?*" The children giggle at the word *mayim* (since the word means both "water" and is the name of their program!), and those who are thirsty raise their hands.

Once the children are settled with a snack, Liron goes around the table and asks each child about his or her day, switching back and forth between Hebrew and English:

> Liron: Ari, *ma nishmah*? [How are you?]
> Ari: *Lo tov.* [Not good.]
> Liron: *B'emet*? [Really?] What was *lo tov* about your day today?

The Evolution of a High-Quality After-School Jewish Education Program

The sketch above provides an introduction to Mayim Tamid. In the pages that follow, we broaden our portrait of this dynamic educational venture and share insights based on the experience of the program's first year. To begin, however, it is important to provide a context by describing both the congregation's current educational landscape and the vision that led us to create a new program to meet the needs of families in our community.

A Reform congregation serving families from Needham and the surrounding cities and towns, TBS has a membership of about 890

2. To protect their privacy, the names of all children and parents mentioned are pseudonyms.

3. *Shin-shin* is a Hebrew acronym for "*Shanat Sheirut.*" *Shin-shinim* are young Israelis who have just completed high school and are completing a year of service between high school and their army service. See: www.jewishagency.org/jewish-social-action/program/2331. TBS was fortunate to host a *shin-shin* during the school year described.

households. The synagogue community has doubled in size since 2002, due in part to demographic shifts that have brought many young Jewish families to this attractive suburb. One of TBS's priorities is to offer high quality learning programs for all of our children and teens. The synagogue is home to a thriving early childhood program, including the TBS Children's Center, a full-day preschool that enrolls over 200 children, and "Bumps, Babies, and Beyond," a series of parenting classes that serve an additional 150 families each year. Our K–12 learning programs include Mayim (kindergarten through fifth grade) and Etzim (sixth through twelfth grade), which, as of the fall of 2017, have a total enrollment of about 540 children and teens.

These programs have evolved over the past seven years, during which the TBS education leadership has developed a dynamic "Vision for Excellence in Jewish Education from Tots to Teens" that is helping us to assess program impact and to think about how to cultivate and sustain a comprehensive educational environment for TBS families. Our vision is built around the central principle:

Sacred Community—קהילה קדושה (*Kehillah Kedoshah*)

Our children's learning takes place within the context of our TBS community, which is crafted with intentionality to deepen relationships so that we can better care for one another and, together, strive to achieve those higher goals we could not accomplish alone.

This central principle is supported by twin core values we refer to as Depth of Relationship and Depth of Learning,[4] which are deliberately fostered throughout our learning programs through the following values:[5]

Depth of Relationship

- Rich Learning Environments—מקום (*Makom*)

- It Takes a Village—מורים חכמים (*Morim Chachamim*)

- Family—משפחה (*Mishpachah*)

---

4. For further explanation of these core values, including their connection to the name of our program being "Mayim," see: http://www.tbsmayim.org/corebeliefs.

5. For a graphic display of this "Vision for Excellence," including definitions of the values listed here, see: http://www.tbsmayim.org/visioninlearning. The English and Hebrew names of the values listed here were written to convey the spirit of the terms, rather than serving as direct translations of each other.

Depth of Learning

- Living Torah—תורת חיים (*Torat chayim*)
- Deep Learning—לימוד (*Limud*)
- Acting on our Jewish Values—דרך ארץ (*Derech eretz*)

It is with full intentionality that we have chosen to put equal emphasis on the core values of Learning and Relationship. In this, we look to sources such as education writer Ruth Sidney Charney, who makes the point that, though it is sometimes easy to think of teaching as being only for offering academic content—and that addressing children's social behavior is time spent away from this essential endeavor—in fact, "helping children learn to take better care of themselves, of each other, and of their classrooms"[6] is central to providing the skills needed for academic success. Charney comments that building relationships between teacher and learner, and among the learners themselves, promotes empathy, structure, and the creation of community[7]—and that these, in turn, lead to students' confidence, motivation, and, ultimately, to "educational mastery."[8] In this way, our goal is essentially to educate our children for "citizenship" in Jewish life in an almost Deweyan sense[9] and, ultimately, for full participation in their Jewish community. Indeed, we are not educating only for future enrollment in Jewish community, but rather for a sense of belonging, responsibility, voice, and empowerment *right now*.

In this endeavor, the work and philosophy of Ben Mardell from Project Zero at Harvard University resonates deeply with us. Mardell writes that children "are citizens, not potential citizens, not citizens in training, but citizens, with rights and obligations like all citizens ... Children must be recognized not just as growing unfinished beings, but also as true thinkers and doers, as active participants in their education."[10] While Mardell's work focuses on younger children (ages 3–5), we believe that his philosophy extends into our work as educators of older children as well. Our ultimate goal is to educate our learners to become active contributors to Jewish community and Jewish life, both now in age-appropriate ways, as well as in the future.

6. Charney, *Teaching Children to Care*, 18.
7. Charney, *Teaching Children to Care*, 18–19.
8. Charney, *Teaching Children to Care*, 27.
9. See Dewey, *School and Society*.
10. Mardell, "The Rights of Children," 43.

From Mayim to Mayim Tamid:
One Thing Leads to Another in Jewish Education

In the fall of 2012, after a multi-year change process, TBS launched May-im, our synagogue's answer to what some communities call "religious school" or "Hebrew school." Grounded in a project-based and experiential learning curriculum, Mayim includes once-a-week classroom sessions and integrated opportunities for family learning and relationship building. Led by a full-time faculty whom we call Jewish Learning Guides (JLGs), children come once a week to small groups for a program that offers ongoing exposure to and exploration of Jewish holidays, prayers, and Hebrew, as well as our distinctive "Exploration" curriculum, through which children and JLGs partner to investigate big questions and engage in hands-on, long-term projects.[11]

About three years after Mayim took hold in our community, several participating families inquired about having their children attend the program more than once a week, either because they needed after-school care for their children and were interested in having their children in a Jewish setting during those hours, or because their children loved Mayim and they wanted more frequent connection to TBS, or both. In 2015, the TBS Children's Center had extended its hours to include a full-day program in which preschool children could stay until 6:00 pm. We knew that, as the preschoolers got older, their families would likely continue to need late afternoon childcare coverage. Moreover, since these parents had shown a strong commitment to having their children in a Jewish setting in their preschool experience, these families were a prime target audience for an everyday Mayim-like experience. Our success with the Mayim approach emboldened us to think creatively about how to expand and extend our programming and whether this might potentially attract additional families to our congregation. It seemed we were being given a chance to reimagine a multi-day-a-week Jewish supplementary learning experience after many years away from such a model.

In the fall of 2016, we launched a new form of Mayim called Mayim Tamid ("Mayim Always") as an everyday after-school model intended to meet this demonstrated need in our community. Since our original Mayim model was not built as a multi-day program, and most TBS families were happy with having their children attend once per week, we knew

---

11. For a fuller description of Mayim, see: http://www.tbsmayim.org/. Our sixth to twelfth grade program, Etzim, can be found at: http://www.tbsetzim.org.

we didn't want to change the mainstream program. Rather, we created Mayim Tamid as an alternative path, one that would meet the needs and desires that were emerging among certain families in the congregation.

In designing Mayim Tamid, we were influenced heavily by the vision and experiences of two Mayim JLGs, Liron Reiss, who grew up on a secular kibbutz in Israel, and Sarah Kanigsberg, a former day school student and teacher. Both of these educators joined with us as we reflected on the limitations and untapped opportunities of traditional multi-day-a-week synagogue supplementary religious schools, and we collaboratively challenged ourselves to think specifically about the needs of our constituent families. We were inspired by independent models of after-school care and Jewish learning such as Kesher in Cambridge, Massachusetts, and the Jewish Enrichment Center in Chicago, in their purpose and function of meeting the needs of families with working parents while providing children with Jewish education and community. Since most Jewish after-school models we were aware of were community-based and unaffiliated with particular synagogues or denominations, in creating Mayim Tamid we needed to think about what it would look like to create a similar model within the walls and structures of a congregation. In doing this, we were aware of the factors that Rob Weinberg describes as the "distinctive positive characteristics of congregational education that give it a unique place in the Jewish educational lives of children, teens, adults, and families."[12] Weinberg identifies six such characteristics in discussing synagogue-based Jewish education: community embeddedness, intergenerational/ family learning, longevity of relationships/engagement, continuity and regularity, whole person learning, and flexibility. In creating Mayim Tamid, we sought to harness and build on these unique characteristics, to create a program that would both meet the needs of our families and elevate their experience within our vibrant community.

We were also influenced by the results of the *2015 Greater Boston Jewish Community Study*,[13] which outlines patterns of engagement and affiliation among adults and families, as well as participation in and attitudes toward Jewish education. The study confirmed what we were sensing about our community: that if parents are going to opt for their families to be involved in Jewish organizations and behaviors, they are

---

12. Weinberg, "The Unique Place of Congregational Education," para. 2.

13. Saxe, *2015 Greater Boston Jewish Community Study.*

most likely to do so if there are high-quality options that fit family logistical needs (such as location, schedule, and cost).

As the first year of Mayim Tamid got underway, we began to see what we intuitively understood to be success in our new program, but we did not yet know what accounted for that success or even what that success was. We initiated a systematic documentation process to help us capture the experience of Mayim Tamid as it was evolving. Over several months in Mayim Tamid's first year, we observed classroom activities, tracked student behavior, interviewed staff (Liron Riess and her co-JLG Julia Zinn), engaged parents in evaluative conversations, and identified dynamics and patterns that seemed to distinctively characterize this new initiative in Jewish education. As we describe below, this data collection led us to identify within our program core elements that we believe have helped our children see themselves as full participants in their own Jewish lives and in their Jewish community.

The Day Continues

While JLG Liron provides after school snacks to the hungry Mayim Tamid first- and second- graders, the group hears about everyone's day. Then Liron reminds the children that Passover is coming and that they are going to practice a special part of the Passover seder. Millie exclaims, "The Four Questions!" Liron replies, "That's right! The Four Questions. What is special about the Four Questions?" A few of the children respond, "I'm going to say them at my seder!" Liron says, "Yes, that's right, usually the responsibility for asking the Four Questions falls to a child at the seder. Sometimes the youngest child, sometimes any child who knows them and wants to say them." While the children are finishing their snack, Liron distributes laminated sheets with the Four Questions in both Hebrew and English. She asks "Who can start us off?" Meirav raises her hand and begins to sing, "*Ma nishtanah . . .* " and all of the children join in.

As they are singing the Four Questions together, Ari (the brown-haired talker) gets up from the table and wanders over to the writing center to continue working on a book he is creating. While working, he sings and hums along with the Four Questions. Nisso quietly moves to that area to sit with Ari while he works. Throughout the song, children get up from their seats to get more snack or water, or to take weaving looms from their cubbies to continue working on their potholders, all the while continuing to sing along with the group. Some of the children begin to giggle and point to their friend, Lylah, every time the words "*ha-lailah hazeh*" ["this night" or "this Lylah"] come up in the song. Liron points to the laminated sheets to redirect children whose attention has wandered, chuckles when they point to Lylah, and sings along enthusiastically, all the while observing the children to notice who is singing, who has mastered the song, and who needs a little extra help or encouragement. She stops them periodically to ask questions: What does that mean—"*kulo matzah*"? Why are we asking about dipping twice? What do we dip? "*Maror*"—what's that? Why do we recline? The children answer the questions—even Ari, from across the room at the writing center—and Liron takes note of who readily knows the answers and who looks confused. She'll use this information later in her planning.

Later, at 4:30 p.m., the children are spread throughout the room, working at several stations. Eleanor, Samantha, and Meirav are sitting at a table, sewing their Passover pillows. Millie, Lylah, and Spencer are in the dramatic play area, setting up for a pretend Passover seder. Ari is still at the writing center, working with Nisso on his book of Hebrew words. Sydney is sitting on the couch with Liron, having some one-on-one instruction on the Hebrew letter of the week, which she missed when she was absent earlier in the week. Liron announces to the group, "Remember, the Passover pillow station is a 'must-do' station today. When Eleanor, Samantha, and Meirav are done, then Millie, Hannah, and Spencer should go and finish yours." When she finishes working with Sydney, she walks over to the writing center and says, "Ari, can you show me your book?" He smiles and proudly shows her the pages he has created, and she exclaims, "Wow! It looks like you have been learning some new words with Nisso! Don't forget that you need to finish your Passover pillow, too." She then walks over to Hannah, whom she pulls aside for some one-on-one reinforcement of Hebrew letters.

At 5:00 p.m., Liron announces, "OK, if you are still working on your pillow, you can keep going. The blocks are also available now for anyone who wants to build." She walks over to Meirav and says, "Do you have homework today? It's time to work on that." Meirav starts to protest, but Liron says, "Remember, we promised Mom that you would have it done each day when she picks you up." Meirav goes to her cubby, gets her homework and sits at one of the tables to work. Ari and Spencer start to build with the blocks. Liron also announces, "If anyone wants to play

Hebrew Bingo, I'll be starting a game at this table." Eleanor, Samantha, Hannah, and Ari come to play bingo. Millie goes to the block station with Spencer. A few minutes later, there is a kerfuffle in the block area, and Liron goes to investigate.

> Liron: Spencer and Millie, what is going on over here with the blocks?
>
> Millie: He hit me with a block!
>
> Spencer: It was an accident!
>
> Liron: How did it happen?
>
> Millie: Well . . . we were playing a game where we threw the blocks into the air . . .
>
> Spencer: . . . and I threw it too hard.
>
> Liron: OK, it sounds like you are both upset about this. What can we do to work this out?
>
> Millie: Say we're sorry?
>
> Liron: I won't tell you what to say, but I know you care about each other and you're good friends. If you're feeling sorry, then saying it might be a good idea.
>
> Millie and Spencer (simultaneously): Sorry.
>
> Liron: Now, how can we make sure it doesn't happen again?
>
> Millie: Maybe we should have a rule about the blocks staying on the rug?
>
> Liron: That's a very good suggestion, Millie. Spencer, do you agree?
>
> [Spencer nods]

At 5:20 p.m., Liron announces that it is time to clean up and get ready for *tefillah* (prayer services). The children help to put away the supplies from the stations, place unfinished projects on the drying rack in the corner, change from their slippers into their shoes, and gather their backpacks and jackets from their cubbies. They walk as a group down the stairs, past classrooms of children in the once-a-week Mayim program, through the synagogue's lobby, and into the sanctuary. They place their backpacks in the designated area in the back of the room and go to the *siddur* (prayer book) cart to take a copy of *T'filoteinu*, the Mayim prayer book. Ari says, "I'm going to take a blue one today, that's my favorite one." Millie says, "I like the red one" and takes one with a red binding: each color *siddur* has different original artwork, created by the Mayim fourth- and fifth-graders during the previous school year, and the Mayim Tamid children know which version's illustrations they like best. They walk to their seats in the front row and settle in. Stephen, a local twenty-something songleader who leads Mayim *tefillah* twice a week, greets each child by name and then says, "OK, Mayim Tamid, any special requests for today?" The children point to pages in the *siddur* and ask, "Are we going to do this one today" and "Can we do the tune for *Mi Chamocha* that goes 'Lai lai lai . . . '?"

Soon, they are joined by the rest of the children from Mayim and *tefillah* begins. The children chant or read along with each prayer. When it is time to recite *V'ahavta*, Stephen asks for volunteers to come up and lead hand motions. Ari asks Liron if he can go up, and Liron reminds him about a conversation they had last week about how leading the hand motions is a responsibility and not a time to be silly. Ari nods and goes up to lead hand motions, along with Millie and Hannah. A group of sixth-grade boys joins them to help lead. At the end of the prayer, one of the sixth-graders fist-bumps the children from Mayim Tamid on their way back to their seats and they beam.

Throughout *tefillah*, parents of Mayim and Mayim Tamid students enter the sanctuary and join the group, often accompanied by the children's younger siblings, who are finishing a full day of preschool at TBS. When Spencer's father, Andrew, who attends the service daily, enters the sanctuary, Spencer moves from his seat to sit with him. When Millie's father, Saul, comes in with Millie's younger brother, Millie turns and smiles at them, but remains in her seat near her friends. After *tefillah*, as the children line up for dismissal, Liron approaches Andrew to ask how his wife Kathy is doing, since she recently broke her leg. Then, Liron gives him an update about Spencer's day, and Andrew shares information about what Spencer's teachers have been reporting about how things are going for him at his elementary school. The children leave with their parents or walk out to the carpool line to be picked up at the end of their day.

Unpacking the Mayim Tamid Experience

The portrait we are painting here is of one spring Thursday in 2017 at Mayim Tamid. In it, the children have been coming to Mayim Tamid multiple afternoons a week since September. Some, like Ari, have grown up here as students in the TBS Children's Center full-day preschool program. Others, like Spencer, came just once a week on a Sunday morning or weekday afternoon in past years when they were in kindergarten and first grade for "regular" Mayim. Now, as the above account shows, the nine children in Mayim Tamid arrive on the bus from their respective public elementary schools around town.[14] Led by Liron three afternoons a week and Julia Zinn the other two days, these children come to their after-school program to relax, do homework, work on projects, participate in daily *tefillah*, and play in an immersively Jewish environment.

Their classroom has been deliberately furnished as a living room. The couch, books, play area, and slippers have been chosen to help students feel at home in this space in which many of them spend as many weekday waking hours in a week as they do in their own homes. Likewise, the learning that happens is intentionally crafted to feel not like school but, instead, like the kind of experience one might have growing up in a committed, knowledgeable, liberal Jewish home, with a parent who has the time and energy to plan holiday-connected cooking and art projects, speaks bilingually in English and Hebrew, and can allow time for both individual and small-group exploratory play.

We do not assume that robust Jewish living is happening for these children and their families at home or in their neighborhoods. We know that many of the parents of children in our programs have limited Jewish knowledge or lack confidence in the Jewish knowledge they do have. Many of our families include one parent who is not Jewish. Moreover, most Mayim Tamid families have two working parents whose primary focus when at home is on the basics of household life and morning and bedtime routines. Weekends are spent running errands, attending birthday parties and children's sporting events, visiting friends or relatives, and spending a few hours of quality time together as a family, which may or may not include Jewish ritual and practice. Additionally, many of the children who attend our programs have the experience of being the only Jewish child on their block or in their class at school. Beyond the widely marked celebrations of High Holy Days, Chanukah, and Passover, the traditional cycles of synagogue attendance, holiday celebration, mindfulness about eating (*kashrut*) and rest (Shabbat), etc., are unfamiliar to most of our families, since many of these parents did not grow up with those cycles and practices themselves. Unlike many of their Jewish grandparents or great-grandparents, our children are not surrounded by Jewish neighbors within walking distance. The bulk of their Jewish life

14. In this pilot year of Mayim Tamid, nine students were enrolled. Of these, three attended two days a week, two attended three days a week, one attended four days a week, and three attended five days a week.

takes place within the walls of the synagogue, not through immersion in a Jewish setting in their homes and neighborhoods.

In creating Mayim Tamid, we dreamed of a program that our families could look to that would provide opportunities not only for children to learn about Jewish living but to experience it within our walls—as children and as families. We soon discovered that parents were seeking the same thing. As Ari's mother, Alicia, says:

> I wanted his Jewish learning to be part of the fabric of who he was as a student and a child, and for that just to be part of his life, not just be this after-school thing that he did, this occasional thing that he did, this extracurricular thing that he did. Being Jewish is not extracurricular. It's everything.

> You know, it's hard to impart that on your children when you're exhausted at the end of the day. And even weekends when you have the sports and the birthday parties and all the other life stuff going on, to know that that Jewish teaching part is taken care of is just such a peace of mind. You know, that's going to carry with him for the rest of his life. So I was just very excited about that. I never had that opportunity. And I'm a working parent, so he would have to go to after-school anyway somewhere, in some way.

When we first conceived of Mayim Tamid, we thought largely in terms of what the academic curricular content of the program would be. We focused on the idea of teaching Hebrew and year-cycle events, based on the opportunities we saw in expanding Mayim to an everyday program. In Liron's words, "Hebrew is the focus. Hebrew and holidays. Hebrew is my baby." But, whereas in a stereotypical "Hebrew school" classroom Hebrew might be taught through frontal teaching of decoding (sounding out of Hebrew letters and vowels, with little or minimal understanding) or, more creatively, using Hebrew Through Movement and other embodied approaches that help to teach understanding of contemporary Hebrew,[15] we wanted a space in which Hebrew was absorbed but not formally taught. In fact, though before the beginning of the year Liron had planned to teach letters frontally to the group as a whole, she quickly discovered that in this homey setting, with these particular chil-

---

15. See the remarkable work described at: http://www.hebrewthroughmovement. org/, created at the Jewish Education Center of Cleveland by Nachama Skolnik Moskowitz, as well as Nicki Greninger's chapter in this volume.

dren, dynamics quickly devolved into sibling-like bickering among the group.

Instead of insisting on a more formal approach, we decided to support Liron in drawing on her experience as a teacher (as well as a mother) of both preschoolers and middle school students to create an environment in which children could unwind in the aftermath of their school day. She actively expresses affection and love for the children, knows them well enough to see what they need individually, and purposely makes space for them to let down their guard—to read a book on the couch, rough house on the playground, or even have a needed tantrum. She says:

> The things I say to them, I find, are things I tell my own children. If I see a kid who's really tired, I tell them to go lie down on the sofa and read a book. Last week, Sydney was having a temper tantrum because she was losing in a memory game. I just let her have [the tantrum], and I said to the other kids so she could hear, "She knows sometimes people lose in a game, and she'll come when she's ready." I care, and sometimes I do what's beyond our curriculum. It's more than a relationship you have with a [student]. I say, "Yeah, my love."

Content instruction takes place largely one-on-one or around the snack table in what might seem to the children to be incidental conversation. As illustrated above, Liron will call a student or two over to a table to teach them about a Hebrew letter, give them play options that happen to have a holiday or Hebrew focus, or build on her use of patterned Hebrew conversation to surreptitiously throw in a new phrase or concept. For example, when doing a cooking project, Liron counts the ingredients in Hebrew. Through repetition, the children pick up the numbers and can count along. As Liron reflected at the end of the year:

> We would count some of the cups and the spoons in Hebrew, and I noticed when we made the chocolate balls, as I was counting, the kids just kept counting in Hebrew. It was really so pleasing to me, because I was like, "Did I teach them that? How does Millie know [how to] to count until ten?"

The curriculum has focused on the year cycle in the sense that all of this is the Jewish environment that the children find themselves in. That is, there have rarely been defined lessons about holidays, but instead, the children learn what they need to know in order to make holiday-related objects: *sukkah* decorations, Chanukah presents for their families, Purim masks. Liron thinks about this as parallel to her experience growing up in a secular Israeli environment:

> If they're here every day as an after-school program, then they need to feel that the holiday coming up is a big thing, just like I did in the kibbutz, and every child in Israel does. The holiday is coming. We are here. That's the big thing that is coming to our lives right now.

With regard to Hebrew and teaching about Israel, Liron has attempted to normalize the use of Jewish language and connection to Israel by weaving them into the fabric of the classroom. She makes a point of speaking in Hebrew whenever other Israelis are in the classroom and tells a particularly illustrative story about a moment when the children questioned this:

> The other day, someone says, "Why do you speak Hebrew to him all the time?"
>
> I said, "That's our language."
>
> They say, "Yeah, but you know English," and I said, "Meirav, when you lived in China and you met someone who speaks English, did you speak in Chinese or English to them?"
>
> "English."
>
> I said, "It's the same thing. It's important for us to talk Hebrew to each other." They kind of got that.

Liron has also made a point of speaking Hebrew at speed. Rather than attempting to instruct the children *about* Hebrew, she has simply used it, in intentionally simple forms, and used repetition and body language to help the kids keep up:

> During *kibud*, I don't even try to slow down and/or make an American accent, and I just say it right away, and they have to figure it out. By now, they've become attuned to all that.

Through these small immersions, we've found that when the children speak Hebrew, they, too, use Israeli accents. Since they are not exposed regularly to conversational Hebrew spoken with an American accent, it doesn't occur to them that the words they hear could be pronounced any differently; they just repeat what they are hearing daily from Liron and Nisso, exactly as they are hearing it—whereas in the highly structured *tefillah* setting, they say words with the same Americanized pronunciation as the song leaders and other students and teachers around them.

In addition to Hebrew and year-cycle, an unexpected but central theme of the year emerged around *chesed* (acts of lovingkindness) and the children's sense of connection and responsibility to the greater TBS community, including to those children in the Mayim program who come only one day a week. At the beginning of the year, as an optional Rosh Hashanah activity in the Mayim Tamid classroom, Liron gave the children the chance to work on "Shanah Tovah" artwork to hang at the top of the stairs to the Mayim floor. To her surprise, every child wanted to work on the poster, and when she suggested creating a sign to go next to the poster that said, "Create[d] with love by the children of Mayim Tamid," the students came up with a plan together for how each of them could contribute to the sign.

When the High Holy Days were over, the children asked what they were making next for the community. Liron saw this and seized on it as an opportunity for a yearlong project, charging the students with the responsibility for helping Mayim students celebrate the Jewish year and helping the greater TBS community where needed. Though at first she was responsible for much of this initiative, she says,

> They took it on for the few months after and just kept asking, "Can we make this for such and such? Can we make this for ... ?" It was not on my plan, but it became my plan because it came from them. They became so excited about taking it on. There were just so many things that they wanted to do. I saw an interest, and I just let them ride with it.

This turned into a meta-goal for the group: ownership for taking care of the greater TBS community:

> In the beginning of the year, very early on, we established that we are here every day, and so we right away kind of defined our purpose as giving back to the community. It was pretty early on a realization that that's what this group is all about: We're here all the time, so we're welcoming. It just kind of coincidentally started and then we just took it on—like, this is actually our space to welcome everyone, because we are here all the time. It's our responsibility.

The children made signs for the Mayim entrance for every holiday. They made Purim *mishloach manot* (gifts of food) for TBS staff. When they cooked as a group activity, the plan became to cook for others in the building, and the kids became increasingly aware of who those people were. Liron's co-JLG Julia described how the the children ended up with a sense of responsibility to those who work in the building and serve the community:

> We were cooking, and they would say, "We should bring some to Rachel! We should bring some to Rabbi Jordi!" Then, they'd always say, "We should bring some to the janitors," because they realize that those are important people in our community also, and they help us in these ways. So, while we're baking, the kids say, "We should bring them muffins." Even if it's not for an occasion. We baked and we gave it to everyone. When we'd bring it to people in the temple, they'd ask, "What is this for? What is the occasion?" And, the kids would say, "We just wanted to make you something, just to be kind."

Another emergent goal of the program has developed around support for parents. Though we originally dreamed of creating a space within our greater Mayim program in which parents could learn and feel comfortable alongside their children, we have found that Mayim Tamid families feel particularly integrated into the TBS community through their children and this program. Some of the parents who started coming to *tefillah* just to support their children talk about how this has become a spiritual practice of their own. Spencer's parents, Andrew and Kathy, explained:

> Andrew: I'll be honest with you. I love coming to the service at the end. I come three times a week. It's good for me spiritually. I see people I know. I like Rabbi Jordi's stories on Friday. I learn.
>
> Kathy: I feel like I'm part of the temple community. I'm not Jewish, but I'm so glad he's taken to a faith. Asking questions. He's a curious kid, and he's teaching me too. There's something about how you close the day [*tefillah*] that's so peaceful. That calming down. That reflection time. Everything else is go, go, go, and it's that time to be grateful. My peaceful time.

We realized that this did not only need to be passive on our part but could be a goal for teaching parents and helping them bring more engaged Jewish life into their homes. Andrew and Kathy described the ways that Spencer has been bringing his Jewish learning and life back home:

> Andrew: I was watching him the other day. He can only read a little Hebrew. But, he knew the first half of the *V'ahavta*, without

looking down. He came home with *Sh'ma*, and he taught me about why we whisper the second line.

Kathy: On Shabbat, he'll start the prayers. He enjoys learning it and enjoys practicing it.

We have also found that many of the parents of Mayim Tamid students look to the teachers and professional staff for support and partnership. For example, Meirav was struggling to do her homework in the evenings after a long day at school and Mayim Tamid. As we mentioned above, her mother, Yael, and Liron came up with a system to support Meirav doing homework at Mayim Tamid, and with language that they could use consistently between home and TBS. As Liron reflects:

> The approach is that Meirav has options. She's one of the first kids to arrive, so she has an extra fifteen minutes in the playground, and she doesn't like it. She often asks to come in, so we said that now that the weather is nice, she has a choice of playing for fifteen minutes, then—she'll tell me when—we're setting a little corner for her in the playground on a picnic table with snacks and drinks, and she will bring her homework packet and work on it. If, for whatever reason, she really wants to continue playing, then she can do her homework before *tefillah* instead of a station, or during *tefillah*, and we will find a table in the lobby where she would sit. Since she comes to *tefillah* nearly every day, we feel okay with her missing it from time to time.

> I'm responsible for her arriving home with her homework done, one way or another. They tell her it's a must from home, that they ask me to tell her to do it; then I tell her it's a must here, so we're all together in this. She was struggling with me before that. She said, "No, I'm not gonna do it," or "I don't want to do it." Once she got that Mom and I are in cahoots on that, she stopped the struggle. Last week, she finished her whole packet.

Another parent told Liron that her son's teacher at school was reporting some troubling behaviors in class, and she asked if we were seeing the same behaviors in Mayim Tamid. She asked Liron how she handled them, so that she could tell the school what we were doing that was effective. We understand this as evidence that parents see the teachers and other staff as partners and rely on them for support beyond the walls of TBS.

What We've Learned So Far

When we reflect on the pilot year of the Mayim Tamid program, we see that the children emerged with something that we had not named as an explicit goal of the program, but which is central to our beliefs and assumptions about the core goals of Jewish education in particular: education for active participation in community. These students have been given voice and choice in their learning and in the synagogue world that they are a part of.

Though we do not have systematic evidence that the children in Mayim Tamid learned more, or more deeply, than children do in our once-a-week Mayim model, we believe that in its pilot year the Mayim Tamid model has had a strong effect on its students across a wide range of domains, including in supporting their Hebrew language acquisition, social-emotional learning, and connection to the synagogue community. Above all, we see these children as having especially gained, in an age-appropriate way, a sense of their own integration into, responsibility toward, and ability to make active choices within Jewish communal life.

What was it about our approach that enabled this learning? After reflecting on what we have seen from the students, heard from parents, and reflected on together as a team of educators, our working hypothesis is that there are three key elements that contributed to this understanding.

1. The people in the Mayim Tamid classroom feel like family.

One of the core elements of our once-a-week, "regular" Mayim program has been our dual emphasis on "depth of learning" and "depth of relationship." In starting that program, one of our premises was that Jewish content learning is not enough, but that Jewish content is meant to be lived out in community, and that it should be integrated with active social education that encourages social knowhow, interdependence and knowledge of each other's needs and interests.[16] We believed that Jewish educa-

16. Though by no means specific to Jewish content and Jewish community, this understanding reflects the approach of the Center for Responsive Schools, an organization whose materials and trainings we have turned to on a regular basis. The Center's approach to building "responsive classrooms" is grounded in six guiding principles that we hope are reflected throughout our work in our Jewish setting:
- Teaching social and emotional skills is as important as teaching academic content.
- How we teach is as important as what we teach.
- Great cognitive growth occurs through social interaction.

tion for Jewish content also needs to express and cultivate shared cultural values.[17] In the Mayim setting, we have attempted to deliberately disrupt the false dichotomy often drawn between "formal" and "informal" learning settings[18] and instead to foster both *relationships through the building of content knowledge* and *content knowledge through the building of relationships.*

The Mayim Tamid setting takes this to a new level in terms of the intensity of the social curriculum. Because of the amount and quality of time that children spend in this setting, we have found an opportunity for encouraging a family-like atmosphere that is warm and that allows children the time and space to learn and grow at their own pace. Here, the relationships between child and JLG and between child and child belie the norms of traditional school and supplementary settings. They are much more like the bonds one might create in one's home in an extended family.

The parent-like relationships between Liron and her students help her to help them feel empowered and are intended to give them a sense of responsibility in their environment.[19] Liron and Julia's planning takes into account the relationship they each have with particular students. In the length of hours in the after-school day—where the immediate goals are those we set together to be responsive to the needs and interests of the children in the classroom—time can stretch to accommodate needs for intimacy and to give children a sense of agency in the class's learn-

---

• What we know and believe about our students—individually, culturally, developmentally—informs our expectations, reactions, and attitudes about those students.

• How we work together as adults to create a safe, joyful, and inclusive school environment is as important as our individual contribution or competence.

• Partnering with families—knowing them and valuing their contributions—is as important as knowing the children we teach.

Source: https://www.responsiveclassroom.org/about/principles-practices/

17. As Barry Chazan writes: "Teaching groups is not simply about transmitting knowledge to all the individuals gathered in one room, but rather is very much about the dynamic role of the collective in expressing and reinforcing values that are part of the culture of the society that created the group" (Chazan, "The Philosophy of Informal Jewish Education," para. 32).

18. See Chazan, "The Philosophy of Informal Jewish Education."

19. Speaking to this point, Allison Gopnik states: "The particular love that goes with caring for children is not just restricted to biological mothers and fathers, but includes all the people whom academics call caregivers and the British, more elegantly, just refer to as carers. It's a form of love that is not limited to biological parents, but is at least potentially part of the lives of us all" (Gopnik, *The Gardner and the Carpenter*, 9).

ing, and thus in their own Jewish life. The message is: we are creating this classroom home—and what happens in it—together; it is our shared space and our shared learning.

Meanwhile, in this intimate environment, the amount and quality of time the children spend together has fostered relationships among the Mayim Tamid children that are almost sibling-like, in all the positive and negative interplay that that implies.[20]

Supporting the sibling-like relationships in this classroom environment can be challenging because, at the end of the day, the children go home to their own families. Though Liron says that she says things to the children that "are things I tell my own children," of course the Mayim Tamid children are not her own children. They will go home to their parents who have their particular parenting styles. At the same time, the opportunities afforded in this family-like setting are powerful. The children are learning about the needs of others and developing skills of self-regulation they will need for full participation in this and other places.

We believe that this family-like setting has helped each child in Mayim Tamid feel that he or she matters, that each of them has rights and responsibilities as part of the group, and that, as in a healthy family, they are in this together.

2. Judaism is woven into children's everyday life and living.

The Mayim Tamid day is bookended by certain daily routines that are distinctively Jewish in terms of language and content. At the beginning of their afternoon together, the children sit down for *kibud*, and Liron uses Hebrew exclusively. At the other end of the day, each afternoon ends in the sanctuary or Beit Midrash with *tefillah*. The week has a distinctive ending of its own: every Friday involves *challah* baking, candle lighting, and *kiddush* over grape juice, in addition to a special Shabbat service in the sanctuary for Mayim Tamid students and their families.

These things stand out as Jewish touchpoints in the day and in the week. But the fabric of life between them is intended as an apparently

---

20. According to Jeffrey Kluger, "Our brothers and sisters are our collaborators and co-conspirators, our role models and cautionary tales. They are our scolds, protectors, goads, tormentors, playmates, counselors, sources of envy, objects of pride. They teach us how to resolve conflicts and how not to; how to conduct friendships and when to walk away from them" (Kluger, "The New Science of Siblings," para. 5).

seamless weave of things that are "Jewish" and things that are "regular" so that there is no boundary between where one ends and the other begins.

Stations around the room offer options each day, some of which are related to Jewish content or to Hebrew language and others of which could be found in any after-school setting. A given day might find children at one table making cards for an upcoming Jewish holiday, others at the sensory table playing with water beads, a child sitting on the couch reading a book, and another practicing Hebrew letters or working on a craft project. On one day they may be supported by an American, non-Hebrew-speaking teen *madrich* (teaching assistant); on another, by the Israeli *shin-shin*, Nisso.

The idea here is to make Jewish rhythms, awareness of Israel, and use of Hebrew part of the daily fabric of the children's experience. The children explore and play, pursuing their own interests, but the things planted in the environment for them to find and use are often Jewish or Israeli things. Most of the books on the shelves—many from PJ Library—have Jewish content or characters. If a country is going to be talked about as an example, it will most often be Israel. If there are five minutes to spare, more likely than not, teachers will engage them with Alef-Bet Yoga.[21]

Liron compares this to her experience in an Israeli environment, in which stories and activities are "Jewish" just by virtue of using Jewish names, language, and living in Jewish calendrical rhythms:

> To them, they may not notice it, but they don't know how much they know just by absorbing it while we're here. It's enough that I tell them a story about Shlomo and Rivka. A child in the public school would immediately say, "That's a weird name," but the Mayim Tamid children don't even question those names anymore.

As a parent watching this experience, Ari's mother, Alicia, contrasted this with her experience growing up in a traditional Hebrew school setting. She said,

> As opposed to the way that I grew up, which was basically Sunday school on Sunday—then, maybe a little bit later, it was Sundays and Tuesdays. And, while I did grow to have a Jewish identity through that and through my family, I just feel like this

---

21. See, for instance, Goldeen, *Alef-Bet Yoga*.

is a priceless experience, to truly have that interwoven through his everyday experiences.

In fact, the impact of this immersion in living Jewishly is evidenced in the contrasting backgrounds of Ari and Spencer. Ari attended pre-school at TBS, where Jewish holidays are marked and there are many Hebrew songs and Jewish rituals in the environment; his parents are both Jewish and have spent time living in Israel, defining Judaism as a core part of their identities; both Ari and his brother Ezra have identifiably Israeli/Jewish names. Spencer's family, on the other hand, was less Jew-ishly engaged in the past; his mother is not Jewish (though she is actively supportive of building their family's Jewish identity and experience) and before this year he was not in a Jewish environment for preschool or after-school care. Liron says,

> For Ari, let's say, this came natural and complemented what he knew. Spencer came from a completely different background, where he was completely not exposed at all to—I don't know how much Jewish holidays they even celebrated. For Spencer, everything was new to him. He started two years ago in Mayim, but that was only once a week. Now, Spencer is so immersed in Jewish culture and Hebrew.

Stemming from this experience, Spencer has joined the TBS youth choir, and his parents both talk about how much he has taught them at home. Through Mayim Tamid, Ari and Spencer are now on largely equal footing. JLG Julia says:

> I think the difference is Ari always has had a Jewish identity at home. Spencer didn't have that before, so this is his Jewish iden-tity. That's okay. You wouldn't know the difference now, because they're both so immersed in it.

Incidentally, it is not only the students for whom Judaism has be-come woven into their everyday lives. For many of the Mayim Tamid families, Jewish practice and synagogue participation have become a more regular part of their week. As an example, as we have mentioned, Spencer's participation in Mayim Tamid has led to his parents' regular at-tendance at Mayim *tefillah*, and to his family's regular presence at Friday night services; Kathy has joined the TBS Elementary Learning Commit-tee; and Spencer's younger sister is now enrolled in TBS's daily kinder-garten program.

We believe that the full participation of Mayim Tamid children and their families in daily Jewish life has given them a deeply rooted sense of ownership and belonging in our Jewish community and that this translates into a sense of responsibility, Jewish identity, and citizenship.

3. Mayim Tamid students see themselves as a part of the fabric of the broader synagogue community.

Mayim Tamid's existence within the context of a larger synagogue community mimics an idealized Jewish neighborhood for these students. They have developed a sense of comfort and belonging within the Mayim Tamid classroom, across the Mayim week, and throughout the temple building. The kids are more aware of who is in the building each day and what the rhythms of the week are than many of the professional adults in the synagogue space. The children are connected beyond their classroom experience to a large network of relationships and support within the context of their synagogue community.

Coming to the synagogue space every day and helping to construct the learning that they are engaging in within it means that these children have gained a sense of responsibility for what goes on in the building. During Mayim *tefillah*, they often stand up to help lead prayers and request particular melodies, and Ari regularly volunteers to collect *siddurim* (prayer books) at the end of the service. Likewise, they regularly bake and make presents for synagogue staff. They've taken especial pride in performing acts of lovingkindness around the synagogue.

This sense of responsibility has become so important to the group's identity that Liron is making this a purposeful part of the curriculum for future years of the entering Mayim Tamid class. She says:

> Now that *chesed* came up as a theme of our year, I think I will continue that policy in the future. It gives them ownership . . . We are just constantly seeing ourselves as the ones who are here all the time, and therefore giving back to the community is a very big thing.

Having *chesed* at the core of the Mayim Tamid social and content curriculum means that children not only learn *about* the communities of which they are a part (within their classroom, within the K–12 learning programs, within the synagogue, etc.), they learn about their own power to contribute to and effect positive change in the world.[22]

One of Mayim Tamid's objectives is to create a sense of group identity that reaches beyond the physical walls of the Mayim Tamid classroom. Consistent with the stance asserted by Barry Chazan, we believe that "the groups of which we are part shape our minds, language, and selves in very central ways."[23] Accordingly, we see the children's learning in Mayim Tamid and in the synagogue as a whole as more than the mere acquisition of information.

We believe that, overall, this immersive experience has enabled the children to become "woven into" the fabric of life at Temple Beth Shalom and to see themselves as integral parts of their group, their synagogue, and even the Jewish community as a whole.

Further Reflections About Jewish Learning

Our experience with Mayim Tamid has affirmed our belief that Jewish supplementary education can be a setting for the growth of joyful, positive Jewish identity, deep learning, and relationships. It can be an environment that teaches for integration into Jewish community and for a sense of responsibility and citizenship in Jewish life for both children and their families.

It has affirmed our belief that children are capable of becoming active participants and citizens in Jewish life and community *right now*, and that when we provide the right settings for them to do so, they can take on responsibility for their Jewish community at every age.

It has affirmed—to borrow the wisdom of Rav Kook—that in creating an old Jewish model from scratch, the old can be made new and the new can be made holy. That is, it is possible to take something that many families saw as outdated and impossible in the framework of their busy lives (in this case, a multi-day-a-week Jewish supplementary education program) and turn it into a desired commodity that is in rhythm with families' lives, in line with contemporary sensibilities and research about education, and rooted in Jewish life.

22. See Charney, *Teaching Children to Care.*

23. Chazan, "The Philosophy of Informal Jewish Education," para. 32. See footnote 17 in this chapter.

It has affirmed for us that many families are hungry for Jewish knowledge and opportunities for participation, even if they don't always know what to ask for.

It has affirmed for us that Reform Jewish life for "regular" families can be an active, daily, rich endeavor—and that a synagogue can be a place of vibrant everyday Jewish life for kids and families alike.

It has affirmed that many things sometimes described as the goals of Jewish education (Hebrew, Torah, connection to Israel, etc.) are the means but not the end. They are the who, what, when, and where, but not the why. The why is in who we are as Jews, both separately and when we are together.

Bibliography

Charney, Ruth Sidney. *Teaching Children to Care: Classroom Management for Ethical and Academic Growth, K–8*. Turners Falls, MA: Northeast Foundation for Children, 2002.

Chazan, Barry. "The Philosophy of Informal Jewish Education." http://www.infed.org/informaljewisheducation/informal_jewish_education.htm.

Dewey, John. *School and Society*. New York: Touchstone, 1997.

Goldeen, Ruth. *Alef-Bet Yoga*. Minneapolis: Kar-Ben, 2009.

Gopnik, Alison. *The Gardener and the Carpenter: What the New Science of Child Development Tells Us About the Relationship Between Parents and Children*. New York: Farrar, Strauss, and Giroux, 2016.

Kluger, Jeffrey. "The New Science of Siblings." *TIME Magazine* (July 10, 2006). http://content.time.com/time/magazine/article/0,9171,1209949,00.html.

Mardell, Ben, et al. "The Rights of Children: Policies to Best Serve 3, 4, and 5 Year Olds in Public Schools." *scholarlypartnershipsedu* 5 (2010). http://opus.ipfw.edu/spe/vol5/iss1/5.

Saxe, Leonard. *2015 Greater Boston Jewish Community Study*. Waltham, MA: Brandeis, 2016.

Weinberg, Rob. "The Unique Place of Congregational Education in the Lives of Children, Teens, and Families." http://www.jtsa.edu/the-unique-place-of-congregational-education-in-the-lives-of-children-teens-and-families.

3

"ALL IN!"

Engaging Sixth-Graders
in Compelling Jewish Learning

Nachama Skolnik Moskowitz

SUNDAY, JANUARY 22, 2017. Anyone who peeked into The Temple-Tifereth Israel's sixth-grade room[1] on this winter morning might raise the question of just what, of Jewish consequence, this class of twenty eleven- and twelve-year-olds was learning. One group of students had a number of tongue depressors spread out on a table. A plastic apothecary container, such as one finds at a physician's office, stood empty nearby. Another group sprawled on the carpeted floor; nearby lay a fat book strangely hollowed out to hold a stash of "hand clappers," pairs of small plastic toy hands that clap when shaken. The colorful clappers were commanding this group's attention. And the third group? They had left with their *madrich* (teen assistant) a few minutes earlier after reading a phone's text message that had been pulled out of a *gragger*, that noisemaker one shakes on Purim.

While the sixth-graders' learning space featured an element of chaos, sophisticated learning was afoot. These students were spending several weeks exploring a few of eleven mystery containers that had been

---

1. A video providing an overview of learning in the sixth grade at this congregation may be accessed at: https://youtu.be/gEnbYQP1iys.

made available to them as part of the "All In!" curriculum.[2] Inside each container were eight to thirteen challenges—a code to break or puzzles to solve, each of which would lead these young explorers to a piece of Jewish content: a video, an article, a person to talk with, or a place to visit. Using the clues discovered along the way, their goal was to deduce the container's theme, which was a Jewish value anchored in a traditional Jewish text.

One may ask: What kind of sophisticated Jewish education includes tongue depressors spilled out of an apothecary jar? The group holding them discovered a coded message written on many of the fat sticks. Using a cipher wheel (also in the jar), they found this message: "Ask me why I became a health professional," along with the email address for a member of the congregation who is a doctor. Her spiritually moving email response would arrive next week. It would connect learners to their container's as-yet-undiscovered theme: our partnership with God in being concerned about and taking care of the sick—an interpretation of the prayer for healing found in the *siddur* (prayer book).

How about the children with the hand clappers? They were a bit surprised to find a hollowed-out section in a large yellow book they had pulled out of their container and its stash of fifteen small, noisy toys. Yes, the preteens felt compelled to shake the hand clappers for a number of seconds, which definitely brought on smiles. But the children quickly noticed that on one side of each clapper was a number and on the other side was a letter. After some trial and error, they put all the clappers in numerical order before flipping them over to reveal a URL leading to a website. Their container's as-yet-undiscovered theme? Being satisfied with what one has, based on the text from *Pirke Avot* 4:1, "Who is rich? One who is happy with what s/he has."

And the children who were walking around the building? Earlier they had found a "text message" from Mordecai to Queen Esther asking her to meet him at the front receptionist's desk. At the desk and at other locations that followed, this group found additional text messages that the students were assigned to imagine had flown between these two historical figures thousands of years ago. The theme of this group's container was a bit elusive, but over the coming weeks the students would discover that all items were based on the phrase spoken by Hillel more than 2,000

2. Jewish Education Center of Cleveland, *All In!*

years ago, "Do not separate yourself from the community" (*Pirke Avot* 2:4).

Partnerships and Process

A key responsibility in my position as the Director of Curriculum Resources for the Jewish Education Center of Cleveland (JECC)[3] is to partner with local Jewish educational programs in curricular change projects. These are intensive and site-driven, meaning that the focus and results are created to fit the specific needs and culture of the host institution.

My own involvement in the process of educational change at The Temple-Tifereth Israel (TTTI) began in 2012 when I became the JECC's partner to two experienced, thoughtful, and skilled educational leaders: Rabbi Stacy Schlein (the education director) and Gloria Grischkan (assistant director). Both have served in various capacities at this congregation for over a decade.

Just a couple of years prior to the TTTI-JECC partnership, a seventh through twelfth grade survey was conducted by Cleveland's congregational directors' network. One question, directed specifically to those teens who were no longer enrolled, simply asked why they were no longer participating. The answers were not surprising; transportation logistics were an issue for some, there were activity conflicts for others, and the predictable responses of "it was boring" or "it wasn't interesting" showed up as well. But there was something in the way the teens described their disinterest that made me and a number of congregational education directors look more critically at the content and format of pre-bar/bat mitzvah education in synagogues. Rabbi Schlein was particularly taken by this issue, so she, Gloria, and I started by considering the learning model for TTTI's grade four. We wrote, piloted, and then edited curriculum for the fourth-graders before doing the same for grades five and six. The planning happened in intense weekly leadership team meetings, after which the JECC brought the decisions to life by developing curricular documents and support materials.

---

3. The Jewish educational planning, service, and financial arm of the Jewish Federation of Cleveland.

The Containers in Context

TTTI is a large suburban congregation with a membership of 1,350 families. A 2016 remodel of the campus led to the creation of a learning center designed to place both students and teachers in new roles. The rooms are called "learning spaces" or "work spaces" rather than classrooms. The sixth-grade learning space features six-foot-long worktables spread throughout the room. One table is always reserved for materials accessed during the day by students, *madrichim* (teen assistants), and the teacher: multiple copies of a research/reflection form that students collaboratively fill out after each challenge, three iPad minis for shared use, headphones and "splitters" (octopus-like plugs that allow up to five students to listen simultaneously to a video on one of the devices), and a black composition book labeled "Nachama's Notebook," which is where students record any technical issues that crop up as they work through the explorations during this pilot year.

In spite of available worktables in this flexible workspace, students are often found head-to-head on the carpeted floor or outside of their dedicated learning space, always in the company of a *madrich/madrichah* or their teacher. Sometimes, children go around the corner to the art room when it's empty, or to the hallway outside their door to view a video. But there are also times when they leave the area completely, when the luck of the draw provides an exploration that takes them to another place in the building.

While the room layout and its set-up may be different from traditional classrooms, the eleven containers around the room are the unusual features in this learning environment. Some of these containers are made of corrugated cardboard, like the kind of boxes that once held ten reams of copy paper, a vacuum cleaner, or a family's possessions during a move. But other containers have more unusual shapes. There are, for example, an oversize flowerpot, an orange five-gallon bucket designed to look like an enlarged pill bottle, and a big picnic basket. These containers, described in more detail below, are key to the design of this learning model.

The "All In!" Learning Model

With attention to human-centered design,[4] TTTI's director of education spent several weeks at the start of the curriculum development process interviewing fifth- and sixth-graders.[5] While they didn't answer with these specific words, students indicated that they wanted to know about their role in the universe and about "the world that is" as compared to "the world that ought to be." They were interested in challenges, that is, in learning that had some depth and that focused on real issues. They were open to messy problems, ones that took time to solve. And they preferred active learning in which their teachers served as guides on the side rather than experts.

It was serendipitous that the student interviews took place at a time when some colleagues and I became curious about a currently popular form of entertainment in which players are locked in a room with a series of coded challenges that must be solved in order to escape in an hour's time.[6] Noting that some of these "escape rooms" are thematic in nature, the education directors of TTTI and I wondered whether this model of codes and challenges could capture the imagination of sixth-graders who had already told us that they enjoyed messy, challenging learning.

That said, we had no intention of locking sixth graders in rooms on Sunday mornings! An organization called BreakoutEDU[7] had already taken the escape room model and adapted it to general studies subjects with timed challenges that led students to unlock a box (rather than a room). Our planning team felt we could adapt the model even more, meshing it with our desire to build learning around a big idea[8] and a focus on Jewish texts.

Thus, we created eleven thematic containers, each with eight to thirteen coded challenges. In most cases, the medium was the message— the outside of the container gave a clue to a theme or Jewish value that focused all of the explorations inside. In addition, as much as possible, the individual challenges also fit the container's theme. For example, the tongue depressors placed inside the apothecary jar were familiar to children from their doctors' offices and offered a clue to the container's

---

4. See, for example, https://vimeo.com/106505300.

5. Moskowitz, "Listening to Our Tweens."

6. Chen, "Escape Rooms."

7. For information about this program, see: http://www.breakoutedu.com/about/.

8. Wiggens and McTighe, *Understanding by Design*, 65–70.

theme of sickness and health. The decision to call the curriculum "All In!" reflected the idea that *all* the learning was *in* the containers, that Jewish interdisciplinary content areas had been "all in" integrated (e.g., Bible, Talmud, world and American history, rituals, Israel, peoplehood, Hebrew, etc.), and that it took a group of "all in" students to solve the conundrums reflected by this model.[9]

The Teaching Team

During 2016–2017 (the pilot year of the program), the sixth-grade teaching team consisted of one teacher and three *madrichim*. The teacher, Dr. Ed Magiste, had taught this grade level at TTTI before. In his everyday life, Ed is a professor at a local university with professional foci on social work and education. He has great rapport with middle schoolers, and his interest in and experience with project-based learning made him a perfect match for this experimental learning model. The *madrichim* included two wonderful high school students (Caitie and Cory) and Rob, a talented and thoughtful eighth-grader.[10] All three teens related well to the sixth graders and rose to the challenge of supporting student explorations without giving away answers. Each work group had its own *madrich*, which freed Ed to oversee the learning process, sliding in to support individual groups and *madrichim* as needed, and sliding out again when not. During the pilot year I served as an additional educational resource to the students, occasionally moving out of my observer role and gently guiding informal student conversations.

For each learning block, the *madrichim* were provided with a curriculum guide that matched the container their students would be puzzling through. The guide was printed half brochure-style to fit perfectly in their hands, making it easy to manipulate in the heat of explorations. It included the container's quotation (hidden under an opaque notecard so students couldn't spy it out), an explanation of its meaning, a list of all the explorations in the container and how they related to the theme, details about each of the challenges (including answers to codes), as well

9. And yes, for Clevelanders, it was a nod to the Cleveland Cavaliers basketball team who had proudly declared that they and the city were "all in" the year that they won the NBA championship.

10. The name of the *madrich* and all students are pseudonyms. Actual names have been used for professional staff members.

as guiding questions that could help move students along a productive path of hypothesis formation.

Working with the Containers

In gathering details for this portrait, I decided to spend time during the third learning block with Rob's group of students (three girls and three boys). For this block, Ed and the *madrichim* took responsibility for choosing the container their students would work on, since in the previous blocks too much time had been spent on students debating the selection; teacher intervention was needed to move things along. Because there were some dominating personalities in Rob's group, the teaching team agreed that it would be beneficial to have these particular students work with the container whose anchoring Jewish quote was "Do not separate yourself from the community." When it came time for the *madrichim* to choose, Rob deliberately pointed to the large cardboard box that was ringed with silhouettes of people holding hands.

Session One: First Steps Towards the Theme

Clue 1.

As this session began, the children looked through the container's contents and quickly agreed to select a rectangular box in which they found both a T-shirt and a large mirror. A student named Ruth immediately indicated that she knew the significance of the shirt and started chanting the name that was printed on its front, "Camp Wise, Camp Wise!" (a camp operated by Cleveland's Jewish community center that she had attended for many summers). Indeed, as with other "All In!" container items, this one had been chosen because students could make a personal connection with it. While Ruth was the only one in the group who had attended Camp Wise, everyone else was aware of its popularity among families in the Cleveland Jewish community.

When the children examined the shirt and discovered a code in printed mirror writing inside the neckline, they quickly deciphered it and copied what they had determined to be a URL. A boy named Ryan grabbed one of the iPad minis on the supply table and typed the letters and numbers as others in the group read them aloud. It took a few tries to input the correct URL because the students didn't realize at first that upper and lower case letters needed to be consistent. At the point of frustration, Rob, in his role as *madrich*, used his hands-on curriculum guide to verify the correct code, thus moving the students along.

The URL led to a video featuring the Camp's education director who had been asked to record a camp story that illustrated the idea of "Don't separate yourself from the community." Without explicitly stating the container's theme, but offering plenty of clues, the video told the story of a child at the camp who wasn't happy about going rafting with the rest of his unit. The child had balked, but with the coaxing of staff and campers, he agreed to get into a raft with others and, predictably, had a blast.

After watching this story, the students spent a few minutes filling out their research/reflection forms. Most speculated that "peer pressure" might be the overall theme because staff and other campers had encouraged the boy to go rafting. As Ryan said, "He didn't want to do it, but then he did it because of peer pressure."

At this point, Rob ruminated aloud to his group, saying that he thought peer pressure was a bad thing, i.e., not a positive trait. However, a number of the children responded by saying this kind of pressure could be good.

Clue 2.

With about half the period remaining, the children tackled a second exploration: opening a thin, narrow cardboard box in which they found a toy rowboat with dots and dashes painted on its hull. Ryan quickly identified the dots and dashes as Morse code, and students with smartphones tried to figure out the message's meaning. While three of the five struggled with who would tackle the code ("Me, I'll do it," "No, wait, I can find it"), Ryan quietly entered the dots and dashes into a search engine on the iPad. Another student, Zach, pulled himself out of the group's efforts, wondering aloud why the figures on the outside of their container depicted people holding hands and then ventured, "Because they're friends." One of the girls turned to the box and touched the picture, but soon the moment passed. The box's picture was ignored, and the group turned back to their decoding conundrum.

As with many of the codes they encountered in their containers, students searched the internet to learn the meaning of the dots and dashes. They discovered the words "*Vayikra Rabba* 4:6," the citation for a specific midrash (a rabbinic story) about people together in a boat. Now, more settled than they were a few moments earlier at the height of decoding, the students passed the iPad with the story between themselves, each reading a few sentences. This pattern of high energy and excitement around the decoding process followed by a more serious focus on the content repeated itself in this group each time they engaged a new clue in a container.

The *madrich* invited conversation about the midrash:

> Rob: It's a short story, but what happens?
>
> Ryan: Two guys . . .
>
> Ruth (interrupting): Two guys are in a boat.
>
> Ryan (while a lot of side conversations erupt around him): I think it (the theme) is about friendship because they are a group of people. We don't know they are friends, but we can infer that they are because they seem to be people who know each other . . . .
>
> Rob: Yeah, but how come the man is drilling a hole in the boat?
>
> Nathan: Because he's insane!
>
> Ryan: He feels it's his own place so he can drill under it.
>
> Rob (with an effort to focus the conversation on some ideas related to the container's theme): Is this compassionate? Selfish?
>
> Ruth and Ryan: Kinda selfish.

Using some of the questions offered in the curriculum guide, Rob then asked, "How do you think the other passengers felt about this? How did they react to his drilling?" Ryan responded in part, " . . . he thought it was just about him."

At this point, Ed, the teacher came into hearing range of this group. He asked them about their current exploration and what they had discovered. When one student started to read the story from the iPad, Ed asked that they tell the story in their own words. Rena picked up the research reflection sheet and read what Ruth had been quietly recording all this time, "Some people were in a boat and one said he would drill a hole and then the others said they would drown. One guy is selfish and the passengers were concerned."

Ed said, "So I'm sitting in a boat, we're all sitting in the boat and I decide to drill a hole in the boat. It's my part of the boat. I could do what I want, right?" When Ruth disagreed, Ed retorted, "But it's my part of the boat."

Ed compared this story to the continued issue of noise level in the room. He said, "So here's an example—there are a bunch of groups in the room and the noise is getting louder. Should they be allowed to get louder if they're having fun?" Ed then turned to the entire class and declared a "noise level check." With all eyes on him, he shared the story of the boat and made a clear connection between the man's lack of concern in drilling the hole in the boat, and the groups' lack of concern about their contribution to the noise level in the room. He concluded, "When you get too loud—when you drill that hole under your seat—you affect the rest of us."

When Rob was again alone with his group, he picked up on Ed's theme and said, "Think about it this way. He's technically drilling the hole under his chair. In a way it's his chair, he's sitting on it. So why do you think his actions are affecting everyone else?" Ryan finally stated the as-yet-undeclared point of the story, "But it's not his boat and he's going to make them drown!"

Clue 3.

After completing their research/reflection form, with about fifteen minutes until the end of the period, Rob's group had the opportunity to begin one more exploration. They zeroed in on a paper plate that had been folded to mimic a Purim *gragger* (noisemaker), the kind children often make in preschool with beans stuffed inside a folded paper plate that is then stapled shut. This *gragger*, however, had a small sheet of paper poking out. On it was an image of a text message—the first of four such messages that the students would discover around the building during the course of this exploration. Ryan and Ruth took turns reading the content of this clue to their group:

Rena picked up the sheet, looked closely at the message and said, "Guys, do you realize it says Queen Esther at the top?" Ruth then pointed out that the other respondent had to be Mordecai. When Rob asked which holiday this particular exploration connected to, the students knew it was Purim. Ryan identified the paper plate as a *gragger*; he and one of the others then reminisced about making *graggers* in preschool and again later as older students. The period then ended and students understood they would have to start with this exploration the following Sunday.

Session Two: Becoming Fixed on a Narrow
Interpretation of the Theme

Clue 3 (continued).

Three of the five students working with Rob the first week were in attendance on the second day of exploration: Rena, Ruth, and Zach. When Rob asked what they remembered from the previous session, their responses were snippets of memories. Zach immediately brought up the Camp Wise story, which he identified simply as "peer pressure." In a quick blur of conversation, Rob reminded them of the Camp Wise video, Rena talked about the T-shirt as well as the mirror needed to decode the URL, and then Zach noted, "Yeah, they told him to do it and he didn't." Zach also retold the story of the man and rowboat in succinct kid-like terms: "We did the boat one where he was drilling the hole and he was like, 'I feel like drilling a hole,' and they're like 'no' and the other guy's like 'yeah.'"

Zach was really "on" this week, with questions and comments that flowed in and out of the various explorations. After the group reread the message poking out of the paper plate *gragger*, Zach asked, "Why did they want to kill the Jews?" Later, while walking with the group to find the second clue of the Purim exploration, Zach offered an answer to his own question in a voice mimicking hatred, "We should kill the cool kids so we can be the new cool kids." Subsequently, after the group read the second set of text messages between Mordecai and Esther and brainstormed what they recalled about the Purim story, he expanded on his response:

> Zach: Haman is the bad guy and he tried to kill everyone.
>
> Rob (sharpening Zach's answer): He was trying to kill the Jews. Do you remember why he wanted to kill the Jews?
>
> Zach: Because he didn't like them.
>
> Nachama: Why?
>
> Zach: I dunno, because he was jealous?

Rob then offered a quick and precise summary of the story in which Mordecai refused to bow down to Haman. The students had a short conversation, putting this piece about Mordecai in context with his text message conversation with Esther. Using the clues on the next two text messages, they tracked down other texts with more information.

In the final set of messages between Mordecai and Esther that was awaiting students in the library, Esther referred to specific chapters/verses in "her book." Students were given a Bible and asked to locate and read them. It quickly became apparent that these sixth-graders had little idea of how to find information in an actual Bible. One of Ruth's first comments reflected no past experience holding a Bible (she said that the paper was so thin for such a big book), and then Rena wondered aloud if they should be looking at the book of Genesis. I entered into their conversation:

> Nachama: Does [the text message from Esther] tell you what book it is in?
>
> Rena: Nope. It just says "In the Bible, find my book and then read."
>
> Nachama (taking a naive stance): "Hmm, so who is the person who just spoke, "Find my book"? Who is speaking?
>
> Rena: Esther.
>
> Nachama (asking again a bit naively): Is the book of Esther there [i.e., in the Bible] somewhere? Is there a table of contents?

Zach had been sitting to the side, so I asked if he could help the two girls. Ruth by now had found a table of contents, so when Zach looked over her shoulder he quickly scanned the pages and said, "I remember Joshua, he's cool. Or Jonah. We should read the book of Jonah. He was swallowed by a whale."

It took Ruth, Rena, and Zach a bit of time to locate the section that the text message had suggested they read, but they persisted and finally found the passage in which Mordecai said that perhaps Esther was placed in the palace specifically to help save the Jews. The more Rena looked at the Bible, the more engaged she seemed to become. At one point, she mused aloud that while she previously knew all the Purim characters, she didn't know *about* the characters.

As the session drew to a close, Rob asked the group how their hunt about Esther related to the other explorations for this container. Rena (again) mentioned friendship and Zach retold the story of the man drilling a hole in the bottom of the boat. Rob then put Mordecai and Esther's text messages back in context:

> Rob: Yeah, Esther was completely safe because she was in the palace and nobody knew she was Jewish. If she wanted to, she could have just stayed silent and she would have been fine . . . So why do you think it was such a big deal for her to risk her life to save the Jews?

Zach: Well, she wouldn't want Mordecai and innocent people to die.

Rob: So how do you think Esther protecting all the people connects with what we're doing so far?

Rena: She's kinda being a friend and helping someone else.

Rob: Okay that's a good thought. So how do you think this connects to the boat thing? If this was the boat, who would be drilling the hole?

Zach: Haman.

Rob: And what does the boat represent in this scenario?

Zach: The Jews.

Rob: Okay, so what was Esther's role?

Zach: She was like the other people in the boat, telling him not to.

Rob: That's a good thought.

Nachama (trying to offer some language that could help the students discover the container's theme of "don't separate yourself from the community"): She kinda stayed connected to the other people.

Ruth: I think it's kinda like we're one big family.

Rob: That's cool. And the family has to take care of each other. So Esther was taking care of her family in a way.

Ruth: So maybe it's like the Jews are taking care of their family in a way.

After this the conversation, the students returned to their workspace to fill out their research/reflection forms. They had a good laugh together when their response to the text messages led them to joke that many, many years ago Esther and Mordecai texted each other (Zach hypothesized that they had Snapchat, too). But when Rob asked one more time what they learned from the text messages, the idea of Jews staying connected to and taking care of each other escaped some students. Rena responded, "I still think it's about friendship or helping others."

Clue 4.

On this second day of the learning block, the students had time for one more exploration. They chose an item that Ruth had been hoping to explore: a small metal bucket with a rope tied to the handle. Spaced down the rope were segments of a midrash, a rabbinic story.

Rabbi Hanina said:

Torah is like a deep well full of water whose waters were cold and sweet and delicious, but no one was able to drink from it.

Then a certain person came along, and supplied the well with one cord tied to another, one rope tied to another, and drew water out of the well, and drank from it.

Then everyone began to draw water and drink it.

(*Shir Hashirim Rabbah* 1.1:8)

The students unrolled the rope and copied down the words in a notebook they had been given. When Ed came over to check on them, they read the text from their notebook and then discussed the significance of the story. Ed asked, "Is it actually about *getting* water from the well, or *how* you get water from a well?"

> Ruth: It's like getting learning. Torah was like a deep well and no one could get to it.
> Zach: Then a guy taught everyone how to read Torah.
> Ed: Are you saying that everyone is a length of rope?
> Zach: Yeah.

Session Three: Catching the Theme and Losing it Again

Rob started the session by reviewing earlier learning and conclusions. The group then turned to completing their reflection sheet for the rope and well story. Rena hit the theme on the head when she offered that they learned, "The Jewish people is like one big family. If someone has trouble, then you have to help the other person and you have to help until the trouble is solved."

Nonetheless, as happened many times throughout the unit, Rena's on-target stating of the container's theme was quickly forgotten just moments later. Ruth spoke aloud while she wrote the response to what she thought they learned: "You're drawing information from the Torah like you would draw water out of the well." Once again, the students had lost the core idea. I spoke up, noting that Rena had just said something different. Like deer in the headlights, Ruth said "What?" and then Rena said "What?" Rena seemed to have no idea what she had said.

> Rena: Oh, everyone is like a family, is that what I said?
> Nachama (trying to return her to the idea of community responsibility): Yeah, like working together or something like that.
> Rena: So like everyone works together.

At this point, the group slid into a side conversation about how this container seemed to be harder than their first ones. Zach had gotten completely off task; distracted by some friends in another group, he asked if they liked his hat. Ruth, continued to work on the reflection sheet and finally asked everyone, "What's the box's focus?"

> Zach: To help people, especially Jews.
> Rena: That everyone is a family and should work together.
> Zach: We're ALL one family.

All were close, but then Rena connected her own dots and said, "Which kinda relates to friendship."

Clue 5.

With this as the last full day for the students to explore the container, I suggested that they choose the black lockbox since I suspected it was concrete enough to help them identify the theme. On the bottom of the locked box were two sheets of paper. While both had different photos of hands holding hands, one was a coded message and one was its solution key (e.g., a specific photo of two children holding hands corresponded to the letter H). This challenge had multiple steps. Students used the code's key to match English letters to the different photos of hands to read two English words, "Hillel says." They then used Google Translate to shift the phrase to Hebrew. Finally using gematria (the matching of Hebrew letters to specific numbers), the students discovered the three-digit code that opened the lockbox. And what was inside? A coffee mug from the Jewish Federation of Cleveland.

A number of times during the decoding process, Rena kept hypothesizing that the container's theme could be about friendship, once in relation to the hands-holding-hands picture code ("I think that the hands together have something to do with friendship") and again a few minutes later, "Guys, the theme of our box could be friendship." But she more accurately identified the theme when Ruth read aloud the words on the side of the mug: "Stronger with each *mitzvah* that helps a neighbor or stranger around the corner or across the globe. We are one community . . ." [Rena gasped at this point.] " . . . one world and we can make our world better by working together." It needs to be noted that the first and last words were both in caps, easily being read as "STRONGER TOGETHER."

Rena: I know, I know.

Rob: So what do you think?

Rena: It's about friendship and working together.

Ruth: Everyone's a family. Friendship.

Nachama: It didn't say family.

Rob: It didn't say family or friendship.

Rena read the mug aloud, again, and Rob asked the students what the mug had to do with everything. The group of three reviewed all their written reflection sheets to date. They found on the rope/bucket sheet their earlier words, "being Jewish is like being in a family, you have to help people and work to solve problems."

In spite of this conclusion related to working together, Rena had a very hard time shaking her impression that the container had to do with friendship. When reviewing the Camp Wise story of the boy who didn't want to go rafting she said, "He didn't want to go and his counselor and camper-friends thought it would be fun. They didn't make him do it but they wanted him to do it. So I feel that's kinda like friendship."

Nachama: How does that idea fit with the mug?

Zach (reading from the mug): Each *mitzvah* helps a neighbor.

Rena: Kinda like a community helper.

After some further discussion about the mug and the man who drilled the hole in the boat, Rena seemed to grasp a broader understanding of the theme: "The guy was selfish, so that's not working together!"

At that moment, Rabbi Schlein, the congregation's Director of Learning, walked into the room. Rob encouraged the group to tell her about the container's theme. At first Rena and Zach both said "friendship," but then Rena corrected herself and said, "Oh, everyone's like a family." This container's theme, a bit more complex than some of the more straightforward texts, had slipped out of her grasp again. So, Rabbi Schlein lifted up the item that matched each clue and asked the students to share what they learned from it. After they told her each story, she put the object in the center of the table, asking, "So what do these two [and then these three, and then these four] have to do with each other?" Slowly, just as Rob had done earlier, she took them through the meanings behind the explorations and connected their discoveries to one another. Students were showing understanding, but still appeared to have a hard time grasping the nuance of the text's use of the negative phrasing ("Don't separate yourself from the community").

As the session drew to a close, to keep things from bogging down, Rob "revealed" the text to the students and asked them to quickly share how "not separating yourself from the community" might apply to their own lives, something that he would return to in the fourth and final session.

Session Four: Integrating and Sharing the Theme

Clue 6.

On this, the final day for the container, Rena, Ruth, and Ryan were in attendance. Rob chose the final clue for his group, a game loosely constructed on the popular children's game, "Hot Potato." In the container's version of the game, students sat in a circle and passed around an envelope filled with slips of paper. When signaled to stop, the person left holding the envelope took one slip from inside and followed its directions on the next turn. Examples were: "Play normally," "Put your head down and refuse to play," "When the envelope comes to you refuse to touch it and say, 'I'm not playing.'"

After playing a few rounds, Rob asked, "So how does the game deal with our theme? You guys remember our theme, yeah?"

> Rena: Working together.
> Rob: Yeah, the theme was working together, so how does that, like . . . ?
> Rena: It's like the opposite.
> Ruth: Oh, I know. It's like if you're on a sports team you have to want to play because if the ball comes to you, you can't just be, "I'm not gonna play," you have to pass it down.

The group thoroughly enjoyed the game and decided that it would be great to play with the rest of the class when it came time for them to share at the end of the day.

Rob then asked students to read through the conclusions written on each of the research/reflection sheets. The old thematic hypotheses reappeared, but thankfully Ryan shared the page that read, "Don't separate yourself from the community." The dialogue that followed contains only the salient student responses, with Rob creating threads back to the container's organizing Jewish text:

> Rob: So after reading all these things, what is the connection between the activities?
>
> Ruth: We all have to work in a group, it's teamwork, it's friendship . . .
>
> Rob: Do you remember what it said on the mug?
>
> Rena: It was "stronger together."
>
> Rob: Yep. What about the boat?
>
> Ruth: It was the opposite because the guy was being selfish.
>
> Rob (finally catching the need to bring the actual text into the conversation): He was separating himself from the community because he was drilling a hole in the boat.

Rob continued this conversation by asking the students about the other clues, each time reinforcing the theme and its message. As the session neared finishing time, he presented each of the students with a final souvenir of their work on this container, a key chain. One side had the Jewish text, "Hillel said, Don't separate yourself from the community" and the other side had a drawing that, when scanned with an augmented reality app, animated into a short example/explanation of their quote. The students took time to read the exact quote aloud and a few of them animated their picture using an iPad or smartphone. As they played with the key chains, Rob asked the students for examples that showed how the theme connected to their lives. Rena and Ruth applied the idea to team activities:

> Ruth: In school we have team tests. You have to work on math problems together and the teacher grades different questions from each paper. We have to make sure that everyone has an answer that we all understand.
>
> Rob: So say this was a team test right now and we were working on a problem, but I decide to sit by myself and not saying anything to you guys. How would that affect our grades?
>
> Ruth: That would make it so other people fail because they didn't know what was going on.
>
> Rena: Just like in a sport like soccer you can't necessarily control what other people do, but you control what you do.
>
> Ruth: I play volleyball and you have to say "mine" so teammates know you're going to hit it.

The conversation then shifted to how the theme might apply to their dynamics with schoolmates:

Ruth: Maybe if you're in school and you see someone is having trouble, maybe you can help them. If someone is getting bullied, you can tell an adult. Let's say there's a new student, you could go sit with them.

Rob: Have you ever seen someone separate themselves from the community? Like the rowboat example, any real world examples of that?

Ruth: So one time when I was in my team test and I saw one kid try and do it by himself in another group.

Rob: How did you feel about that?

Ruth: Angry. He's not enjoying the class and he's sometimes rude.

Ryan: Yeah, if someone's having a bad day at school they might go sit by themselves at lunch.

Rob: How can you improve that? How do you think you can help get him get himself back into the community?

Ryan: Go sit over by them and say hey, here are some of your friends
. . .

In the final part of this last day, the students taught the hot potato game to the others in their class. Each clearly explained their box's theme and one gracefully summarized the Jewish angle:

Ruth: So we had one activity that had to do with (Queen) Esther and so it kinda relates back to when they were going to kill all the Jews. Nobody knew she was Jewish so she could have just separated herself and say that she didn't have to help with the situation. But Esther decided to speak up and say something so that nobody else would get hurt. She didn't separate herself. If she had separated herself then there may have been a different outcome and maybe we wouldn't even be here today.

Thinking about the "All In!" Learning

While at times messy and chaotic, "All In!" offers middle school students Jewish learning embedded in hands-on challenges that take time to solve. It is active learning that introduces students to compelling and engaging stories and dilemmas of Jewish life. While exploring the "Do not separate yourself from the community" container, students were involved in rich conversations that exposed them to elements of Jewish life with which they had previous experience (like key ideas in the Purim story) and others they did not (like the midrash of the hole drilled in the bottom of the boat). They learned stories in which they could imagine themselves or their friends as central characters (like the one of the boy from camp) and others that provided insights into Jewish and general life (like the rope, the well, and the water bucket). Jewish learning became relevant and meaningful, pushing to depth-of-learning, as compared to merely breadth.

As with all curriculum created by the Jewish Education Center of Cleveland, "All In!" uses the Understanding by Design (UbD) curricular model[11] in which all learning is focused around an Enduring Understanding (EU), a big idea or a conceptual proposition. In normative UbD units, the EU is known up front—a teacher posts it in the room, introduces and discusses its meaning early and often, and offers learning activities that enable students to gain a nuanced understanding of the big idea that organizes all else.

However, in the case of "All In!" the UbD learning process is turned on its head. Each container's EU is a Jewish quotation—from the Torah, Talmud, midrash, or even a key text from modern Jewish life (as with Theodor Herzl's Israel-focused statement, "If you will it, it is no dream"). But unlike the normative UbD learning model, "All In!" students are not told the EU in advance—it is their challenge to deduce the big idea by exploring items that introduce them to a variety of interesting and engaging aspects of Jewish history, philosophy, current events, people, and texts.

In the pilot year of "All In!" this group displayed characteristics of intellectual development appropriate to middle school students.[12] As might be expected, some students stretched easily to engage in abstract and complex thinking (Zach), while others were still anchored in concrete thinking (Ruth). However, even the most sophisticated of these sixth-grade learners needed time to analyze and synthesize multiple images and stories that provided examples of a Jewish text's meaning. As these students navigated their understanding of ideas behind one Jewish quotation (e.g., "don't separate yourself from the community"), they repeated a discernible behavioral pattern—with various students "getting it" one minute, losing the central thread a few moments later, and then regaining it again. This dynamic was observed multiple times, not only with this group but (according to the teacher and other *madrichim*) with the other groups as well. The universality of this behavioral pattern, even in the time span of one class period, surprised both the teaching staff and

11. Wiggens and McTighe, *Understanding by Design.*

12. Caskey and Anfara, "Developmental Characteristics of Young Adolescents," third section.

me. I offer three speculations about why this pattern may have been part of the "All In!" students' learning experience:

1. *Overt and consistent student participation.* In a more traditional classroom,[13] where the teacher initiates and leads discussion with the entire class, the "getting it-losing it" dynamic would have been masked by the active participation of a handful of students while the others sat quietly. However, in the small group experience of "All In!" all the students had multiple opportunities to contribute verbally to the discussions, which exposed their faulty thinking and connections more clearly.

2. *Random sequencing of concepts.* In more structured learning settings, new ideas are presented sequentially,[14] often to intentionally move students from concrete to abstract thinking over time. Although the "All In!" containers explored earlier in the year had been organized around relatively concrete EUs, this container introduced an especially challenging and complex theme—one made even more difficult because it was worded in the negative ("don't separate yourself"). In addition, because "All In!" clues are typically chosen in random order by the students, sometimes more abstract ones are picked before those that are easier to solve. In this instance, some of the initial clues required far more sophisticated interpretation capabilities than those chosen later, which may have led to the students' inconsistent—perhaps impulsive—responses. Consider, for example, how they responded to the more abstract camp rafting example as compared with how they reacted later on to the Federation mug with its "Stronger Together" label.

3. *Constructivist learning, but with support.* As with other constructivist models,[15] "All In!" puts meaning-making in the hands of the students. Recognizing that sixth-graders need scaffolding from teachers to help them synthesize complex concepts,[16] Rob (the *madrich*), Ed (the teacher), and I worked hard to provide prompts that would help the students grasp the theme more easily and consistently. Indeed, as one would expect in a constructivist learning

13. Groshell, "Why Teach Like This?"
14. Morrison et al, *Designing Effective Instruction,* 137–42.
15. Brooks and Brooks, *In Search of Understanding,* 15–22.
16. Scales, "Characteristics of Young Adolescents," 62–63.

environment, the "All In!" students produced original ideas (e.g., that the team aspects of volleyball was an example of not separating oneself from the community) and raised insightful questions (e.g., why would Haman have wanted to kill the Jews?). Nonetheless, in exploring the clues, they were not fully on their own. There *was* a targeted answer they were being asked to deduce and specific Jewish concepts they were encouraged to articulate, even embrace (e.g., that Jews need to be attentive to the community, that it's not just about us as individuals). In the end, the open-ended, exploratory features of "All In!" genuinely engaged and empowered these students, but when asked to apply their thinking to big ideas they still needed considerable guidance and support from their teachers.

Further Reflections About Jewish Learning

For decades, with their behavior, spotty attendance, and voices ("I'm bored"), students have complained about Jewish educational experiences that are not meaningful or sufficiently engaging. In the past, many Jewish educators have metaphorically patted these children on the head and indicated that their perception was faulty ("Look at all the cool games you played today!"). But, in my year-long observation of the "All In!" pilot year, and especially through consistently documenting the students' experience with the "Don't separate yourself from the community" container, I came to a new understanding of the dynamics of Jewish learning and of the potential of well-trained educators to help students find excitement and relevance from Jewish life. Although not every community can mount the kinds of initiatives that have been developed by collaborating Jewish institutions in Cleveland, I am gratified by the commitment of the JECC to sharing its "All In!" curriculum via free download[17] so that our experimental approaches can be adopted or adapted by educational institutions across the Jewish world.

17. Educational programs that wish to introduce "All In!" to their students will find the curriculum guide available for free and immediate download from the JECC Marketplace: http://www.jeccmarketplace.com/all-in/. Included are shopping lists and ordering information for each container's materials, instructions for assembly, and supports for student learning. A video showing this curriculum in action is available at: https://youtu.be/gEnbYQP1iys.

That said, I want to call attention to several take-aways from my inquiry—points that I encourage educational programs to consider as they grapple with how to improve students' Jewish learning experiences:

- In many congregations or other part-time programs, a teacher is generally responsible for a class or two, with the support of one or more *madrichim*. Yet, in many cases, the *madrichim* are underutilized: handing out supplies or trouble-shooting technology, then sitting to the side with no clear direction. In contrast, Ed's three *madrichim* were integral to the "All In!" students' learning and success. I view the "All In!" portrait as an outstanding example of highly and meaningfully engaged *madrichim*, a model that could be emulated by other programs that utilize teens.

- While Ed and his three *madrichim* were charged with primary responsibility for their students' education, the children consistently interacted with additional learning resources. They consulted with a congregant (the doctor) who offered a personal story, met with a Jewish camp education director, discovered and debated Jewish texts, grappled with the slogan on a Federation coffee mug, and spoke with the congregational education director when she dropped in intermittently to see how the program was progressing. The students also had reason to walk around the synagogue to locate information and interact with others, including the congregation's librarian and receptionist. Watching these sixth-graders explore, I was reminded that lifelong learners do not confine their Jewish education to "Sunday mornings, 9:30–12:00." In this sense, "All In!" affirmed the importance of breaking down the walls of traditional, formulaic part-time synagogue classes, so that students can benefit from learning resources beyond just one teacher and a single classroom environment.

- Many teachers assume that their students are learning when they appear to be engaged in an activity or when one student gives a correct answer to a question posed to the entire class. However, throughout the "All In!" sessions, the iterative checking-in process opened my eyes to the need for a more concerted effort by teachers (even in part-time settings) to probe and shape student thinking as it develops.

- Finally, this experience reinforced for me that we cannot assume that teachers are the sole source of Jewish learning for our students. Nor can we assume that students don't bring their learning forward from year to year. As seen in this portrait, learners don't leave at the door their experiences from Jewish summer camp, holidays, and earlier learning in our programs. Our learners are *integrators*, with the potential to make connections between their past and present learning and experiences. My time with this group of students helped me see that we should more consistently encourage and deliberately applaud how learners in Jewish educational programs connect the dots.

Bibliography

Brooks, Jacqueline, and Martin Brooks. In *Search of Understanding: The Case for Constructivist Classrooms*. New York: Pearson, 2001.

Caskey, Micki, and Vincent A. Anfara, Jr. "Developmental Characteristics of Young Adolescents: Research Summary." https://www.amle.org/BrowsebyTopic/WhatsNew/WNDet/TabId/270/ArtMID/888/ArticleID/455/Developmental-Characteristics-of-Young-Adolescents.aspx.

Chen, Evelyn. "Real-life 'escape rooms' are new US gaming trend." http://www.cnbc.com/2014/06/21/real-life-escape-rooms-are-new-us-gaming-trend.html

Groshell, Zach. "Why Teach Like This? When Learning is This?" https://educationrickshaw.com/2017/12/02/after-100-years-of-the-same-teaching-model-its-time-to-throw-out-the-playbook/.

Jewish Education Center of Cleveland. *All In!* http://www.jeccmarketplace.com/all-in/.

Morrison, Gary R., et al. *Designing Effective Instruction*. Hoboken, NJ: John Wiley & Sons, 2012.

Moskowitz, Nachama Skolnik. "Listening to Our Tweens." http://ejewishphilanthropy.com/listening-to-our-tweens/.

Scales, P.C. "Characteristics of Young Adolescents." In *This We Believe: Keys to Educating Young Adolescents* by National Middle School Association, 62–63. Westerville, OH: National Middle School Association, 2010.

Wiggens, Grant, and Jay McTighe. *Understanding by Design*. Alexandria, VA: ASCD, 2005.

4

A PORTRAIT OF THREE PARTNERS

Orit Kent and Allison Cook[1]

Dear Seventh Grader,
As a member of the seventh grade of Temple Emet[2] you are being
invited to participate in an exciting research project as a part of
your regular Hebrew School experience on Wednesday nights. Orit
Kent and Allison Cook, teachers and researchers from Brandeis
University, will be creating with you a "beit midrash" or "house
of study" in which we will learn together particular ideas and
skills of studying Torah with one another. In order to learn more
about how teachers teach and students learn, we will be video and
audio taping these classes as well as collecting photographs and
in-class artifacts—such as writing or art projects. This beit mi-
drash project will last for eight weeks. After the eight weeks, each
participant will be interviewed. Each participant will also receive
a certificate from Brandeis University, Mandel Center for Studies
in Jewish Education, to honor your helping in this effort to better
understand teaching and learning in Jewish education.

1. Thank you to Susan Fendrick and Meir Lakein for reading and commenting on earlier drafts of this paper and to participants in the Mandel Center lunch seminar series for their comments on our presentation of many of these ideas. Thank you also to the many teachers who have engaged with these ideas in our workshops and helped us think about them more deeply. This project was supported by the Jack, Joseph and Morton Mandel Center for Studies in Jewish Education, Brandeis University, to which we are grateful.

2. This is a pseudonym.

THE FOLLOWING PORTRAIT EMERGES from the work of a cohort of seventh-graders who readily signed on to participate in creating this experimental *beit midrash* (house of study) with us. On eight Wednesday evenings from 6:00–7:30 p.m., students finished up their communal dinner and schmoozing time in the synagogue social hall to join us for what we hoped would be a different kind of Hebrew school learning experience. Synagogue educators in this suburban congregational school were eager to experiment with strengthening their students' skills for closely reading Jewish texts and they, along with the seventh-graders' parents, were pleased to entrust us with the winter term of the seventh-grade course of study which we would set up as an action research[3] project. Our research aim was to test out and document how and to what effect students could be inducted into a particular "havruta partnership" model of Jewish text study in which students learn to regard and draw upon both one another and the text they are studying as full partners in learning.[4] [5]

Havruta learning is a form of Jewish learning in which two students sit together as partners to study a sacred text, independent from the direct mediation of a teacher. Havruta learning in many permutations has found its way into a variety of Jewish (and even some non-Jewish) educational contexts as a go-to classroom or program structure that educators may incorporate into their course of instruction for many different reasons. Generally speaking, however, few students have any direct instruction or opportunities for *learning how to learn* in havruta. As a result, the great potential that havruta learning could afford students—including ethical and spiritual growth, in addition to intellectual and social learning—is often left unrealized. For this action research project, we crafted

3. See Zeichner and Noffke, "Practitioner Research," 298–330, and Carr and Kemmis, *Becoming Critical*.

4. This chapter is based on an earlier publication. See Kent and Cook, "Leveraging Resources for Learning through the Power of Partnership," 1–31.

5. The "Seventh Grade Beit Midrash" action research project is one of a suite of research efforts that make up the "Beit Midrash Research Project" at the Jack, Joseph and Morton Mandel Center for Studies in Jewish Education at Brandeis University. To learn more about the Beit Midrash Research Project, see: http://www.brandeis.edu/mandel/projects/beitmidrashresearch/index.html.

To learn more about Pedagogy of Partnership, the professional development initiative that has grown out of this body of research, see: https://www.hadar.org/pedagogy-partnership.

a curriculum in which learning how to learn in havruta constituted the explicit architecture for the students' course of study.[6]

We based the curriculum and pedagogy of the Seventh Grade Beit Midrash on the partnership frameworks developed through previous research: (a) the framework of the "three partners of havruta"[7] also called "the havruta learning triangle;"[8] (b) a model of six paired havruta learning practices,[9] and (c) the framework of "havruta-inspired pedagogy," which includes a particular teaching and learning *stance* (attitudes and beliefs), a set of learning *practices* (skills), and learning *structures*.[10]

The foundational partnership framework, "three partners of havruta," is captured in the following diagram, which we introduced and explored directly with our seventh-grade students:

The Three Partners of Havruta[11]

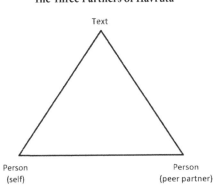

In this framing, havruta partnership is not a partnership merely between two people, but a partnership of three among two people and the text. In our conceptual and pedagogical work, we use the language of "partnership" to underscore the idea that each person *and* the text are all subjects in their own right, and they must be *in relationship*. Students must treat each other and the text as subjects, each with its own integrity.

---

6. This explanation of havruta learning in the context of this particular project first appeared in Cook and Kent, "Learning Torah Through Partnership," 1.

7. Kent, "Interactive Text Study and the Co-Construction of Meaning," 10.

8. Holzer with Kent, *Philosophy of Havruta*, 52–54.

9. Kent, "Interactive Text Study and the Co-Construction of Meaning," 213–20; Kent, "A Theory of Havruta Learning," 215–43.

10. Kent and Cook, "Havruta Inspired Pedagogy," 230–31.

11. Kent, "Interactive Text Study and the Co-Construction of Meaning," 10; Holzer with Kent, *A Philosophy of Havruta,* 55.

This means that each partner, including the text,[12] is a living resource[13] that has something worthwhile to offer to the learning relationship, and that this contribution can come to light when listened to closely. Further, the idea of partnership implies that there is a mutual *responsibility* to try *to understand the other* instead of merely treating the text and one's peers as objects to be used in pursuit of one's own goals or, as one seventh-grader later reflected about typical group learning experiences, "just to get work done." In order to actualize this partnership ideal among people and texts, students must work on both the skills and attitudes that enable them to build and take responsibility for the relationships among self, other, and text.[14]

The havruta learning structure of pairing two people with a text maximizes this approach by providing the most concentrated and accountable grouping through which students can practice particular partnership skills and attitudes most intensively. When there is only you,

12. Holzer, "What Connects 'Good' Teaching," 191; Kent, "Interactive Text Study and the Co-Construction of Meaning," 229.

13. For an earlier discussion of partners as resources, see Kent, "Interactive Text Study and the Co-Construction of Meaning," 77–124.

14. Our previous research as well as the current study is grounded in scholarship that tends to each relationship—the reader to text and person-to-person relationships—depicted in the "the three partners of havruta" framework respectively. For scholarship on the *reader-text relationship* that understands the reader to be an active agent in constructing meaning in interaction with the text and that readers must be given an opportunity to engage with the text and supported in developing the skills necessary for constructing meaning through that interaction, see Langer, *Envisioning Literature* and "The Process of Understanding;" Scholes, *Textual Power*; Iser, *The Act of Reading*; and Rosenblatt, *The Reader*. See also Haroutunian-Gordon, *Interpretive Discussions* and *Learning to Teach* for an example of an approach to teaching that works on these reader-text skills with students. Scholarship grounded in the sociocultural view of knowledge, in which learning is viewed as socially constructed and mediated, informs our understanding of the *person-to-person relationship*. See Vygostky, *Mind in Society*; Rogoff, *Apprenticeship in Thinking*; and Tharp and Gallimore, *Rousing Minds to Life*. This scholarship provides some of the theoretical underpinnings to the scholarly work on the potential benefits of well-designed collaborative learning such as Cohen, "Restructuring the Classroom" and Cohen et al., "Can Groups Learn?;" Johnson and Johnson, *Cooperation and Competition*, *Learning Together*, and "Energizing Learning;" Webb, "Peer Interaction;" and Webb and Farivar, "Promoting Helping Behavior." All of these literatures taken together underscore the idea that it is important for learners to engage both with texts and people in pursuing understanding of texts. Our study builds on these literatures by drawing connections between the reader-text relationship and the learning relationships among peers and holding these important dimensions of learning together through a unifying conceptualization of learning as relationship-building.

me, and the text, both the opportunity and the requirement to show up fully as a partner is intensified—as opposed to a bigger grouping of "me, *many others*, and a text," in which it is easier to withdraw and also more difficult to draw out and manage the many voices that must be balanced in the learning partnership. We therefore designed this beit midrash with havruta learning as a central feature, accompanied by full-group and smaller-group discussions, games, and exercises. In preparing the students for havruta practice, we emphasized that the partnership skills and attitudes they would be developing are meant to be applied throughout their different learning experiences (not just in pairs and not just in Hebrew school) and that they can be applied even in their personal lives.

In this portrait we provide one view into the Seventh Grade Beit Midrash and will present the story of one particular havruta pair whose learning we were able to video-record over the course of the eight weeks. By looking closely, we are able to cast light on how these students learn to recognize and access not only their peers as learning partners but also the text as a partner; further, we can discern how these students intentionally put these partners into relationship in order to see what effect this had on their learning.[15]

Learning in the Seventh Grade Beit Midrash

In preparation for the project we consulted with synagogue staff to choose the textual focus—or the "third partner"—of our beit midrash. We chose to focus our text learning on the Jacob and Esau narratives in the Bible because they were developmentally appropriate and potentially interesting thematically to middle school students. In addition to the text content, the course focused on three necessary components to support students' partner learning: learning a partnership stance (a set of attitudes), learning skills of engagement for accessing their human and textual partners, and developing capacities for reflecting on learning with others.

At the beginning of the beit midrash, we introduced students directly to the three partners of havruta framework (the partnership between two people and a text) and the idea that, for the partnership to come alive, a stance of exploration and deep listening is required. Then, through in-class discussions, games, and exercises, students explored how their own

15. This chapter reports findings of one aspect of this action research.

stance toward their peers and the text could affect their partnership. A poster of the triangle diagram remained visible in our beit midrash space throughout the project as we continued to build on its meaning with students and turn back to it regularly as a basis for reflection on learning.

In addition to envisioning the meaning of partnership learning and exploring what kinds of attitudes we can bring to our partnership to make the ideal come to life, we had to teach our students specific skills and strategies to help them learn to access their partners as resources in learning. We did this by teaching them a series of talk moves[16] or, as we called them, "Torah study speech prompts." We taught these prompts to the students over time in order to help them better draw out each other's ideas, elicit the similarities and differences in each other's thinking, and better attend to and understand one another. The prompts included:

- Attentive silence

- "Tell me more about what you mean."

- "I don't understand. Can you say that in a different way or give an example?"

- "I don't think you are understanding me. Let me explain . . . "

- "My idea is different from yours in the following way . . . "

Students also learned talk moves to help them better attend to the text, such as,

"What's your evidence?"

and

"Is there another way to understand that?

16. Talk moves are words, phrases, or sentences that one uses in the course of speaking in order to affect something or someone. In this context, students were taught particular talk moves in order to have particular effects on their partnership learning. Research by Resnick et al., "How (Well Structured) Talk Builds the Mind," 179–80, helps us understand that not all classroom talk is equal in its learning benefits, and that certain kinds of talk moves allow for more intellectually productive work than others. They have spearheaded a line of research and practice focused on what they call "Accountable Talk®." For more information, see: http://ifl.pitt.edu/index.php/educator_resources/accountable_talk. Our work represents a related stream of work but grows out of different research and foci. Our "Torah Study Speech Prompts" grow out of our work on Jewish text learning.

We also embedded these talk moves and reminders about the partnership stance in text study guides to support their use.

Importantly, in the early classes of the beit midrash, we taught that the stance and skills to access both the text and human partners were often parallel. For example, we explored with students what it means to listen to a peer and to listen to a text, and to become aware of the similarities (and differences) in doing each. We emphasized to students that the core relational stance and skills that they were learning and practicing needed to be directed on all sides of the three partners of havruta triangle.

Finally, through in-class exercises and written assignments, we gave students regular opportunities for meta-cognitive reflection, to look at what they were each learning and how they were learning with others so that they could more intentionally utilize their new knowledge and skills and make mid-course corrections.[17]

The Story of Nate and Jim

At the beginning of our beit midrash, with the input of the synagogue staff, we assigned havruta pairs. We considered social and academic factors with the intention that these pairs would stick together for the majority of the beit midrash sessions. Nate and Jim were the pair for which we collected the highest number of recorded sessions, allowing analysis of their learning trajectory as partners together with the text. Our intent here is not to argue that Nate and Jim's learning typifies—or for that matter exceeds—other pairs. Rather, their case offers "images of the possible"[18] for how students' text learning can develop and grow deeper as they recognize the havruta learning partners of self, other, and text and get better at putting them into relationship.

In this portrait, we will present such an image of partnership learning by exploring Nate and Jim's final havruta session in which they engaged with both textual and human partners productively. In order to highlight their process of *learning to learn* in partnership, we will provide two snapshots from Jim and Nate's earlier peer-learning sessions in order to develop a picture of their evolving learning patterns over time, followed

17. While a complete description and analysis of this pedagogy is beyond the scope of this article, see: http://www.brandeis.edu/mandel/projects/beitmidrashresearch/havruta.html for a video and written narrative about our pedagogy.

18. See Shulman, "Visions of the Possible."

by a close analysis from beginning to end of their aforementioned final text-based peer-learning session. The close analysis of this session serves to show how far they have come from the earlier working patterns, and provides a context for showing how their growing attention to the three partners of the havruta triangle changed both their learning process and their textual and person-based understanding.

In each preceding snapshot, we will provide some context, present excerpts of the students' havruta discussions, and examine their learning conversations in light of the three partners of havruta framework. Through our analysis, we invite the reader to see how Jim and Nate are more or less able to form the "points and lines" of the partnership triangle in a given episode of their learning together. We explore the extent to which each partner is present and connected to the others and, importantly, what the quality of this partnership presence and connection seems to be in order to promote or, in some instances, prevent, maximizing opportunities for learning and understanding.

Nate and Jim's Prologue: The need to "share power"

Before jumping into havruta text learning, we facilitated a partnership warm-up exercise based on a questionnaire through which students could reflect individually on their experiences both with learning Torah and with learning (and playing) with others. Jim and Nate's first assignment as a havruta pair was to share these reflections with one another, get to know one another as learners, and to think about how their previous experiences with texts and working with peers may impact their particular partnership.

In their pre-course reflection questionnaire, both Jim and Nate stated that they know the basic facts of the Jacob and Esau narratives. Both wrote that they like to participate in group work. Nate explained that what helps him work better with a partner or group is when "I'm in charge and they listen to me." Jim said that a challenge for him in group work occurs when people in the group have different ideas. Given this background, it is no surprise that at Jim and Nate's first havruta meeting, when they discussed what would be important to their efforts to learn together as partners, they came up with the idea that they would need to "share power"—in the sense of giving each other space and respect to be a full participant in the work. Learning to "share power" was one of the challenges they would face as a pair. Keeping their self-identified goal in mind through the lens of the three partners of havruta, let us touch down into two of Nate and Jim's learning sessions.

Snapshot #1: Beginning to try to intentionally listen to one another and the text.

Context: In the classes preceding this snapshot of Nate and Jim's havruta, the students already had the opportunity to explore the practice of "listening," discussing what it means, what it sounds like and looks like, and what we can each do to listen to another person as well as to the text we are studying. In this snapshot of an early learning session, we gave the students a havruta assignment to practice the skills of listening—to the text and one another—specifically by identifying details in the text and pointing them out to one's peer partner. When the following interchange between Jim and Nate occurred, we had just wrapped up a lesson in which we explored with students how the close consideration of textual details may open up the possibility for multiple meanings in the text, and by so doing, help us better listen to the texts by preventing us from rushing to premature judgment about its meaning. In this excerpt we see Nate and Jim beginning to try to listen to one another and the text with some success as well as with some missed opportunities.

Excerpt of the havruta *discussion:*

Nate [reading the text]: "His father, Isaac, said to him 'Who are you?' And he said 'I am your son Esau; your firstborn.' Isaac was seized with a cry, violent, with very violent trembling. 'Who was it then' [reading in an angry sounding voice] he demanded 'that brought, that hunted game and brought it to me? Moreover I ate of it before you came, and I blessed him. Now he must remain blessed!'"

Jim: Nate, you know, you're kind of making assumptions by the way you're saying it; that he was really mad.

Nate: He sort of is. He's trembling. He's violently trembling.

Jim: But he might be sad.

Nate: And he's demanding. I mean, I'm not going to just go and demand that we—

Jim: But Ms. Connor [their middle school English teacher] demands things and she's really cool about it.

Jim: So we can't really be—

Nate: I mean, I know nobody's going to walk in and demand that they stop videoing us on the iPad; if I demanded something like, "I demand that you turn these microphones off," that's angry. I'm frustrated. I want these gotten rid of.

Jim: Okay, keep going [with reading the text].

Analysis

Both Jim and Nate attend to the text by reading it aloud and tap into themselves as partners in relationship to the text by suggesting two different ideas about Isaac's emotional state at this time: Nate suggests that Isaac was mad and Jim suggests that Isaac could have been sad. Jim's challenge of Nate's early interpretation—that Isaac was mad—seems to suggest that Jim is trying to make the text a partner by closely listening to it and considering different interpretive possibilities (the subject of the previous lesson). However, Nate does not probe Jim's idea—that Isaac was possibly sad—to help him understand it better and consider its merits. He just continues with his initial idea, which he seems to base on the fact that the English translation says, "he [Isaac] demanded" and which he understands as reflecting anger. Nate is not tapping into his peer partner as a resource: he is not really listening in a sustained way to Jim, nor extending him the power of being a full participant with ideas worthy of engagement.

Jim also falls short by not making it clear to Nate what he does not understand or agree with in Nate's suggestion that Isaac is angry—that is, by not making a sustained effort to serve as a partner. He tries to suggest that "demanding" doesn't have to mean "angry" by bringing a counter-example of a teacher they both have, but then when Nate pushes back, Jim does not attend to his own idea and pursue it; he just tells Nate to keep reading.

As they move forward with their reading of the text in this session, Jim calls attention to six details in the text, compared to Nate calling attention to one. This is consistent with Jim's other peer-learning sessions: he stays close to the text, looking at single details and trying to understand their significance but not necessarily developing an understanding of the larger whole. Nate does not seem to stick as closely to the text and, as demonstrated in the dialogue above, moves fairly quickly to drawing conclusions about what the text means.[19]

19. For this session, we assigned students the task of recording "three details my partner helped me notice in the text." Interestingly, Nate writes that Jim helped him

We see in this snapshot that Nate and Jim begin to attend to their partners in an effort to seek understanding, though, in important ways, not fully so. They are also starting to develop a pattern of engagement with one another and the text which, as we will see in the next snapshot, proves to be a challenge for them in their learning partnership.

Snapshot #2: The challenges of holding all three partners in conversation.

Context: The relational dynamics among Jim, Nate, and the biblical text came to a head a couple of sessions later. They read the part of the biblical narrative that explains that Rebekah is sending Jacob away from home, saying she does not want him to marry a Canaanite. The next thing the text says is that Esau saw that his father did not approve of his sons marrying Canaanite women and marries one of the daughters of Ishmael, his uncle.

In the havruta, Jim tried to probe the text as they are reading it. He asked Nate what he thought and volunteered his own ideas. Nate does not want to stop and probe the text in the middle of reading it. Even when Jim got Nate to stop and respond to the question he has raised, Nate was the one who decides how much time they will take exploring the question before going on.

In this excerpt, we see that when Nate brings up an interpretation of part of the text, it is not based in textual evidence. Jim challenges him, using speech prompts he learned in class.

Excerpt of the havruta *discussion:*

> Jim: I don't see what you're trying to say, Nate. Could you explain that in a different way [speech prompt]?
>
> Nate: Esau is trying to be a jerk to his father.
>
> Jim: Where does it say-?
>
> Nate: Because he didn't get the [blessing], that's my interpretation.
>
> Jim: Where's your evidence [speech prompt]?
>
> Nate: I don't have evidence. It's just an interpretation.

---

notice that Isaac wasn't necessarily angry, and Jim writes that Nate helped him notice that a demand is usually a form of anger. They both retained what the other one has said, but because during their havruta they did not treat their partners' ideas as resources for learning, they lost out on the opportunity to probe the ideas and see how that probing might have enriched their understanding of the text.

> Jim: Then, then it's, oh well, show me where your interpretation is.

Nate has simply misread the text. He mistakenly assumes that Ishmaelites are Canaanites. And based on this assumption, he assumes that Esau's marrying someone from Ishmael's family is an attempt to intentionally go against his father's wishes. Nate is so sure of his reading of the text that he is unable to re-listen to it and unwilling to point to specific evidence, and therefore cannot even see his misreading. Nate's retort, "I don't need evidence; it's just an interpretation," stands in direct contradiction to what we have taught students explicitly about interpretation—that interpretation *must* be rooted in textual evidence and that havruta partners have a responsibility to hold one another accountable to the text. It seems likely that Nate's momentary reaction may come out of frustration rather than an outright misunderstanding about the nature of interpretation, given that Nate has demonstrated in the past that he draws on evidence, particularly when prompted. Jim continues to challenge Nate, using speech prompts and trying to hold him close to the text, but Nate understands these challenges to be proof that Jim simply does not understand him, rather than an invitation to explore the merits of the interpretation together. A little further into their havruta, the following exchange takes place:

> Jim: No, but I don't understand what you're trying to say because here [in a hypothetical example Nate just offered about a father and son in order to explain his point] the dad is deliberately making it bad for you [for the son in Nate's example].
>
> Nate: That's the point. That's my point. Esau is deliberately making it annoying for Isaac; that's my interpretation.
>
> Jim: But it doesn't—
>
> Nate: He's deliberately doing that, that's my interpretation.
>
> Jim: It doesn't, but, but, no. It doesn't say anywhere in the text that Ishmael, any of Ishmael's ladies or cousins or whatever are Canaanites.
>
> Nate: See, that's also my interpretation.
>
> Jim: Wait. So, you're just thinking that Esau married her just to annoy him, but it doesn't say anywhere that he did?
>
> Nate: I'm trying to make an interpretation.
>
> Jim: Yeah, but you don't have any, you're, no. You're predicting. You can't, you can't—

Nate: I don't think you're understanding me. Let me not explain because you still wouldn't understand it.[20]

Analysis

At this point in their learning experience, we see evidence that Jim is trying to hold the text in relationship; he is respecting the text as a full partner and a necessary resource by sticking close to it and trying to explore its multiple meanings. He is using speech prompts[21] he learned in class to try to get his partner to elaborate his interpretation and point to evidence in the text to back up his ideas. He challenges his partner's idea twelve times in this havruta session alone. Jim is still spending a great deal of time reacting to Nate instead of proposing his own ideas, and focusing on discrete details in the text instead of looking at it as a whole. Nate, too, is trying to work with the text as a partner by taking seriously his role to make sense of the text, but his tendency to draw large conclusions before fully exploring the text undermines his ability to listen to it. He also continues his tendency to not listen to his havruta partner's ideas and challenges (ignoring the important contributions his peer partner brings to their learning) and this gets in his way. Nate gets frustrated because he thinks Jim is not trying hard enough to understand him, but it is at least as significant that Nate is not trying hard enough to understand the text.

In this learning episode, Nate and Jim's patterns of engagement among the three partners of their havruta blossom into a palpable partnership challenge—and learning opportunity. This challenge of how to attend to all three partners and hold them in productive conversation, even when it is hard, is a learning process, and bumps in the road should be expected and seized upon for further learning. We will see as we present Nate and Jim's final havruta session the following week how both boys were able to recognize and learn from their challenges in order to bring their partnership of three to life.

---

20. Nate's comment is a subversion of one of the speech prompts we taught them which is, "I don't think you are understanding me; let me explain in a different way . . . "

21. This is an example of how the speech prompts operate in allowing Jim to both attend to the text as a resource and to tap into his partner as a resource.

A Portrait of Three Partners:
Bringing the Partnership of Three to Life.

Nate and Jim entered into their final havruta discussion together after one of the many different kinds of reflection exercises we conducted regularly with the whole class. In this penultimate beit midrash class session, we sought to synthesize and reflect on the partnership attitudes and skills the students had been exploring and practicing throughout the project. Since this exercise had particular significance to Nate and Jim's havruta partnership in particular,[22] we will describe it here.

To set the whole class up for their havruta work, we created a continuum across the floor of the room in order for students to self-assess how they were doing with particular partnership skills. One end of the continuum represented the idea of "needs work," the other end, "doing well," and the middle meant, "working on it" to different degrees of success. Students placed themselves physically along the line of the continuum in response to our calling out discrete skills we had taught them such as, "Asking for clarification when you don't understand," or "Supporting your partner's understanding by finding further evidence for it in the text." Students had an opportunity to share why they were standing where they were standing in order to initiate further reflection and to learn from their peers. At the end of this exercise, each student named one thing they were going to try to work on in their upcoming havruta session. Through their own self-assessments, Nate and Jim came to recognize salient features of their partnership dynamics on their own and identify how they each could make some adjustments. Nate wrote that he was going to work on "attentive silence," (a critical listening move we taught them) and Jim wrote, "I'm working on trying to talk because I need to talk," by which he meant not merely a need to say more words but rather the need to contribute his own ideas to the partnership.

Nate and Jim's ensuing havruta session was markedly different from their earlier sessions. From the start, they articulated to each other how they were going to try to shift their pattern from one in which Nate develops theories about the text and often ignores Jim's questions (and even the text), sticking to his original idea, and in which Jim reacts to Nate's

---

22. In his interview weeks after the course ended, Nate specifically points to this exercise as a turning point for him.

ideas (generally by raising textual challenges to Nate's ideas) rather than developing his own ideas or building off of Nate's (at least for exploratory purposes). This pattern has left Jim feeling like Nate is doing all of the real talking and none of the listening, and has left Nate feeling like Jim doesn't understand what he says. To be sure, each has certainly learned something through the course of their previous sessions, and through the course of their interchanges noticed many details in the text. Some might even view their previous sessions as strong models of partner learning, since they are talking to each other and drawing on the text to varying degrees in their discussions. If one were to watch their havruta videos with the sound turned off, one would see what appears to be a lot of talk and activity directed at the central players of the peer learning session, the text and the two individuals.

However, talk and activity alone are not enough. To be effective, they need to enable learners to draw upon the contributions of all of their learning partners. Nate and Jim's learning patterns have meant that they have not been fully utilizing the potential of their partners—themselves, the other person and the text—and working together to explore what everyone is bringing to the table. They are sitting next to each other, talking to each other and trying to interpret the text, but their words and actions are not sufficiently intersecting or building anything more substantial than the initial ideas each poses. Jim has practiced noticing details in the text, but has not built them into a larger whole. He often reacts to Nate's ideas rather than posing his own. Nate has developed some of his own big ideas, but often does not adequately ground them in the text, explore other textual interpretive possibilities, or consistently consider his partner's questions and suggestions.

To highlight their attempt to shift the dynamics, at the start of their conversation they each made it clear with the other that they were going to try on different roles in this particular havruta session. Nate says to Jim, "I won't be the one talking," meaning that he recognizes that he tends to talk a lot and that he will try harder to make room for Jim's ideas and not just his own. In return, Jim says to Nate, "This time I will [talk]," meaning that while Jim has talked in past havrutot,[23] in this one he will try harder to share his own ideas about the text while also responding to Nate's.

---

23. Havrutot is the plural of havruta.

In the following excerpts and analysis of this havruta session—in which students were given back the entire Jacob and Esau narrative text to look at as a whole—we will explore how the boys were able to draw upon one another as full partners (connecting the person-to-person line of our partnership triangle), how they were able to draw upon the text as a full partner (connecting the person-to-text lines of the triangle), and how they were able to pull the entire partnership of three together in order to arrive at the co-construction of new questions, insights, and interpretations.

a. Drawing on one another as partners

In this havruta session, while Nate and Jim each say an almost equal number of words, this fact alone could not tell us whether they were engaging with each other or using each other to explore ideas and build them together. However, a close look at the transcript from their conversation shows that they are also completely responsive to each other in this session. Each utterance follows up on a previous utterance. They answer each other's questions, never ignore a question that is raised, and check for understanding along the way. In the following exchange, we see an example of this after they read the verses in which Rebekah was told by God that she has two nations in her womb and that the older will serve the younger, years before she helps her younger son get the blessing meant for the older.

> Jim: Okay. Okay, so where it says where God gives Rebekah the prophecy sort of thing?
>
> Nate: Yeah.
>
> Jim: How did this come to happen? Because Rebekah knew this was going to happen, right? Because God told her.
>
> Nate (Looking at the text and then at Jim): Are you asking what, which parts of this came true in the story?
>
> Jim: No. How did it happen that Rebekah, did God, because God doesn't control people's minds? So how did it come that Esau, that, that Jacob would get the birthright when Rebekah already knew? Had Rebekah been like waiting?

Jim starts to ask a question and Nate encourages him to finish asking his question. Jim's question—"How did this come to happen?"—isn't completely clear to Nate. While in past sessions, Nate might have moved on, ignoring Jim's question altogether, in this session he stops and checks to see whether he understands what Jim is asking. Nate then pauses to let Jim tell him if his understanding is correct. Nate gives Jim an opportunity to confirm or negate Nate's own understanding of Jim's words. This is an example of a talk move, a word or phrase, in this case "Are you asking . . . ?" that affects the peer interaction. This particular talk move helps keep the partners in sync and makes sure they are understanding each other. Nate's invitation to Jim to confirm or negate Nate's own understanding of Jim's words gives Jim an opportunity to clearly tell Nate that he has it wrong, and to then try to reformulate his question more clearly. He makes three different attempts to do so, giving us more hints to what he is trying to sort through. It is only because Nate has given Jim the space to talk through his idea—in the language of the class, Nate used the practice of "attentive silence"—that Jim is able to elaborate upon his earlier question. While in past sessions Jim might have let his idea go, in this session, where he is more attuned to utilizing himself as a contributing resource to his partnership, he takes advantage of the space created by Nate and tries to pursue his idea.

Jim's question seems to get Nate thinking about his theory of what is going on. However, unlike previous sessions where Nate alone has elaborated theories, this theory comes out of his interaction with Jim and his interaction with the text. He is drawing on both as partners, and connecting them to his own thinking.

Nate's Theory

Nate: So it says "So God tells Rebekah what's going to happen." [Looks at text and reads.] "Two nations are in your womb. Two separate people shall issue from your body. One people shall be mightier than the other and the older shall serve the younger." She knows that now but she thinks that, my theory is that she doesn't think that that can happen without her making it happen . . .

According to Nate, Rebekah doesn't think the prophecy will happen without her making it happen. Therefore, she is the cause of all that occurs thereafter. (In articulating his theory, Nate responds to Jim's questions: "Has Rebekah been waiting?" and "God doesn't control people's minds."[24]) Jim tries to unpack Nate's idea and they continue to work hard to understand each other as they try to develop the big ideas they are weaving.

b. *Drawing on the text as a partner*

It would have been so easy at this point for these students to simply move into the land of abstract discussion and share ideas back and forth, never looking back at the text and possibly leaving it far behind. But to do so would have been a missed opportunity to engage with the text as a full partner and delve into it more deeply. Jim returns them to the text to see how Nate's theory reads within the text itself, and through this move uncovers an important point: If Rebekah is really the cause of events, how do we explain the scene when Esau comes in starving from hunting and sells his birthright to Jacob for food? In Jim's words: "Rebekah didn't make Esau starving." The question that Jim frames becomes: Why is Esau hungry on that particular day of all days, since his hunger seems to set a whole chain of events in motion? In making this move, Jim has attended to the text, drawing on it to ask a question that responds to the conversation that preceded it and moves their discussion forward.

This is but one of the many examples of the ways in which the text is present in their conversation. Jim and Nate closely examine this incident in the text, and Jim's conclusion is, "I feel like there's something that the text is leaving out . . . because what is the cause of him selling his birthright and being really hungry?" They spin out the details in the text, imagining Esau as a hunter, working hard and coming home hungry on other occasions too, which only strengthens the question: Why on this day of all days did Esau come home hungry? As Nate says, "It wasn't just coincidental." By attending to the text in this case, they allow the text to challenge their own idea that Rebekah is the cause of all that has unfolded. In that way, the text is also a partner in their study. They use the text's details, its resources, to deepen their exploration.

c. *Making the learning partnership (of three) come alive*

As they shift their study to a focus on Jacob (their assignment was to consider the text in its entirety through Jacob's eyes and to consider

---

24. In human speech, not all questions are phrased as questions. Jim often makes comments about ideas that he is questioning and wondering about. This is one such example.

Jacob's character), their exploration becomes a full-fledged theological discussion. They are no longer focused on one or two details in the passage, but are considering all of the text they have studied up to this point to explore their big question: What or who is the cause of how this narrative unfolds? This question has emerged through Nate's and Jim's bringing themselves in relation to the text and to each other. They are exploring what is truly important to *them*, what Sophie Haroutunian-Gordon calls "a genuine question."[25] Neither is wedded to a single answer to this big question; they are working together to explore it based on what they have learned in the text and from their own and each other's knowledge and beliefs. Nate suggests that the birth story of Jacob and Esau is the cause of all that unfolds, because their birth order affects everything to come: "The effect of those two being born the way they are is the cause of the prophecy." This suggestion shifts their conversation to an explicit theological discussion about the nature of God's role in humanity.

> Jim: But God said that He does, He doesn't control people. He created them since they'll have their own minds just like any living thing because the whole world is what he wanted. Now He wants people who can have their own decisions.
>
> Nate: Yeah, but at the same time God knows what's going to happen.
>
> Jim: He does but He can't change it.
>
> Nate: Yeah, He may not be able to change it but He can know what's going to happen.
>
> Jim: But I feel that God isn't being honest here. He knows that something's gonna happen so he tells Rebekah so that she can sort of—
>
> Nate: Intervene and make it happen.
>
> Jim: Is God, does God favor Jacob?
>
> Nate: In, in a way. I think that God is the cause of this entire dispute. If that prophecy hadn't happened, my theory is if that prophecy had never been given to Rebekah then she wouldn't have helped Jacob . . .

Jim suggests that while God might know everything that happens, He can't make it happen. As he gets to the crux of his argument—that God is not being honest in this narrative since He tells Rebekah the prophecy, knowing full well what that will set in motion—he and Nate are in sync, with Nate revoicing Jim's idea with a slight shift of emphasis ("Yeah, He may not be able to change it, but He can know what's going to happen.") and finishing Jim's sentence ("intervene and make it happen").

---

25. Haroutunian-Gordon, *Learning to Teach Through Discussion*, 178.

Each concludes this part of their study with a new idea:

> Nate: In, in a way. I think that God is the cause of this entire dispute. If that prophecy hadn't happened, my theory is if that prophecy had never been given to Rebekah then she wouldn't have helped Jacob [points to text repeatedly] steal the birthright.
>
> Jim: Yeah, because, because Ja—
>
> Nate: Because she wouldn't have known that one of, that the older will serve the younger.
>
> Jim: And—
>
> Nate: So she wouldn't have tried to get Jacob the spiritual power.
>
> Jim: And, you don't hear, in this text [points to text] you don't hear, see Jacob telling Rebekah. Rebekah just gets involved all of the sudden.
>
> Nate: She just says "Oh he's gonna get the birthright. Go get some skin. Go get some hairy stuff on, and we'll get that birthright for you." [Jim looks at text]
>
> Jim: Yeah, and I feel like God favors Jacob here.
>
> Nate: In a sense—
>
> Jim: Do you see that? Because—
>
> Nate: In a sense, I mean, in a sense, yes.
>
> Jim: You know, God knows but that doesn't make sense now because God could have just had Jacob come out first not Esau. Was, was God trying to make it hard for Esau?
>
> Nate: Well, we'll never know.

Nate gets more definitive as he speaks, suggesting that God is really the cause of all that unfolds in the narrative (and not Rebekah or the prophecy, as he earlier suggested). Jim provides textual support to Nate's idea ("And, you don't hear, in this text, you don't hear, see Jacob telling Rebekah. Rebekah just gets involved all of the sudden."), as Nate continues to revisit his idea and develop it further. Jim frames his own new idea initially as a question: Does God favor Jacob? While he could easily have stopped with this question, he continues to develop his idea based on their discussion of the text and frames the following question: "Was God trying to make it hard for Esau?" since if it was just a matter of favoring Jacob, God could have had Jacob be born first.

As we consider this havruta session overall, we see that Nate has used it as an opportunity to listen and respond to his partner's ideas in a way that he has not previously. And while Jim has raised many questions, they do not come out as attacks on Nate's ideas but as explorations of the text itself. Jim has moved away from focusing solely on this or that textual detail to being able to explore the text as a whole and put forward his own ideas about it (often in the form of a question), even at times supporting Nate's ideas in the process. The tone of their havruta has the quality of focused exploration. They are focused on a big question: What is the cause of this narrative? What is the power behind it? And they pursue a number of points to try and respond to that question, maintaining an open quality in their consideration of new ideas and new evidence as they move along in their discussion. Even Nate's theory comes across as less heavy-handed than in previous instances, as he is more ready to explore the underpinnings of his theory, consider Jim's response to it, and revise it based on what he hears from the text and from Jim.

In this session Nate and Jim have succeeded in meeting the overall learning goal of activating and connecting all sides of the three partners of havruta triangle and made their partnership of three come alive. They have done this by keeping themselves, the text, and their human partner ongoing parts of the conversation and they have learned to "share power," putting all three in relationship by really listening to each partner, by giving space to each to articulate or share ideas, by supporting the building of each other's ideas, and by challenging ideas for the purpose of sharpening their understanding.

There is a sense of "focused wondering"[26] in their discussion, a focus on a big idea (what is the cause of the particular chain of events in the story of Jacob and Esau?), a focus on the details in the text and how the text supports or challenges their interpretations, and a focus on each other. This focus is balanced by their wondering stance—their willingness to explore different ideas and interpretations and not simply settle on the first idea that comes their way. Their work is undergirded by what appears to be a deep respect for each other and the text, as reflected in how they treat each partner.

During this session, Jim and Nate have been jointly constructing knowledge. While each raises and pursues his own ideas, the development of these ideas is distributed across them so that their ideas become shared and integrated within each other's developing trajectory of thought. Each starts the session with a particular idea or question that is developed and changed through their interactions with each other and the text, and they move from trying to fill gaps in the text through close textual analysis

---

26. See Kent, "A Theory of Havruta Learning," 233, for a further discussion of "focused wondering" and its role in partner learning.

(already a more advanced way of working with the text than merely reading the plot) to having a theological discussion grounded in the details of text. Their increased attention to each partner heightens their ability to dig more deeply into the text.

In interviews conducted three weeks after the beit midrash ended, Jim and Nate reflected on what they perceived to be their partnership learning gains. These perceptions were consistent with what we observed in the data. Both comment on some specific ideas and skills that they have learned about the practice of partnership itself and ways in which they have already used some of those skills in other contexts. Jim starts off his interview explaining that this class gave him an opportunity to go "close into the text" and notice "new interpretations . . . that I would never have thought of." [27] He eloquently talks about learning to understand the idea of the text as a partner, and learning to use the prompt, "What is your evidence?" to make the text a partner and "not judge" it, which to him means not reading it quickly and not going with his first understanding. He explains, "I think that the text is telling you something, so that makes it a partner, but you have to listen to what it's telling you . . . and just like you . . . can't judge a person by their looks, you can't do that with the text either just by scanning it." He provides a specific example of how he made the text a partner in one of his study sessions with Nate. "I was really looking in [to the text] to see where he [Nate] was coming from, and I thought he might be right, but then I realized that I had just scanned over it. [I] went back and I looked really closely at it, and I found a couple of things that I had skipped over—it was actually a whole line that I skipped over that had important information in it."[28]

Jim also gives a nuanced description of what a good human partner/havruta looks like: "somebody who really cares about what the other person thinks, and . . . how they feel about what they're looking at; even

27. He does not specifically list those new interpretations and due to time constraints for conducting these interviews, the interviewer protocol prioritized trying to elicit information about students' learning new skills and ideas about the work of partnership, rather than fully assessing what new content ideas they gained. (However, an examination of his student work indicates some of the new details in the text that he notices and some of the interpretations he develops.)

28. It is noteworthy that Jim also points to examples outside of class where he has begun to work harder to listen to the text. Specifically, he talks about learning *parshat hashavua* (the weekly Torah portion) with his family and using the speech prompt, "where is your evidence?" and more generally, re-reading what he reads in books and not merely skimming.

if the other person completely disagrees, they should both look at each other's evidence, and somebody who, I guess, really . . . is thoughtful about the other person's idea, even if it's not what they believe." While he says that the practice of "attentive silence" was the hardest thing for him to practice in terms of working with his human partner, Nate, his nuanced discussion of how he used this practice in his havruta work points to his understanding of this concept and his ability to use it intentionally at important points during his partnership work. For example, "I listened to him and I got his point and then I let him keep going but once he went too far and I said, 'wait . . . I don't think that's right.'" Overall, his comments reflect an understanding of the importance of considering both the other person and the text in order to make the most of the Torah learning experience, and he is able to provide details of his experience to illustrate his understanding.

In his interview, Nate indicates that his most clear partnership learning gain was that he is able to recognize himself as someone who has trouble listening to his human partner and then turn this around to become a better listener. "I definitely got better at attentive silence because I was always the talker and by the end, I was letting my partner talk."[29] He specifically talks about how this turnaround came about through the course of the reflective exercise in class, described above, and we see evidence of this in his last havruta session. "I was, most of the time, in the not good at all area [on the self-assessment continuum] and it just came to me like I need to turn this around and get on the other side. And so I said 'All right,' I sat down with my partner Jim and I said 'All right, I've done the talking. What do you want to say?' And I let him talk and I responded." He highlights the quality of being a good listener in his description of what makes for a good havruta: "I think it [a good havruta] is someone who isn't just a talker but they also listen, and when they're listening, they use attentive silence, they ask questions, and when they're talking they let the other person respond."

He also says that he is doing a better job of listening in his relationships outside of class as well. "I have always been the talkative person . . . and I've been talking a lot in places that I should have kept quiet. I [am

29. Interestingly, during most of their havruta sessions, Jim and Nate uttered an almost equal number of words. This highlights the fact that being a good listener and practicing attentive silence isn't just about the number of words one utters but about one's stance towards one partner and whether one really makes space for his or her ideas to flourish.

now] attentively listening, using attentive silence and paying attention, learning what I need to. And when I don't understand, then I ask a question, and I ask them to explain. And if I don't get how they're explaining it, I ask them to explain it in a different way."

Later in the interview, Nate shows his understanding of the three partners of havruta triangle by explaining that it emphasizes the importance of not just working together with another person, but also working with the text too. "There's the person and the person and they work together, which makes the bottom of the triangle. And then you're working, in a sense, with the text, and it's not that you and your partner are reading the text. You and your partner are working *with* the text so you have your partner, the two people connected, and they're both connected to the text . . . ." There is certainly evidence in the last havruta session that Nate does more listening to both the text and his havruta. It is interesting to note that he does not yet seem to consciously connect the fact that, by pressing him for evidence, his havruta partner helped him treat the text as a partner and to listen to it.[30]

Conclusion

This portrait illuminates what the learning process looks like as students activate their most elemental partners in learning—themselves, their human partner, and the text—and the subsequent gains that they make as a result.[31] As Jim and Nate learn to recognize these partners, attend to them productively, and put them in relationship, their learning can be described as "going deeper." The analysis of Jim and Nate's havruta helps show that it is not enough to activate each of the three partners separately; "parallel play" among the partners does not on its own generate the most productive learning. That is, mere turn-taking or speaking the same amount of words does not produce deep learning or productive talk

30. This would be the next step to pursue with him if the beit midrash had continued.

31. Another study might focus the lens more broadly to look at all the student work that this class generated and/or all of the student interviews; we hope to conduct such an analysis in the future, in particular to help highlight all of the students' learning gains. This fine-grained analysis of one pair's learning process and learning gains has had the advantage of illustrating with some specificity what students need to do within their text-based discussions to bring about those learning gains, and identifying some of the factors that make them possible.

among peers and does not on its own create a partnership. Rather, it is when Jim and Nate are able to access their partners and bring them into productive relationship that their partnership of three comes alive, and their discussion reaches new levels of insight.

Jim and Nate come away from their Hebrew school's Seventh Grade Beit Midrash program—only eight sessions at 6:00–7:30 p.m. in the evening—with several gains. They raise new and sophisticated questions and insights into the meaning of their textual partner. They can articulate a new conception of and commitment to what it means to learn in partnership with another person and a text and express an accompanying awareness that how one seeks to understand another person is connected to how we seek to understand our sacred texts. Finally, they learn to exercise a set of relational skills that they both report using inside and outside of their havruta partnership.

Jim and Nate did not just learn to regard and draw upon themselves, one another, and the text as full partners in learning because they were given the opportunity to do so by having ample time to participate in havruta study with one another. Nor were they able to form their partnership of three incidentally due to a match that enjoyed good chemistry. Rather, they learned to "share power" and to hone intentional attitudes and skills that would allow them to co-construct meaning out of the resources that each of them and the text brought to their particular learning partnership of three. Through a systematic and explicit curriculum designed to explore and cultivate a set of *partnership attitudes*, a set of *partnership skills* operationalized through concrete talk moves, and through regular and targeted *meta-cognitive reflection* on the process of learning in relationship, Jim and Nate demonstrate the potential that this relational approach to teaching and learning in partnership holds for learners and Torah alike.

Further Reflections on Jewish Learning

The story of Jim and Nate's partnership and that of their fellow seventh-graders demonstrated the impact of teaching a particular set of partnership attitudes and skills to empower these students to achieve deeper learning. In the Seventh Grade Beit Midrash, we taught partnership attitudes of listening, wonder, empathy, responsibility and reflection, and then we taught students how to put these attitudes into practice with each other and the Torah text through the use of the partnership skills of listening, articulating, wondering, focusing, supporting, and challenging. The attitudes provided them with a different vision of what their learning was really about and the skills gave them the tools to actualize that vision and, in their words, "go deeper."

The theme of "going deeper" came from the students' reflections in their interviews after the beit midrash ended. Many students talked about the beit midrash experience as having been different from their usual experience studying texts and how they learned a new way to learn that required them to slow down, re-read, consider alternative ideas, get up close to the text, connect with each other, and go deeper. As teacher-researchers, we saw the students going deeper by developing and exploring multiple interpretations grounded in the evidence and gaps in the text, learning and utilizing skills and tools for studying together, and developing a stance toward one another and the text that supported this learning process.

From the work and reflections of the seventh-graders we see that it is possible to build with students a collective vision for learning in partnership with one another and the Torah text, and to inspire a certain quality of relationship with one another and Torah that can result in rich, student-driven interpretive discussion and stronger bonds with peers. By framing Jewish learning as building partnership relationships and by teaching the skills to do so, we learn that Jewish educational programming need not choose between the affective social goals we have for our learners and rigorous content goals, but that the two sets of aims are linked. This insight may be particularly salient for educators working in congregational schools or informal contexts where the pressure to appeal to students' social interests often overrides efforts to go deep into content. Conversely, educators in formal contexts, where there is pressure to cover content (sometimes at the expense of the social-emotional curriculum) need not choose between these critical and complementary sets of goals for Jewish education. When partnership attitudes, skills, and tools form the core of learning, students are motivated and equipped to bring themselves to the learning, access and regard their peers and Torah text as resources for learning, and thereby arrive at insights about the text, themselves, and their peer partners that they can carry with them in the classroom and beyond.

Bibliography

Carr, Wilfred, and Stephen Kemmis. *Becoming Critical: Knowing Through Action Research*. Victoria, Australia: Deakin University Press, 1986.

Cohen, Elizabeth. "Restructuring the Classroom: Conditions for Productive Small Groups." *Review of Educational Research* 64 (1994) 1–35.

Cohen, Elizabeth, et al. "Can Groups Learn?" *Teachers College Record* 104 (2002) 1045–68.

Cook, Allison, and Orit Kent. "Learning Torah through Partnership: A Viewer's Guide." http://www.brandeis.edu/mandel/pdfs/2014-10-24_Video-companion_Learning_Torah_through_Partnership.pdf.

Haroutunian-Gordon, Sophie. *Interpretive Discussion: Engaging Students in Text-Based Conversations*. Cambridge, MA: Harvard Education Press, 2014.

———. *Learning to Teach Through Discussion: The Art of Turning the Soul*. New Haven, CT: Yale University Press, 2009.

Holzer, Elie. "What Connects 'Good' Teaching, Text Study and Hevruta Learning? A Conceptual Argument." *Journal of Jewish Education* 72 (2006) 183–204.

Holzer, Elie, and Orit Kent. *A Philosophy of Havruta: Understanding and Teaching the Art of Text Study in Pairs*. Brighton, MA: Academic Studies, 2013.

Iser, Wolfgang. *The Act of Reading: A Theory of Aesthetic Response*. Baltimore: John Hopkins University Press, 1978.

Johnson, David T., and Robert W. Johnson. *Cooperation and Competition: Theory and Research*. Edina, MN: Interaction, 1989.

———. "Energizing Learning: The Instructional Power of Conflict." *Educational Researcher* 38 (2009) 37–51.

———. *Learning Together and Alone: Cooperative, Competitive, and Individualistic Learning*. Boston: Allyn and Bacon, 1999.

Kent, Orit. "Interactive Text Study: A Case of Hevruta Learning." *Journal of Jewish Education* 72 (2006) 205–32.

———. "Interactive Text Study and the Co-Construction of Meaning: Havruta in the DeLeT Beit Midrash." PhD diss., Brandeis University, 2008.

———. "A Theory of Havruta Learning." *Journal of Jewish Education* 76 (2010) 215–45.

Kent, Orit, and Allison Cook. "Havruta Inspired Pedagogy: Fostering an Ecology of Learning for Closely Studying Texts with Others." *Journal of Jewish Education* 78 (2012) 227–53.

———. "Leveraging Resources for Learning through the Power of Partnership." http://www.brandeis.edu/mandel/pdfs/2014-10-24-Kent_and_%20Cook_Leveraging_Resources_for_Learning.pdf.

Langer, Judith. A. *Envisioning Literature: Literary Understanding and Literature Instruction*. New York: Teachers College Press, 1995.

———. "The Process of Understanding: Reading for Literary and Informative Purposes." *Research in the Teaching of English* 24 (1990) 229–60.

Resnick, Lauren, et al. "How (Well Structured) Talk Builds the Mind." In *Innovations in Educational Psychology: Perspectives on Learning, Teaching, and Human Development*, edited by David D. Preiss et al., 63–194. New York: Springer, 2010.

Rogoff, Barbara. *Apprenticeship in Thinking: Cognitive Development in Social Context*. New York: Oxford University Press, 1990.

Rosenblatt, Louise. *The Reader, the Text, the Poem: The Transactional Theory of the Literary Work*. Carbondale, IL: Southern Illinois University Press, 1978.

Scholes, Robert. *Textual Power, Literary Theory and the Teaching of English*. New Haven, CT: Yale University Press, 1985.

Shulman, Lee. "Visions of the Possible: Models for Campus Support of the Scholarship of Teaching and Learning." In *Teaching as Community Property, Essays on Higher Education*, edited by Pat Hutchings, 9–24. San Francisco: Jossey-Bass, 2004.

Tharp, Roland, and Ronald Gallimore. *Rousing Minds to Life: Teaching, Learning, and Schooling in Social Context*. Cambridge, UK: Cambridge University Press, 1991.

Vygotsky, L. S. *Mind in Society: The Development of Higher Psychological Processes*. Cambridge, MA: Harvard University Press, 1978.

Webb, Noreen M. "Peer Interaction and Learning in Small Groups." *International Journal of Educational Research* 13 (1989) 21–39.

Webb, Noreen M. and Sydney Farivar. "Promoting Helping Behavior in Cooperative Small Groups in Middle School Mathematics." *American Educational Research Journal* 3 (1994) 369–95.

Zeichner, Kenneth, and Susan Noffke. "Practitioner Research." In *Handbook of Research on Teaching*, edited by Virginia Richardson, 298–330. New York: MacMillan, 2001.

5

Movement, Motivation, and Fun
An Alternative Portrait of Hebrew Education

Nicole M. Greninger

It's a Tuesday afternoon and the sun is shining. Fourth grade students begrudgingly sit at desks in a synagogue classroom, trying to sound out Hebrew words they don't understand while wishing they were playing outside instead. The teacher asks students one by one to sound out words in their workbooks, but it is a slow and tedious process. A student struggles to sound out a word from V'ahavta: "eh ... eh ... ehl ... ehlo ... ehlo ... ehlo ... ehloheh. ehloheh ... ehlohech ... ehlochecha?" The other students are restless. Most are fidgeting, a girl twirls her hair absentmindedly, another girl rolls her eyes, two boys are snickering, and several are whispering to each other. One student wanders around the room, looking for something to do, or someone to pester. The teacher knows her lesson is boring, but she wonders how else she can help her students learn to sound out Hebrew words if they don't practice it in class. They surely aren't working on it at home!

THIS SCENE—OR ONE QUITE similar to it—plays out in synagogues all around the country on a regular basis. Hebrew learning is the elephant in the room of synagogue-based education: educators know that they must teach students to read (or more accurately, decode) Hebrew, but due to limited classroom time, inconsistent student attendance, the inability to assign homework, long summer months in which Hebrew gains are lost, inexperienced teachers, and perhaps most importantly, lack of student motivation and interest, it can feel like a Sisyphean task. Most students in synagogues everywhere do eventually learn to read Hebrew, but at what cost? Is there a better way to help kids feel enthusiastic about learning Hebrew?

Rethinking Temple Isaiah's Hebrew Education Program

This question was on my mind seven years ago when, as Director of Education at Temple Isaiah (a large Reform synagogue in Lafayette, California), I spent time with a college student whom I hired to help me do some filing in my office. Molly[1] had been one of the most active high school students in our congregation, serving as a teacher's assistant in our religious school, working as an aide in our education office, staffing junior youth group events, singing in our teen choir, and participating in our high school youth group. As we were going through the materials to be filed, we came upon a lot of Hebrew resources. Molly asked me how I thought things were going with our new Hebrew program (she knew we had started using the Union for Reform Judaism's Mitkadem program[2] about three years prior), and I said that while I thought it was better than what preceded it, I was still not satisfied.

On a whim, I asked Molly what she remembered from her own Hebrew learning, and she told me that while she eventually learned how to sound out Hebrew words (i.e., basic decoding skills), she didn't really get the hang of it until her one-on-one tutoring began in the months before her bat mitzvah. To my surprise, Molly had left religious school at the end of second grade because of her negative experiences learning Hebrew. The class was learning the *aleph-bet* (the Hebrew alphabet), but Molly recalled having a difficult time keeping up with the other students and said she felt lousy about herself as a result. Moreover, she didn't have any good friends in the class, which made her feel lonely *and* bad about her Hebrew skills—a double whammy. She quit for a little while but returned to religious school about a year later.

Thinking back to her later years of learning Hebrew, Molly remembered a teacher who would conduct Hebrew games with the kids that

---

1. I use pseudonyms for all individuals from Temple Isaiah mentioned in this paper, whether children or adults.

2. See: http://www.behrmanhouse.com/mitkadem/home.

were competitive in nature. One was a fast-paced classroom quiz called "Around the World." Molly said she hated those games; she is not a competitive person and the pressure of needing to come up with quick responses reinforced the insecurity she already felt about her Hebrew skills. She also found it frustrating that the Hebrew she didn't "get" was simply sounding out letter/vowel combinations, especially when she realized that even if she learned how to do that, she wasn't really learning Hebrew as a living/spoken language.

Molly's experience mirrors what has occurred in many American synagogues for the last few generations. All too often I have observed that students spend several years learning to decode Hebrew, and by the time they become bar/bat mitzvah, they have developed a negative attitude toward the language. For some, this has led to negative feelings about Judaism as a whole. Although recent studies of the American Jewish community report some decline in enrollment in synagogue education for students post-b'nai mitzvah,[3] to date there is only limited documentation about the bar/bat mitzvah experience and even less about students' experiences learning Hebrew or the impact of Hebrew education programs.

§

When I arrived at Temple Isaiah in 2008, the challenge of improving the congregation's Hebrew program was foremost on my mind. I was heir to the synagogue's strong educational program, one characterized by dynamic teachers, clear and organized systems, enthusiastic families, and innovative curricula.[4] However, the one area that seemed to need improvement was Hebrew, and I wondered how we could teach it more effectively to our students. First we switched from using a series of different publishers' Hebrew primer workbooks to implementing the URJ's Mitkadem program for all third- through sixth-graders. After three years of using Mitkadem, however, it seemed to me that we had not made significant improvements, and I began to consider next steps. Around that time I began conferring with a small group of educators, led by Isa Aron and Nachama Skolnik Moskowitz, who were all asking the same question: How might our students learn Hebrew in synagogue settings in ways that are more engaging and motivating?

3. For example, see the 2000–2001 National Jewish Population Survey: http://www.jewishdatabank.org/studies/details.cfm?StudyID=307.

4.. With compliments to educator Debbie Enelow.

In the summer of 2011 I convened a Hebrew task force at Temple Isaiah, comprised of parents and teachers who worked with me to improve the way our students learn Hebrew in JQuest, our religious school.[5] As a result of an extensive change process, and after experimenting with small adjustments to our Hebrew program over the course of two years, we implemented a new approach to Hebrew education for children in grades K-6 in the fall of 2013.[6]

As we overhauled the way students would learn Hebrew, we wondered how our new approach would affect students' feelings about learning Hebrew and possibly toward their overall Temple Isaiah educational experience. Over four years, we observed classes, interviewed students, and conducted annual surveys of students and parents in order to better understand our students' competence, confidence, and attitudes about Hebrew. Our b'nai mitzvah tutors began completing an intake assessment each time a student began his or her tutoring. Although we have accumulated a great deal of data from those years, the most challenging question that people continue to ask me about our new program is, "does it work?" In other words, do students learn adequate Hebrew skills for b'nai mitzvah with our new approach? And if so, what other changes or improvements have we seen to be able to call our program "successful"? How does one define success in Hebrew education? Finally, if we claim our program is successful, what contributes to its success? In this paper, I examine what we have learned to date about our students as they transition from JQuest to b'nai mitzvah tutoring. I focus especially on what the b'nai mitzvah tutors have observed about their students' attitudes toward learning Hebrew and consider the implications for the field of Jewish education.

5. In this paper, I use the term "JQuest" when referring to our synagogue's part-time educational program for children in grades K-7, as the name of our program was changed from "Religious School" to "JQuest" in 2015. Meanwhile, I refer to other part-time synagogue education programs as "religious schools" because that term is widely understood and less unwieldy than the alternatives. That being said, I do not personally favor the term "religious school" and would advocate for all synagogue education programs to consider new names. See: http://rabbigreninger.blogspot.com/2015/09/why-jquest-instead-of-religious-school.html for more on this topic. We are grateful to Rabbi Stacy Rigler, who came up with the name "JQuest" in her congregation and gave us permission to adopt it.

6. The new approach includes a sound-to-print model of learning starting in kindergarten (Schachter, "Why Bonnie and Ronnie Can't Read"), including pedagogy based on James Asher's Total Physical Response (Asher, "Total Physical Response Approach").

The New Curriculum

Temple Isaiah's goals for our "Hebrew and Prayer" curriculum, as developed by our Hebrew task force, can be found on our JQuest website.[7] Although many of these goals are similar to those of other congregations around the country, our list includes a section dedicated to the students' feelings about Hebrew and prayer, as well as the students' knowledge and skills in those areas. With these goals in mind, the Hebrew task force developed an innovative curriculum that consists of a number of different components: Hebrew Through Movement, Jewish Life Vocabulary, Hebrew Boot Camp, and *tefillah* (prayer/communal worship) (in addition to b'nai mitzvah preparation for individual students and their families).[8] One of the principles underlying the curriculum is that students learn Hebrew (or any language) best with a sound-to-print approach. Students start with an aural foundation of Hebrew (i.e. hearing the language—in our case through Hebrew Through Movement, *tefillah*, music, and Jewish Life Vocabulary), and move to print later on (in the later years of Hebrew Through Movement, Jewish Life Vocabulary, *tefillah*, and Hebrew Boot Camp).

Hebrew Through Movement

Hebrew Through Movement is a language acquisition strategy in which students learn Hebrew by hearing and responding to Hebrew commands through physical movements. It is a Hebrew version of James Asher's Total Physical Response (TPR) method of teaching languages.[9] The approach is explained on the Hebrew Through Movement website:

> The curriculum for Hebrew Through Movement starts with a foundation in modern Hebrew, but in part-time educational settings has as its goal making the prayers in our *siddur*, as well as synagogue and Jewish vocabulary, more easily accessible to those with limited learning time ... Hebrew Through Movement was developed by faculty at Siegal College of Judaic Studies through courses and community workshops. As with other TPR curricula, it introduces Hebrew in a playful and

7. See: https://temple-isaiah.org/education/hebrew/

8. For details about the components of our program, please see our website at: https://temple-isaiah.org/education/hebrew/

9. Asher, *Learning Another Language Through Actions.*

meaningful way, creating a positive first link between children and Hebrew. Hebrew Through Movement is supported by the latest brain research on learning, providing an aural foundation for Hebrew that opens the door to more facile Hebrew decoding and reading.[10]

At Temple Isaiah, students in JQuest begin Hebrew Through Movement in kindergarten and continue with it through sixth grade. In grades K-2 students participate in Hebrew Through Movement with a Hebrew specialist for ten to fifteen minutes once a week. Older students (grades 3–6) participate in this program for ten to fifteen minutes twice a week. Our main goals in using Hebrew Through Movement are that all children will develop a strong aural/oral foundation of the Hebrew language including knowledge of a core vocabulary of Hebrew words, and that children will feel that learning Hebrew is fun, since brain research suggests that "fun is not just beneficial to learning but, by many reports, required for authentic learning and long-term memory."[11]

A Hebrew Through Movement Lesson

So what does Hebrew Through Movement look like in practice? Here is a portrait of a class of fifth-grade students I observed in the spring of 2017:

A teacher stands at the front of the room. She is a woman in her sixties who smiles a lot and speaks with a warm, gentle tone of voice. Several fifth-grade boys sit at a table. Affixed to the back of one of the chairs is a label with the word *kisei* (Hebrew for chair) along with a picture of a chair. Affixed to a table is a label with the word *shulchan* (Hebrew for table) with a picture of a table. There are magnetic Hebrew words on the board, divided into words and phrases:

- *L'hadlik ner shel Shabbat*
- *Ha'motzi lechem min ha'aretz*
- *Borei p'ri ha'gafen*

In addition to the tables and chairs for students, a table has been set up with various Passover-related items on it, such as a haggadah, a fake piece of matzah, a Kiddush cup, and a seder plate.

10. See: https://www.hebrewthroughmovement.org; for curriculum details, see Schachter, "Hebrew Through Movement."

11. Slade, "Why Fun is Important in Learning," para. 10.

The teacher asks the boys (in Hebrew) to stand up ("*lakoom*")[12]. They stand up. She instructs them to run quickly. They begin running around the room. Continuing in Hebrew, she instructs them to walk quickly. They slow from a run to a walk and then proceed to walk quickly around the room. The teacher asks the students to walk slowly to their chairs and to sit down in the chairs. They do so. The teacher now speaks to one particular boy, calling him by name (Jake). As she gives instructions, he follows them:

- Jake, stand up.

- Jump to the board.

- Point to the word "Shabbat"

- Point to the blessing for bread (*ha'motzi*)

- Spin (*l'histovev*) to the map of Israel (Jake spins around himself while heading to the map of Israel on the other side of the room)

- Touch the word "Israel"

- Touch the word "Syria"

- Touch the word "Jerusalem"

- Run to the chair (i.e., his chair). Sit down.

The teacher says to the other boys with a big smile: Clap your hands for Jake! The boys all clap for Jake.

While Jake has been following commands without much trouble, the other boys have been watching intently. The teacher now calls on another boy, Matt, and begins to give Matt instructions, which he follows:

- Matt, stand up.

- Jump on one foot to the map of Israel.

- Touch the word "Egypt."

- Walk to the Pesach table.

- Lift the haggadah (in Hebrew she says, "*haggadah shel Pesach*").

- Put the haggadah on your head (he does so and laughs).

12. Hebrew Through Movement uses verbs in their infinitive form. For ease of following, I employ the English equivalent to describe what is happening in the Hebrew Through Movement lesson. However, the reader should note that all of the commands are given in Hebrew. In Hebrew Through Movement lessons, the teacher uses no English at all.

- Take a second haggadah from the table. Walk to Jake. Give it to Jake.
- Jake, put the haggadah on your head.
- (Both boys are listening and smiling, waiting to see what request the teacher will make next.)
- Jake, walk to the Pesach table. Matt, walk to the Pesach table.
- (The two boys walk to the Pesach table. Each boy is still holding a haggadah on his head, while waiting for further instructions).
- Matt, lift the matzah.
- Put it on the belly of Jake.
- Jake, lift the *chametz* (a plastic piece of bread).
- Put the *chametz* on the belly of Matt.

The boys are now in a somewhat awkward/silly physical position—each boy is holding a haggadah in one hand, with the haggadah on his head, and is holding something else (a piece of matzah or bread) which is touching the belly of the other student. They are smiling and laughing, as the teacher proceeds to tell them to "jump and spin." They begin jumping and spinning around each other until they both dissolve into a fit of giggles. The teacher is also laughing.

The teacher asks the boys to put the haggadot, the matzah, and the *chametz* on the Pesach table. She calls to the other boys:

- Boys (*banim*), stand up.
- Dance over to the Pesach table. (Now all the students are standing near the Pesach table.)
- Simon, pour wine into the Kiddush cup. (Simon pours imaginary wine from the pretend wine bottle into the Kiddush cup that is on the table.)
- Simon, put the bottle on the table.
- Boys, sing the blessing for wine. (They all sing the blessing for wine.)

Of course, this is a description of just a short piece of one Hebrew Through Movement lesson, and that is only one component of Temple Isaiah's new approach to Hebrew learning. Nevertheless, it gives a window into the students' experiences, which are quite different from a typical Hebrew lesson in a synagogue classroom.

Jewish Life Vocabulary

According to socio-linguist Sarah Benor,[13] one of the important ways that American Jews connect to the Hebrew language is through key Hebrew words and phrases that are part of contemporary American Jewish life. With this in mind for JQuest, we created a new component of our Hebrew curriculum in which teachers consciously integrate "Jewish Life Vocabulary" into all classes and programs, with particular Hebrew letters, words, and phrases highlighted each week. Each week at JQuest is "brought to you by the Hebrew letter (such-and-such)," à la *Sesame Street*, along with words and phrases that go along with that letter. For example, when the letter of the week is *yud*, students learn the words *yad*, *Yisrael*, *Yerushalayim*, and *yayin*, and the Jewish Life Vocabulary phrase of the week is *yasher koach*. Teachers integrate the Hebrew letter, words, and phrases of the week into their classes in different ways depending on their personal strengths, the type of JQuest class they teach, and their students' ages.[14] Over time, students in JQuest hear, use, and explore Hebrew terms (such as shalom, *mazal tov, tikkun olam, tzedakah, derech eretz*, and more) frequently, and are, therefore, immersed in a Hebrew-rich environment.[15] The purpose of adding Jewish Life Vocabulary to our program is to help the students at Temple Isaiah learn to experience the world through Jewish values and come to appreciate Hebrew as a sacred Jewish language. Through the use of Jewish Life Vocabulary, we also seek to develop what language socialization expert Netta Avineri calls a Hebrew-oriented "metalinguistic community"[16] in which students feel connected to one another and to Judaism through shared Hebrew greetings, words, and phrases. This process of language-learning, in which group identity is built through exposure to fragments of the group's special language (in this case, Hebrew), is what Benor describes as "ethno-linguistic infusion."[17]

13. Benor, "Do American Jews Speak a 'Jewish Language'?" See also: Benor, "Yiddish, Ladino, and Jewish English."

14. One teacher may use yoga, another uses art, another plays a short game with the letter and words; it is up to each teacher to teach the letter and words in whatever way suits them and their students. These mini-lessons usually take no more than a few minutes of class time.

15. Schachter, "Why Bonnie and Ronnie Can't Read," 84.

16. Avineri, ""Heritage Language Socialization Practices in Secular Yiddish Educational Contexts."

17. Benor, "Hebrew at Reform Jewish Summer Camps."

Hebrew Boot Camp

One of the biggest differences between learning Hebrew at Temple Isaiah and learning it at other synagogues is that, at Temple Isaiah, students learn to decode Hebrew in a twelve-week-long "Hebrew Boot Camp" as a precursor to their b'nai mitzvah tutoring. They work one-on-one with a volunteer mentor from the congregation (or with one of their parents) using a program called "Let's Learn Hebrew Side-by-Side."[18] Students begin the Hebrew Boot Camp ten to eleven months before their bar/bat mitzvah date (outside of and in addition to their JQuest classes) and work on it for one hour per week for twelve weeks. When the Boot Camp is completed, students move on to six to seven months of bar/bat mitzvah tutoring. By the end of the Hebrew Boot Camp, students are expected to know all Hebrew letters and vowel signs, be able to comfortably sound out Hebrew words, and be able to read (for meaning) Hebrew words they know (such as frequently used prayer words and words from Hebrew Through Movement and Jewish Life Vocabulary).

Tefillah

Because so much of Jewish prayer is in Hebrew, *tefillah* education and Hebrew education are intentionally intertwined at Temple Isaiah. *Tefillah* is a vehicle to learn Hebrew and an important outcome of our curriculum; one of our educational goals is for our students to know and value *tefillah* for its own sake. We believe that the best way to learn *tefillah* is to participate in *tefillah*.[19] Therefore, students attend *tefillah* every time they come to JQuest. *Tefillah* is usually 30 minutes: students in grades K-2 attend once a week, students in grades 3–6 attend twice a week, and students in seventh grade attend (and co-lead) every week. *Tefillah* is led by Temple Isaiah's rabbis, cantor, and other song-leaders, using Visual T'filah[20] on Sunday mornings and the Mishkan T'filah siddur (prayer book) on weekday afternoons. In every *tefillah*—whether the words are projected on a screen or in a printed siddur—there is Hebrew, transliteration, and English translation for everyone to use.[21]

18. See: www.Letslearnhebrew.org.

19. Greninger, "Believing, Behaving, Belonging," 412.

20. For more about Visual T'filah, see: https://www.ccarpress.org/shopping_product_list.asp?catID=3756 .

21. See Hoffman's "The Role of Transliteration" for the importance of transliteration

The Affective Dimension of Student Learning

When rethinking Temple Isaiah's Hebrew and prayer curricula, one of our goals was to improve the affective component of our students' learning experiences. While hoping that the students' competency in decoding Hebrew and recitation of Hebrew prayers would ultimately remain at the level it had been in the past (or improve, of course!), we wanted to see meaningful improvement in our students' attitudes toward learning Hebrew as well as their confidence with the language. Numerous scholars have established the connection between mood and performance: Positive mood increases students' cognitive abilities such as memory (including both short-term and long-term memory), creative problem-solving, and learning new rules or categories.[22] Put another way, when students feel positive about their experiences in religious school, it is an improvement because they are enjoying the learning and because they are actually better equipped to learn.

Furthermore, over the last two decades the Jewish community has placed a renewed emphasis on positive feelings about Jewish learning. As education scholar Jack Wertheimer puts it, "Today, the rules of the game [for synagogue-based education] have changed: schools are valued not only, or primarily, for the skills they teach—ritual observance, participating in religious services, decoding Hebrew texts—but for the good experiences children have, the Jewish memories they create, and the positive tone of interactions between parents, children, and school staff."[23]

With the affective dimension of student learning in mind, we set out to create a program in which our students feel positive toward learning Hebrew. So far, we seem to have had some success in that realm. A 2018 survey of 112 JQuest students in grades 3–6 revealed that the overwhelming reaction to the Hebrew-related aspects of their learning was in fact positive (roughly 80 percent indicated that they "liked" or "loved" Hebrew Through Movement and learning Hebrew in general). This positive attitude toward learning Hebrew has also been reported by a wide cross-section of parents in surveys and anecdotal comments. While our findings are preliminary, they point us toward a conclusion that our

---

in *tefillah* for youth.

22. See, for example: Nadler, "Better Mood and Better Performance;" Pitt and Rose, "The Significance of Emotions in Teaching and Learning;" Ashby et al., "A Neuropsychological Theory."

23. Wertheimer, *Schools that Work*, 5.

program is "working" in terms of improving students' attitudes toward Hebrew, and they provide a basis for further inquiry about the changes we are making in Temple Isaiah's approach to Hebrew education.

Observations from the B'nai Mitzvah Tutors

In developing this portrait of Jewish learning, I was particularly interested in how the new Hebrew education program might affect students as they approached their b'nai mitzvah preparation. I wondered what characterized their attitudes as they moved from their JQuest and Hebrew Boot Camp activities to the more focused experience of one-on-one b'nai mitzvah tutoring where they would be expected to decode Hebrew and to take on the demands of their upcoming bar/bat mitzvah services.

To get a better understanding of this transition, I conducted in-depth interviews with Temple Isaiah's b'nai mitzvah tutors, Carrie and Sharona, asking them to reflect on their recent tutoring experiences. Both women are seasoned tutors with extensive experience in Jewish education. Carrie has served as the director of education at multiple Reform and Conservative synagogues. Sharona is an Israeli woman who made her home in the United States as a young adult, served as the assistant director of education at a Reform synagogue for a long time, and currently teaches Hebrew at a pluralistic Jewish day school. Between them, these women have more than sixty years of experience in Jewish education and tutoring students for their b'nai mitzvah.

Several themes about the students' attitudes emerged from the interviews. Both tutors asserted over and again their surprise and delight in how willing the Temple Isaiah students were to take risks as new Hebrew readers, how at ease they seemed to be with prayer, and how comfortable they seemed with their Jewish identities. For example, Carrie commented on the students' readiness to engage in the tutoring experience, contrary to many students she has tutored at other synagogues:

> I think the strongest impression I have is that when the kids come in and I ask them to read [something in Hebrew], very many of them—almost all of them—have a really nice, positive relationship with the challenge of reading Hebrew. You say to them, "So, here, try to read this," and they—you know, they'll smile and hunker down and focus on it, and do their best. It's not a roll your eyes "You're asking me to read Hebrew?!"— which perhaps some other kids who are prepared in a different

way might have. But what really has struck me is most of them have an "Okay, let's get down to it" positive reaction when asked to read.

Carrie noted, as well, that the students willingly embraced the opportunity to study the prayers they would be chanting at their b'nai mitzvah services:

> It's very simple. It's "okay, we're gonna try this prayer. Can you give it a shot?" And usually the answer is "Sure, I'll give it a try." Right? Or, "Let's sing it through, now can you give it a shot?" And usually the answer is, "Okay, I'll try!" It's not the eye roll. They're smiling, they're nodding, they're engaged, they're positive about it, they're not turned off. That's impressive. That's really impressive.

Similarly, Sharona mentioned that even though as many as half the students weren't able to decode well when they began tutoring, their attitude toward prayer was so positive that they were able to progress quickly to competent reading:

> I get kids who are not necessarily fluent in decoding, but they are very enthusiastic about their Jewish identity. They feel very strong—I feel—about their Jewish identity. Especially, for example, when we start doing prayers: they are really into it. They do it with hand motions, they ask me, "Should I close my eyes? Should I stand up now?" They take it literally, the ritual part is very strong in them. It's beautiful to see that they are "in it," they feel part of it, it's not alienating for them.

For the students at Temple Isaiah, *tefillah* is a regular and natural part of their Jewish life, and by the time they begin tutoring for bar/bat mitzvah, they demonstrate a strong connection to prayer. Moreover, Sharona was gratified by how well-integrated the students' Jewish identities seemed to be:

> They feel very authentic to me, they don't feel like it's two separate parts of their life—it brings tears to my eyes! They are here! It's their second home. They feel very comfortable with the culture. They feel supported by the culture, they feel a strong identity, they don't feel like this is it, and then I go home and I'm doing something else. I feel like they are really themselves doing it. Some deep connection that I feel coming from them.

She further explained that while as beginning Hebrew readers the students often confused "the look-alike letters: *dalet* and *resh*, *bet* and *vet*," their connection to the content moves them quickly along:

> For me, as a tutor, it pays off. It's almost better that they come confused about the *dalet* and the *resh* but [already] feel *really* connected to the prayer and really know the melody. They *love* the melody. Because then it's easy to do the other part when they feel connected to it. Already. They come to me already connected.

As Sharona makes clear, Temple Isaiah students may not know the correct pronunciation of every sound of every word when they begin b'nai mitzvah tutoring, but they already feel deeply connected to the prayers and melodies of the community because of their *tefillah* experiences in JQuest, and that leads to an easier experience for the tutors in helping students to fine-tune the words. In some congregations, memorizing prayers—knowing prayers by heart—is somehow seen as "cheating" for b'nai mitzvah preparation. However, as Rabbi Stacy Rigler puts it, "Why wouldn't we want our students to know the prayers by heart, to have the prayers in their hearts?!"[24]

Both tutors asserted that bringing the students up to speed with decoding and reading did not require months (or years!) of tutoring, as is generally the pattern in other synagogue Hebrew programs. As Carrie described it, for most of the Temple Isaiah students who have completed Hebrew Boot Camp, acquiring solid Hebrew reading skills takes only a few weeks:

> In terms of facility of actually being able to read . . . When they first come to me, I make sure to say to them, "I know you're a beginning reader. You're going to forget some things and mix some things up. I want you to know that's okay. I want you to ask me—if you get confused or you forget a letter, don't sit there and worry. Ask me! I'll tell you. I'll tell you fifty times. I don't care. You're a beginning reader."

Given her longer view of how learning occurs, Carrie is able to reassure her students and to help them relax when they occasionally experience lapses:

---

24. Statement made at #OnwardHebrew meeting, Cleveland, Ohio, November 2017. For more information, see https://www.onwardhebrew.org/

So with the recognition that they're a beginning reader, that they're going to get better, that we know they're gonna get better, but for right now, at the very beginning, they're gonna need a little support—that helps them relax into making a good effort.

And usually, within a few weeks, they're pretty confident readers. So all of them—most of them—need reminders of one letter or another, things that look alike, or a vowel here and there, but with those reminders, that's kind of the frosting on that cake. After that, they can read unfamiliar words, even longer words. So with that little bit of individual practice, the program is working.

The Motivation Factor

Of course there are some kids at Temple Isaiah for whom this new approach does not work. There is still a small percentage of students who do not like learning Hebrew, are not motivated to learn, and are not really "prepared" when they begin their b'nai mitzvah tutoring (though all do eventually learn what they need to in order to become bar/bat mitzvah, even if it is in the eleventh hour and with a great deal of extra help from their tutors). Carrie described such situations:

> The kids that I see—which are very few—that come in and it doesn't work with them are usually those kids that are not motivated, not self-motivated to learn Hebrew. And I am not sure that any program on this earth would make them learn Hebrew . . . I don't think it's a fault with the program, I think it's a challenge for those kids . . . it's not important to them, they don't see the relevance in their lives. They don't wanna!

This brings up one of the most important factors leading to the success of our program for the majority of our students: motivation. Motivation can be defined as "a readiness to learn," which means that students have an easier time learning, and enjoy it more, when they are motivated.[25] One of the biggest barriers to success in Hebrew education in synagogues is that many (perhaps a majority) of our students are not particularly motivated to learn Hebrew. Some students may lack motivation because they do not see how learning Hebrew makes a difference in their lives (for example, they do not know anyone who speaks Hebrew); others lack

25. Ostroff, *Understanding How Young Children Learn*, 7.

motivation because they think learning Hebrew is inherently boring or because they believe that knowledge of Hebrew is not necessary for a meaningful Jewish life.

So what might motivate these students who may not otherwise be motivated to learn Hebrew? Cognitive psychologist Wendy Ostroff argues that "humans are motivated by newness, change, and excitement."[26] The Hebrew Through Movement program is designed to feel new and exciting with each and every lesson. The teachers are supposed to be creative with their commands—to give unexpected commands, to ask students to do silly things—to keep the students' attention and help students remain motivated by mixing it up frequently. Ostroff expands on this point:

> Habituation, the tendency to lose interest in a repeated event and gain interest in a new one, is one of the most fundamental human reflexes . . . Habituation is important to understand in relation to children's motivation, because if children are habituating to the learning situation of the classroom, their attention and interest will decline.[27]

This perhaps helps to explain why the usual way of teaching Hebrew tends to lead to less positive outcomes. First, the methods for learning Hebrew in the "old" way (through workbooks, reading aloud, etc.) may not be intrinsically fun or exciting, particularly after the thrill of learning a new language wears off. Moreover, when we begin to teach students to read Hebrew starting in third grade or younger, and repeat the same types of Hebrew reading exercises for years, students habituate to it and lose interest.

Of course, students could habituate to the way Hebrew is taught at Temple Isaiah, too, in which case they may lose interest and therefore motivation. It seems that the key is to keep the Hebrew learning new and fresh to the best of our ability. Hebrew Through Movement lends itself well to that goal as it involves physical movement and can be taught in silly, entertaining, and yet meaningful ways. Jewish Life Vocabulary is formally taught for only a few minutes in each class, in creative ways for each age group, and then it is integrated into the life of the classroom for the remainder of the year. Furthermore, our Hebrew Boot Camp is purposefully taught in the three to four months before students begin their b'nai mitzvah tutoring. In this time frame, students are excited about

26. Ostroff, *Understanding How Young Children Learn*, 15.
27. Ostroff, *Understanding How Young Children Learn* 15.

learning to read Hebrew; at that point, it is a new skill for them, and it is a skill for which they have already developed a basic scaffolding (such as oral/aural language, sight words, a large vocabulary) that makes learning easier. The students are also motivated by the goal of an upcoming bar/ bat mitzvah (which is usually about ten to twelve months after the start of their Hebrew Boot Camp). When students in other synagogues begin learning to read Hebrew in third grade (or earlier), I would guess that they do not really see bar/bat mitzvah as a goal. They may enjoy learning Hebrew at first because it is fun to learn a new language, but within a year or two, the novelty often wears off. Although Jewish educators do not want bar/bat mitzvah to be the end goal of Jewish education, many students do understandably view bar/bat mitzvah as a meaningful goal with regard to their ability to read and chant Hebrew. When a bar/bat mitzvah is on the horizon, it feeds a student's motivation for learning to read Hebrew proficiently.

Another related motivator for learning is the element of surprise. Reviewing the work of Willis[28] and Pogrow,[29] Wendy Ostroff concludes that human brains "have evolved to remember unexpected or novel events because basic survival depends on the ability to perceive causes and predict effects."[30] Therefore, it may be that students are more motivated and may even have a better memory for what they learned when they are surprised. I would speculate that one of the reasons Hebrew Through Movement works so well is because it is designed to delight and surprise the students. When possible, the teacher is supposed to give unexpected instructions; instead of always telling students to eat the matzah, the teacher may tell the students to "put the matzah on your head," for example. Or instead of asking students to sit in a chair, the teacher may ask students to sit under a table. The goal is to surprise the students—in part so they cannot guess the correct action (they have to actually understand the command), but also in part to keep their interest and motivation high for learning more.

There may always be a small percentage of students for whom nothing will motivate them to learn Hebrew, but the approach we are using at Temple Isaiah seems to succeed with a significantly larger percentage of our students than our old approach did. Although we do not have clear

28. Willis, *Research-Based Strategies to Ignite Student Learning.*
29. Pogrow, *Teaching Content Outrageously.*
30. Ostroff, *Understanding How Young Children Learn*, 15.

data to explain our success, we can speculate that some of the reasons include higher motivation, less habituation, and more of the element of surprise.

The Social and Communal Dimensions of Learning

Newness is not the only way to motivate students, and I do not believe it is the only reason Temple Isaiah's Hebrew education program has been successful. Another major component of our program is its social nature. Literature on student engagement highlights the importance of the quality of the relationships in the classroom—the student-teacher relationship as well as the peer relationships among the students.[31] Russian developmental psychologist Lev Vygotsky theorized that collaborative learning is desirable because children who work together can surpass the levels they can achieve alone, and they are more likely to get engrossed in the challenge of learning.[32] Furthermore as Wendy Ostroff notes, "Perhaps the greatest motivator and set-up for learning is the one we notice the least because it is so seamlessly embedded in our daily lives—our desire to join the community."[33]

As we saw in the example of Jake, Matt, and the other boys in the fifth-grade Hebrew Through Movement lesson, students in JQuest stay engaged in their Hebrew learning in part because they are having fun with their peers and want to be part of the community by understanding action-related Hebrew words. The students laugh at one another, they help each other, and they cheer for each other. Hebrew Through Movement is designed to be social in nature and to mimic language learning in its most natural form. Babies and young children learn language by watching and listening to those around them; similarly, students in a Hebrew Through Movement lesson watch each other learn. It is not "cheating" to rely on others—it is how we learn. For example, if the teacher says "stand up" (*lakoom*) to everyone in the class, and a student does not understand the command, he or she can watch the other students and follow their lead.

It is worth noting that Hebrew Through Movement is not only a social, collaborative way to learn Hebrew; it is also a meaningful vehicle

31. Fredericks, *Eight Myths of Student Disengagement*.
32. Vygotsky, *Mind in Society*.
33. Ostroff, *Understanding How Young Children Learn*, 41.

to build community, a "Hebrew-oriented metalinguistic community" (what Benor and Avineri describe as a "community of Jews who have a personal connection to Hebrew"[34]). Hebrew Through Movement is by nature a communal experience, and it allows students to feel positive and connected to Hebrew even when they do not know all the words. By taking social cues, students can be part of the Hebrew learning experience in a fun, encouraging way that enables them to build positive feelings about the Hebrew language as well as about life in the Jewish community. In addition, through the integration of Jewish Life Vocabulary, students develop a common language (including such communal norms and values as *derech eretz* [manners, courtesy] and *g'milut chasadim* [caring for others]) with one another as well as with staff and parents. As Jack Wertheimer points out, "The best [synagogue] schools *intentionally* develop a community among their students, staff, and parents."[35] At Temple Isaiah, Hebrew learning is one of the important avenues for developing a strong sense of community.

The Acquisition of Mastery and Purpose

There is yet another important reason that may explain why the students at Temple Isaiah seem so positive about learning Hebrew, related to Daniel Pink's findings about motivation: that people are most motivated when they have autonomy, mastery, and purpose. In the case of Hebrew learning, students typically have little autonomy and even less of a sense of mastery or purpose.[36] Although our new approach to Hebrew learning does not allow for increased autonomy (students still must follow a teacher's instructions, for example), there is certainly a greater sense of mastery and purpose. Our students develop a fairly significant Hebrew vocabulary prior to learning how to decode Hebrew, so that decoding actually becomes *reading* (sounding out words for meaning). As compared to the "old" way of learning Hebrew, this approach leads to far more light-bulb moments when students sound out a word and realize they know what it means, or when they sound out a phrase from *tefillah* and realize they know what it means and how to sing it. As tutor Sharona observed,

---

34. Benor and Avineri, "Beyond Language Proficiency," forthcoming.
35. Wertheimer, *Schools that Work*, 12.
36. Pink, *Drive*.

> They feel good about [prayer because] they feel good chanting, and [then] seeing something and realizing, "Oh, now I can read it in Hebrew!" . . . When they make a connection between the decoding and the chanting—and they know the chanting [from their experience], they just need to read it. When they make the connection, it feels very satisfying for them.

Students at Temple Isaiah no longer have the frustrating experience of sounding out words that they do not understand or prayers with which they have no connection. Instead, they develop a sense of mastery over the skill of Hebrew reading; they can sound out unfamiliar words but, more importantly, they can truly read a great deal of Hebrew because of their familiarity with Hebrew words, phrases, and prayers. Of course, the students are not fluent in Hebrew and could not pick up a book written in Hebrew and understand everything they decode, but they do feel a sense of mastery over the skill of reading prayers (which they can already recite well by the time they learn to authentically read them, because they have been reciting prayers and learning prayers aurally for years).

Perhaps most importantly, students feel what Daniel Pink describes as "a sense of purpose."[37] They learn to read Hebrew just before they embark on an intense process of individual tutoring for bar/bat mitzvah, so the learning feels relevant, timely, and important. They also learn to read Hebrew at a complicated developmental time: early adolescence. As Urdan and Klein point out, "Research has consistently shown that early adolescence is a period marked by negative changes on a variety of motivational indices," including decreasing intrinsic motivation, declining self-esteem, and a decline in perceived competence.[38] It is precisely at this fraught developmental stage that students have an experience of learning to sound out letters in a foreign alphabet, understand what much of it means, and develop the skills to put it all together to read or chant it in front of their family and peers. The timing of bar/bat mitzvah at the onset of adolescence perhaps explains why it is such a deeply meaningful ritual: it gives students an opportunity to shine right when they feel most vulnerable, giving them a sense of purpose in the midst of great developmental change.[39] At Temple Isaiah, that same sense of purpose that

37. Pink, *Drive*.

38. Urdan and Klein, *Early Adolescence*, 12.

39. According to Dr. Isa Aron, Director of the Union of Reform Judaism's B'nai Mitzvah Revolution project, this is an issue of great interest, but it has not been systematically documented.

comes from the bar/bat mitzvah experience is extended to the students' Hebrew learning, in part because students have already developed positive associations with Hebrew and have not spent years learning to sound out meaningless words.

In Summary

In 1997, in *Succeeding at Jewish Education: How One Synagogue Made it Work,* ethnographer Joseph Reimer devoted a chapter to the topic of Hebrew education at "Temple Akiba" (a pseudonym for the real congregation he studied). He described how this synagogue went through a process of transformation in its education program; the account included a chapter entitled "The 'Mandatory Hebrew' Controversy," that depicted significant controversy about Hebrew learning. It is fascinating—more than twenty years later—to read about a synagogue community that was so deeply conflicted about the role of Hebrew that it questioned whether learning Hebrew should be mandatory for all students in its education program. Reimer noted that after much deliberation the temple's Religious School Committee decided to make the learning of Hebrew "a mandatory requirement for all the students in the religious school," and that this decision "ran into fierce, unforeseen parental opposition."[40]

To understand how far we have come since then in Jewish education, and to appreciate how far we have to go, we need look no further. I would guess that there are very few synagogues today that do not include Hebrew as a significant part of the curriculum for their children's education, and I would be surprised if there were synagogues arguing about whether Hebrew learning should be mandatory. However, it seems that many synagogues still view Hebrew as a subject to be taught, as a dedicated class that is part of a school program. In this model, Hebrew is an optional part of a school that can be deemed mandatory—or not. In such settings, questions about Hebrew education abound, but they typically are focused on curricular decisions rather than bigger questions about Jewish learning.

In contrast, at Temple Isaiah, the question of whether to make Hebrew learning mandatory is irrelevant because Hebrew is integrated and interwoven into the very fabric of JQuest. In the words of educator Cyd

---

40. Reimer, *Succeeding at Jewish Education,* 133.

Weissman, Hebrew is not "a subject to be taught."[41] It is not offered as a separate class on a separate day of the week. For Temple Isaiah's students, Hebrew is part and parcel of their overall experience of Jewish learning.

Further Reflections about Jewish Learning

Educators reach out to me frequently to ask what we are doing with Hebrew learning at Temple Isaiah and how it is working. While the research we have conducted is limited, there is evidence that our new approach to Hebrew learning, based in sound-to-print methodology, has been successful in helping our students build positive feelings about Hebrew while enabling them to achieve the level of competency we expect for prayer recitation and Hebrew decoding. The transition from JQuest to b'nai mitzvah tutoring, as described by our tutors, is characterized by students' upbeat attitudes, openness to trying, deep connection to and familiarity with prayers, and motivation to learn. We have begun to create a Hebrew-oriented metalinguistic community through our new approach to Hebrew learning, and it seems that students are generally enthusiastic about how they are acquiring the language. Moreover, our approach to Hebrew learning is less time-consuming than before, which means we have more time for other types of Jewish learning in our JQuest program overall. [42]

The shift in our approach to Hebrew education has shown me that it is best for students to learn to decode (and read) Hebrew when they already know a great deal of Hebrew vocabulary (by ear, by heart, by movement), when students feel connected to prayers (through the words and the melodies), when students feel part of the community, and when students are motivated to learn. As a Jewish community, it is time to change the conversation about what it means to "learn Hebrew." The approach we have taken at Temple Isaiah has reinforced my appreciation of holistic Jewish education, one in which Hebrew is integrated into all aspects of a child's learning rather than as a separate class or subject to be taught. Hebrew learning binds the community together, builds relationships, and helps to transmit the values of our community to the next generation. It becomes a source of fun and motivation—and a link for positive Jewish identity for years to come.

41. Weissman, "Hebrew is Not a Subject to be Taught."
42. See https://temple-isaiah.org/education/3rd-6th-grade/ for more information.

Bibliography

Ashby F. G., et al. "A Neuropsychological Theory of Positive Affect and Its Influence on Cognition." *Psychological Review* 106 (1999) 529–50.

Asher, James J. *Learning Another Language Through Actions.* Los Gatos, CA: Sky Oaks Productions, 2000.

———. "The Total Physical Response Approach to Second Language Learning." *The Modern Language Journal* 53 (1969) 3–17.

Avineri, Netta Rose. "Heritage Language Socialization Practices in Secular Yiddish Educational Contexts: The Creation of a Metalinguistic Community." PhD diss., UCLA, 2012.

Benor, Sarah Bunin. "Do American Jews Speak a 'Jewish Language'? A Model of Jewish Linguistic Distinctiveness." *Jewish Quarterly Review* 99 (2009) 230–69.

———. "Hebrew at Reform Jewish Summer Camps—Ethnolinguistic Infusion." https://limmud.org/publications/podcasts/limmud-conference-2015/hebrew-american-jewish-summer-camps-ethnolinguistic-infusion/.

———. "Yiddish, Ladino, and Jewish English." http://jdov.org/talk/yiddish-ladino-and-jewish-english-do-american-jews-speak-a-jewish-language/.

Benor, Sarah Bunin and Netta Avineri. "Beyond Language Proficiency: Fostering Metalinguistic Communities in Jewish Educational Settings." In *Beyond Jewish Identity: Rethinking Concepts and Imagining Alternatives*, edited by Jon Levisohn and Ari Kelman. (Boston, MA: Academic Studies, forthcoming).

Fredericks, Jennifer Ann. *Eight Myths of Student Disengagement: Creating Classrooms of Deep Learning.* Thousand Oaks, CA: Corwin, 2014.

Greninger, Nicole Michelle. "Believing, Behaving, Belonging: Tefillah Education in the 21st Century." *Journal of Jewish Education* 76 (2010) 379–413.

Hoffman, Joel. "The Role of Transliteration in the Synagogue." http://blog.joelmhoffman.com/2009/12/09/the-role-of-transliteration-in-the-synagogue/.

Nadler, R. T. "Better Mood and Better Performance: Learning Rule-Described Categories is Enhanced by Positive Mood." *Psychological Science* 21 (2010) 1770–76.

Ostroff, Wendy L. *Understanding How Young Children Learn: Bringing the Science of Child Development to the Classroom.* Alexandria, VA: ASCD, 2012.

Pink, Daniel. *Drive: The Surprising Truth About What Motivates Us.* New York: Riverhead, 2011.

Pitt, Alice J., and Chlöe Brushwood Rose. "The Significance of Emotions in Teaching and Learning: On Making Emotional Significance." *International Journal of Leadership in Education* 10 (2007) 327–37.

Pogrow, Stanley. *Teaching Content Outrageously: How to Captivate all Students and Accelerate Learning, Grades 4–12.* San Francisco: Jossey-Bass, 2009.

Reimer, Joseph. *Succeeding at Jewish Education: How One Synagogue Made it Work.* Philadelphia, PA: The Jewish Publication Society, 1997.

Schachter, Lifsa. "Hebrew Through Movement: A Curriculum." http://www.hebrewthroughmovement.org/uploads/1/0/1/2/10120788/0_htm_final_5_2017.pdf.

———. "Why Bonnie and Ronnie Can't Read (the Siddur)." *Journal of Jewish Education* 76 (2010) 74–91.

Slade, Sean. "Why Fun is Important in Learning." *Washington Post* (June 4, 2010). http://voices.washingtonpost.com/answer-sheet/learning/why-fun-matters-in-education.html.

Urdan, Tim and Steven Klein. "Early Adolescence: A Review of the Literature." A Paper Prepared for the U.S. Department of Education Office of Educational Research and Improvement. https://www.rti.org/sites/default/files/resources/early_adolescence.pdf

Vygotsky, L. S. *Mind in Society: The Development of Higher Psychological Processes.* Cambridge, MA: Harvard University Press, 1978.

Weissman, Cyd. "Hebrew is Not a Subject to be Taught." http://livinglomed.blogspot.com/2012/03/

Wertheimer, Jack. *Schools that Work: What We Can Learn from Good Jewish Supplementary Schools.* New York: The Avi Chai Foundation, 2009.

Willis, Judy. *Research-Based Strategies to Ignite Student Learning: Insights from a Neurologist and Classroom Teacher.* Alexandria, VA: ASCD, 2006.

6

"IF YOU WANT POWER, YOU CAN GET IT"

Orthodox Female High School Students
Negotiating Authority and Autonomy
in Torah Texts

Rafael M. Cashman

WHEN I ENTERED GRADUATE school to study modern religious education, I took for granted a "common sense" inverse relationship between a
person's desire for autonomy and his or her willingness to accept regimes
of authority. I assumed that where there is an increase in one there would
be a decrease in the other, and vice versa; I thought of the two as mutually
exclusive. My doctoral research challenged this assumption. My findings
suggest instead that in practice the results are far more complicated than
I had previously assumed.

In this portrait I describe what I observed when Torah texts are
learned by young, modern, autonomous[1] Orthodox high school girls,
and the way in which, despite their strong sense of autonomy, these students adopt and accept religious authorities associated with these texts.

1. *Autonomy* is commonly construed as the capacity to act with independence and
self-direction, which in a modern context implies freedom from or resistance towards
authoritative constraint, and is thus contrasted with notions of authority. *Heteronomy*,
by contrast, refers to one's being subject to a law, authority, or constraint external to
one's self.

119

Mainstream Modern Orthodox Judaism embraces modern thought and
traditional Jewish learning as epistemologically compatible.[2] In other
words, according to Modern Orthodox theory, a person should be able
to be fully autonomous and fully observant of religious law. In practice,
sociological and educational research suggests that the experience of
Modern Orthodox people (and especially women) may be less straightforward.[3] Typically, contemporary young Modern Orthodox women
are taught the language of "individual rights" and the importance of au-
thenticity and autonomy, while simultaneously being instructed to defer
to religious authorities. They are encouraged to exercise leadership and
self-determination,[4] while being socialized into traditional structures
that tend to essentialize and often domesticate gender roles and identities.[5] Most fundamentally, they are given exposure to core religious texts
that used to be forbidden to study by women and are now permitted.
Nevertheless, they find the impact of gender on pedagogy and the hidden
curriculum[6] to be inescapable, even in those cases where the level of text
study is more equivalent to boys' education.[7]

Given this context, the present analysis sought to probe several
questions about how girls learn Torah texts, including: How do Modern
Orthodox female students use conventional hierarchical and patriarchal
religious scripts in their interpretative framework, and how do they di-
verge from these norms? How do these girls perceive their relationship
to those texts—as authoritative (heteronomous) superstructures in their
very autonomous lives? Does their strong sense of autonomy lead them
to challenge the Torah's authority? If not, why not, and how do they understand or make sense of the relationship between them?

As someone who situates himself within the Modern Orthodox
community, these questions were central to understanding my own surroundings and were ones that I faced in making sense of the two cultures

2. See: Bieler, "Vision of a Modern Orthodox Jewish Education;" Sacks, *Tradition
in an Untraditional Age*; Schacter, "Torah U-Madda Revisited;" Weinberg, *Struggle
From Within*.

3. Tirosh-Samuelson and Hughes, *Tamar Ross*.

4. Levine, *Mystics, Mavericks and Merrymakers*.

5. El-Or, *Next Year I Will Know More*.

6. See: https://www.edglossary.org/hidden-curriculum/

7. See: Benor, "Talmud Chachams and Tsedeykeses;" Cashman, "Conflict and
Creativity;" Charmé, "Gender Question;" Krakowski, "Dynamics of Isolation;" Safer,
"Construction of Identity."

I lived with and between. As an educator in Jewish day schools, including schools which were not Orthodox, I was particularly interested in what our students were learning and how they were making sense of their religious lives and Jewish education(s) in the broader modern context, quite separate from what we as teachers were teaching or intended to accomplish. Without understanding the outputs of our choices, I felt we as educators were at a significant disadvantage as we did not fully understand the impact of our pedagogical and curricular decisions, let alone the implications of the hidden curriculum that exists in all schools.[8] The results of my research, I felt, would be relevant in understanding and making decisions about Jewish education broadly. This would be the case whether the context was Orthodox or not, as all Jewish day schools promote two curricula, which is to say, two sets of values and cultures, to one degree or another.[9]

What became interesting as I explored these questions was less the girls' interpretations of the texts themselves than how these and other biblical and rabbinic texts are understood and mobilized by adolescent female readers today. Recently, other researchers of contemporary religious practice have been looking at the intersection of autonomy and authority in modern religious life, with surprising results. For example, Saba Mahmood notes the challenge of delineating the strictly personal from the authoritative, asking:

> How do we conceive of individual freedom in a context where the distinction between the subject's own desires and socially prescribed performances cannot be easily presumed, and *where submission to certain forms of (external) authority is a condition for achieving the subject's potentiality?*[10]

---

8. Apple, "The Hidden Curriculum and the Nature of Conflict."

9. This follows Peter Berger's understanding in *The Heretical Imperative*, that all religious practice, whether explicitly modern or not, is a response to the modern condition. The Modern Orthodox context, however, has a specific advantage, as it explicitly and fully embraces both "modern" and "orthodox" values and culture, something which neither the more right-wing Orthodox nor the non-Orthodox communities can lay claim to, each one not fully accepting one side of the ledger. As such, the tensions between these two cultural poles can readily be explored in a Modern Orthodox school.

10. Mahmood, *Politics of Piety*, 31, emphasis added.

Mahmood addressed this challenge in the context of religious Muslim women in Egypt, as does Jamal[11] in another Muslim community, with similar questions being addressed in Christian[12] and Jewish[13] contexts as well. In each, the scholars have identified the way discourses of autonomy and discourses of authority have interpenetrated one another, leaving each changed as a result. My research explored a similar theme, with illuminating results.

The Setting

The present inquiry formed one part of my doctoral research, where I spent eight months as a qualitative ethnographic researcher in a Modern Orthodox all-girls high school (henceforth referred to as Neshama). My research followed the twelfth-grade girls, 15 of whom (out of a class of 23) chose to participate in my study.

Neshama is a place that bustles with energy, and one feels this upon walking into the building. The girls play an important role in creating the school culture, with a strong sense that much of what happens in the building is directed or supported by them. And while they take their academic studies very seriously, there is also an informal, camp-like quality in the building that creates both a sense of balance and a sense of empowerment. This can be manifest in the formal structures of school, such as the *va'ad* (committee) structure that runs everything from the lunch programs to student council to *chesed* (volunteer social action) programming.[14] It can also manifest with the girls spontaneously singing and dancing through the halls for no particular reason (at least any reason that seemed to me, and even often to them, enough to justify missing part of a class), or passing doughnuts around the entire school simply to celebrate a birthday, or even a non-event that they deemed worthy

11. See: Jamal, "Feminist 'Selves' and Feminism's 'Others;'" Jamal, "Gendered Islam and Modernity in the Nation-Space."

12. See: Keane, "From Fetishism to Sincerity;" Fabian, *Moments of Freedom*; Seale-Collazo, "Charisma and Freedom."

13. See: Fader, *Mitzvah Girls*; El-Or, *Next Year I Will Know More*.

14. Over time these structures had become ritualized in the school, with traditions built in and around them. At the end of the year I observed a "transition" ceremony, both serious and playful, where the *va'ad* leaders passed responsibility from the present leaders to the next year's leaders.

of doughnuts. Neshama has a positive energy, one which the girls feel themselves both a part of and responsible for creating.

In 2011–2012 I spent much of each day observing the daily life of the school, experiencing its activities and special events, and sitting in on over forty classes. I interviewed each girl according to a set protocol.[15] Some met with me more than once at their discretion; with others, a relationship developed over time where they would notice things around school they thought might interest me and would bring these occurrences and observations to my attention. These then became the fodder for our discussions and reflections about the school and its culture. More than one girl commented on the value of our conversations in clarifying and developing their own understanding of the school and how it operates—a benefit for which I was grateful, but which was unintended.

Building on an ethnographic technique developed by Jo Anne Dillabough,[16] my research design included engaging the girls interactively by presenting them with a familiar artifact as a prompt for discussion. Dillabough used old photographs to enable her informants to confront aspects of the present that, by virtue of the distance in time, would allow them to utilize a perspective of distance that they did not have about their present reality. Instead of photographs, I chose to use an artifact more relevant to the girls' religious experience—a Talmudic text.

The small piece of Talmudic text I read and discussed with the girls would, I hoped, afford me the opportunity to assess how they dealt with issues of autonomy and authority. It was a narrative text that had *halakhic* (Jewish legal) overtones,[17] a text that had the potential to raise issues of both gender and autonomy/authority in religious life. By inviting the

15. I interviewed teachers and administrators as well, using a protocol designed specifically for each group. I had many informal conversations with teachers beyond the formal interview, often using them as a sounding board for my developing ideas and observations.

16. Dillabough, "Exploring Historicity and Temporality in Social Science Methodology."

17. The Talmud is broadly composed of two types of texts—*halakhic*/legal discussion, and narrative (or stories), which are often referred to as *aggadata*. The Bible also has a similar distinction, with both legal and narrative components (but are not referred to as *aggadata*). These distinctions are a useful heuristic for understanding different types of texts in the Bible and Talmud, although in practice the distinction is not always so neat, as narrative can be used to buttress or make a legal point. Moreover, when referring to "Talmud" in an educational context, the implication is generally that legal texts are being studied, not narrative ones.

girls to discuss the text as a group, I hoped to see how they would respond to the content and how they would relate to it as a religious text.

Although I initially intended to set up formal discussion groups outside the classroom for those students who had chosen to participate in my study,[18] a less structured and more organic opportunity arose when a Judaic Studies teacher invited me to meet with her students during class time. Since Torah text-study (including Talmud) was at the core of the girls' Judaic classroom experience, this context seemed of a piece with their normal learning experiences, and therefore the most natural setting in which it could occur. The group discussions occurred about four months into my study, at which point I already knew the girls well, and had already conducted the majority of my individual interviews and observed their normative classroom dynamics. Granted this point of entry, I conducted and recorded the group discussions in the classroom and later analyzed the tapes for discernible themes and patterns.

The Text

The text I introduced raises issues around egalitarianism in marital relationships, subversive uses of power by women in a male-dominated religious hierarchy, and the relationship between how *halakha* is understood in theory and how people use it in practice. In my doctoral dissertation I was interested in seeing how the girls responded to these issues generally. For this paper, I have focused my analysis on their learning process and have discerned a fascinating pattern regarding the girls' relationship to and interaction with this and other Torah texts. In this pattern, traditional texts are not inanimate; rather, my research points to how texts are actively used and framed and suggests that how texts are processed reflects the students' relationship to them, their broader religious commitments, and their deep internalization of a modern autonomous framework.

Here is the text I presented to the students:

> Mishnah: The commandment to procreate applies to the man but not to the woman. Rabbi Yochanan ben Beroka says: [the commandment applies] to them both, as it is written: "And God blessed them, and God said unto them, 'Be fruitful and multiply'" (Genesis 1, 28).

---

18. And during school time as well, since the administration had been very supportive and flexible with my research.

Gemara: Yehudit, the wife of Rabbi Hiyya, experienced *tza'ar leidah* (the suffering of childbirth). She changed her appearance and came before Rabbi Hiyya. She asked, "Is a woman commanded [by Jewish law] to procreate?" He answered her, "No." She went and drank a sterilizing potion. Eventually, the matter became known. He told her: "If only you would have borne me one more bellyful."

This text is taken from page 65b of Tractate *Yevamot*. The Talmud in general, and this excerpt in particular, is composed of two different rabbinic texts. The Mishnah, which is the core text, is a collection of short rabbinic statements, *halakhic* in nature, which was edited in the second century. The Gemara, edited in the sixth century, contain rabbinic discussions recorded subsequent to the editing of the Mishnah, whose primary but not sole purpose is to understand the terse words of the Mishnah. The text presented contained both Mishnah and Gemara, both of which are standard, if minor, parts of the girls' overall Judaic studies curriculum.

Autonomy, Heteronomy, and Personalization

On the whole, in discussing the text, the girls were critical of Yehudit's decision: they did not support what she did or how she did it. What I found distinctive—even intriguing—was *how* they studied the texts and *the relationship they expressed* to them. When I analyzed their responses about moral issues regarding Yehudit's behavior, I was struck by the degree to which the girls used other Torah texts to make sense of the one under discussion rather than evaluating the challenges her behavior presented based on universal moral grounds. They rarely shared an autonomous moral evaluation of the actions described in the story; rather, they used the values they had learned in other Torah texts to make sense of what happened in this one. In this sense, their moral evaluations were embedded within the authority of the Torah's values—they were heteronomous, not autonomous.

I also discerned that, despite their strong sense of individual autonomy and attachment to modern values and culture, the girls found a way to *own* the text as their own, a process that can be deemed "personalizing." Personalizing an authoritative text demonstrates a kind of conceptually complex feat. It demonstrates the ability for someone with a strong sense of autonomy to feel personal ownership over a tradition that is deeply authoritarian and, in doing so, allows him or her to live comfortably with that tradition—because through this personalization, its authority no longer threatens the person's autonomy. This can happen for girls at Neshama because they have some breadth of knowledge of the Torah's textual tradition, knowledge that religious women of previous generations did not have. Because these girls have this knowledge, they can use a variety of texts to generate a variety of moral positions that then become an extension of their personal moral value systems overall.

The girls' responses, therefore, point to the surprising and non-linear way in which autonomy and heteronomy operate simultaneously for contemporary Orthodox students. Their responses reveal the impact that the girls' broad Torah education has had on their understanding of their own moral decisions as well as of other Torah texts. As will become clear as the girls' responses are reported below, their opinions do not seem to happen because they have differentiated between their religious and non-religious moral positions, such that Torah texts would only be evaluated against other Torah texts. Rather, the girls' personalization of the Torah's authoritative texts seems to emerge because, for these students, *the texts themselves have become a personal expression.* The girls have learned to adopt the texts as authoritative and they use the Torah lens to generate moral decisions that are both autonomous *and* heteronomous.

A colleague once described to me Avivah Zornberg's writing about Tanach as post-modern. He suggested that in Zornberg's work, texts that are biblical, rabbinic, modern, literary, and psychoanalytic all operate together and at the same level of interpretive authority, and not in the hierarchical fashion that is the norm in traditional Jewish learning. Whether or not one agrees with this assessment of Zornberg's approach, this seemed to be the case for the girls at Neshama. They expressed a sense of ownership over the texts they know, moving fluidly from the texts to their own understandings and back again. Despite their being deeply personal, however, these texts retained a kind of heteronomous authority for them.

Students in Dialogue: A First Response to the Text

The Talmud is composed of both *halakhic* (legal) and *aggadic* (non-legal) content, with far more of the former than the latter, both in volume and as the focus of commentators. For the most part, students who attend Orthodox Jewish day schools primarily study the *halakhic* portions of the text. Neshama is no exception. As such, the group conversation started out with a conventional dynamic, with the girls responding to the *halakhic* or legal issue in the story, grappling as to whether there was a *halakhic* issue with Yehudit's decision to sterilize herself, a choice that would have prevented her from fulfilling the *mitzvah*[19] of having more children. In the excerpt from the discussion below, when girls refer to a *"mitzvah"* in the text, this is the *mitzvah* under discussion. Also, towards the end of the conversation, the girls operate with the traditional understanding that the *mitzvah* of reproduction only applies to men, not women, and that if one has had a male and female child, he has fulfilled this *mitzvah* and no longer has an obligation to procreate. Here is an excerpt from that part of the discussion.

> Avigail[20]: But did she have a girl to fulfill the mitzvah?
>
> Rafi[21]: Yeah. That I don't know.
>
> Devora: I'm guessing that she clearly didn't fulfill the mitzvah because then he said, "if you only would have borne me one more child" . . . it probably could have been a girl.
>
> Rivki: He just wanted one more kid though. I don't think he was saying, like, you haven't fulfilled the *mitzvah*, like, if only I could have one more child I would have been happy.
>
> Samantha: He didn't say, "if only I could have fulfilled the *mitzvah*."
>
> Rafi: What does it say? What did he answer no to? What was the question she asked?
>
> Cindy: Is a woman commanded to procreate.
>
> Rafi: So what does that mean, when you read the mishnah, you thought the *mitzvah* was on both of them?
>
> Esther: Yeah, but . . . [the *mitzvah*] is not on both . . . Cause she already did her *mitzvah*.
>
> Rafi: She had no *mitzvah*.
>
> Esther: She's stopping her husband from doing the *mitzvah*.
>
> Cindy: If he had a boy and a girl then he's fine.

In this first read, the girls use *halakha* as the frame through which to judge Yehudit's actions. They are not paying close attention to the details

---

19. One of the Torah's 613 commandments that articulate a Jew's religious and moral obligations.

20. All student names in this paper are pseudonyms.

21. "Rafi" here refers to me, the author, for the purposes of transcribing my conversations with the girls, although in person the girls did not call me by my first name.

of the text (otherwise they would have noticed that there is no *halakhic* judgment of her actions by her husband); nor are they analyzing the interaction between husband and wife as a story, which would require a different interpretative lens than that of *halakha*. Rather, they are using their prior knowledge about the *mitzvah* of reproduction and trying to apply it here. That they seem to bring so much knowledge about the issue to bear is revealing with respect to the amount of Torah they seem to know (e.g., the specific requirements to fulfill the mitzvah and to whom the mitzvah does or does not apply). This interaction, therefore, says something both about the level of their Torah knowledge and about what a normative (*halakhic*) first response might be.

And yet, the *halakhic* level of response is ultimately both narrow and short-lived, taking up only a very small part of the beginning of the discussion. Subsequent to this opening set of interactions, the girls quickly pivot and use both Torah and Talmudic narrative (i.e. non-*halakhic*) passages to make sense of the broader moral messages they perceive in the text before them.

Using Torah Texts to Make Personal Moral Decisions

The thirty-eighth chapter of the book of Genesis tells the story of Judah (Yehudah in Hebrew), son of Jacob, and Tamar. Tamar was Judah's daughter-in-law who first married Judah's oldest son. When he died, Tamar married the next son in line—and then he died as well. In both marriages Tamar was childless, and following the biblical law of *yibum* (levirate marriage), she was obliged to marry yet another of Judah's sons. Judah did not want Tamar to marry a third son, fearing that he would marry her and die as well, so he sent her off to live somewhere else, promising falsely that he would bring her back into the family at a later date. Tamar, upset by this, pretended to be a prostitute, slept with Judah (her identity unknown to him), and became pregnant. In the conclusion of the story, Judah admits that he'd treated Tamar improperly and that the sons he has with her are considered legitimate heirs. As such, the Torah ultimately seems to vindicate Tamar's actions, implicitly accepting her duplicity as justifiable under the circumstances.

In the group discussion of the text, the conversation begins with Cindy's quick personal judgment, which is supported by two other girls. However, Ayala moves from the moral problem in the Rabbi Hiyya story as developed by her classmates to quickly identifying the parallel to it in the story of Judah and Tamar, which contains a comparable moral dilemma:

> Rafi: How does she (Rabbi Hiyya's wife) go about getting what she wants?
>
> Cindy: She tricks him.
>
> Rafi: In what way does she trick him?
>
> Cindy: By disguising herself.
>
> Sarah: Cutting her off from being pregnant.
>
> Esther: And pretending she's someone that she's not.
>
> Ayala: It's [like] Tamar and Yehudah.

For Ayala, it seems that simply making a personal judgment about a rabbinic character is insufficient unless it is supported by precedent, which the story of Judah and Tamar is understood to be. As the conversation continues, Batya shares her thoughts on the direction Ayala has taken. A close read of her words (my italics added for emphasis) shows how she personalizes the biblical story and how she claims the moral dilemma for herself:

> *I'm going back* to the Tamar and Yehudah story, which is different, but, *I think* in the Tamar and Yehudah story they don't, she's not a villain, *I mean,* Daveed [King David] comes from her. So if that's ok, and she disguised and everything there, then *I'm thinking* what she did here is okay, unless the sterilization she did is a problem, then *I have a problem* with that. But *I* don't have a problem, *I* don't think *I have a problem* with what she did.

In her comments, Batya fleshes out Ayala's reference to Tamar and Judah, and then takes the analysis a step further. If what Tamar did is acceptable, as evidenced by her progeny being King David (i.e. a meritorious outcome), then the outcome of what Yehudit did should be okay as well, as long as there is not a competing *halakhic* prohibition.

But close attention to Batya's language reveals something deeper about how she is using these texts. She says "I'm going back to the Tamar and Yehudah story" and "I think in the Tamar and Yehudah story . . . she's not a villain, I mean, Daveed comes from her." For Batya, if the actions of Tamar are acceptable—"then I'm thinking what she did here is okay"—then the biblical case justifies her personal acceptance of Yehudit's behavior. This view is placed in contrast with the question of sterilization in the Talmudic case which, although not explicit, "is a problem" only if it is legally forbidden; in fact, if there is a *halakhic* problem with sterilization, then Batya personally endorses that position, as she stipulates, "then I have a problem with that." She invokes her personal feelings, and not just an abstract and demanding law that is the ground for the critique. This seems to be emphasized, and it goes beyond the *halakhic* or biblical when she concludes: "But *I* don't have a problem, *I* don't think *I have a problem with what she did.*" At this point, the decision comes solely from a personal place. On the one hand, the decision comes as a result of turning to biblical and *halakhic* precedent; on the other, it is not just an appeal to authority. Rather, Batya has blended the authoritative and the personal.

What emerges from this part of the conversation is the use of biblical texts as the reference point for judgment. This may not seem entirely surprising, given the educational context. But it is noteworthy, because the biblical texts, which are construed as authoritative, are subsumed into a personalized, autonomy-oriented discourse.

Additional Examples of Authority and Personalization

In the discussion of Yehudit's behavior, the girls also use a further intertextual reference point by bringing in the story of Jacob and Isaac (Yakov and Yitzchak). In this biblical story, Jacob, encouraged by his mother, dresses up as his brother Esau in order to get the blessing of the first born from their father Isaac. While the commentators are mixed about the morality of his actions, there is a tendency to vindicate Jacob's behavior and see his deception as ultimately justified. Like the previous story, this one deals with the permissibility of deception, and in the girls' interpretation it is marked by both authority and personalization.

In the classroom discussion the girls spend twenty minutes considering Yehudit's behavior and I then ask them what her change of appearance might mean. The conversation continues:

> Leah: It kind of reminds me when like with Yitzchak and Yakov and how they ... so like we're learning about that in *chumash* [the five books of Moses].
>
> Rafi: That they were deceptive.
>
> Leah: *I mean,* first of all, *I don't think it's so right* that she [Yehudit] cheated him, but *I guess,* for her to get the honest answer, which is what she felt she had to do ...

Leah turns to the story of Jacob and Isaac, as Batya and Ayala did with the Yehudah and Tamar story, to figure out if deception can be acceptable. Turning to a Torah reference is her first instinct. Yet immediately afterward she pulls back and says, "*I* don't think it's so right that she cheated him." In doing this, she moves away from the biblical narrative as a reference point and toward her own moral compass—making a personal, autonomous judgment of Yehudit's behavior. Yet this move on her part is itself questioned ("but I guess") as Leah sees the redeeming possibility in Yehudit hiding from her husband in order to get an honest answer to the *halakhic* question posed in the story.

Leah's first inclination is to turn to the textual tradition, either because it is proximate and contextual as a school activity and a pedagogical norm, or because it is part of how these girls come to make sense of a moral issue. But she also moves to acknowledge her own moral critique of Yehudit. Finally, representing her unique attempt to justify Yehudit's behavior, she assumes that a *halakhic* truth could be achieved without a disguise and reads Yehudit's deception as an honest attempt to get the most truthful *halakhic* answer. Absent this deception, Leah implies that her human subjectivity would have improperly influenced the *halakhic* decision Rabbi Hiyya would have come to, namely, the one that favored him—continuing to have children.

As with Batya, in Leah we see an emerging discourse in which religious authorities (*halakha* and the biblical narratives) are personalized and thus subsumed within an autonomous framework. The texts are contextualized by personalization, even as the girls' own, quite independent autonomous opinions also play a legitimate and deciding role in how they judge Yehudit's behavior. While Batya and Leah have in a way taken on the texts as their own, thus limiting the sense of it acting as an authority which makes demands on them and challenges their autonomy, I do not think this tells the whole story. They move too easily and smoothly between these personalized expressions of text and their own quite independent and autonomous opinions about Yehudit's behaviors. The girls do not seem to distinguish between their own personal autonomous worldview and one informed by the authorities of God, text, and *halakha*.[22] Rather, for the girls of Neshama, there is a much more fluid

22. This observation builds on a study by Devra Rose Lehmann in her dissertation ("Literacies and Discourses"). She studied the ways students studied (or were trained to study) differently in a Bible class and an English literature class in a Modern Orthodox high school. When studying literature, students felt empowered to express

and overlapping relationship between the values that come from each of these cultures.

This is a significant observation because it challenges the notion that autonomy and authority are mutually exclusive ways of looking at or understanding the world, such that more of one means less of the other. This is clearly not the case for the girls of Neshama, who move seamlessly between one worldview and the other, or alternatively, occupy both within one conceptual framework. Even if their educational experience is bifurcated between two domains and discourses of autonomy and authority, the girls themselves don't experience this bifurcation; they express something new and syncretic. In a fascinating way, they are able to own their learning, or at least the texts of their learning, in a way that would not be possible for someone who revered the text as beyond or above them. Through their personalization, they are able to develop a close identification with the texts in a way that someone from a more traditional Orthodox culture might find challenging, because for them the text is divine in nature and so, by definition, of a higher status. This more nuanced response is made possible by the influence of cultural modernity and the value it places on autonomy.

Beyond these examples are others in which the girls bring in various biblical and rabbinic sources as they try to understand the story. In each case, the intertextual references similarly attempt to mediate the relationship between autonomy and authority. For example, Bracha offers a different biblical reference point wondering if Yehudit was wrong to remove from herself the fate of woman—the dynamic described in the biblical story of Adam and Eve. She muses:

> So now I'm wondering if it was appropriate for her [Yehudit] to do something like that. But at the same time, like, the woman is the one who's going through all the pain, just so the man gets

---

their opinions about the text and that their opinions mattered. Lehmann calls this "a discourse of autonomy." In the Bible classes, the opinions and ideas of students were subservient to the classical commentators like Rashi, or the interpretations of the Rabbi/teacher, with little credence given to the students' own interpretations of the biblical text. Lehmann labels this as "a discourse of authority." While her research found the existence of different ways of learning and thinking in each environment, she did not look at the outcome of these differences in the lives of students. My study, as evidenced in this example (and through many others in my full thesis), built on Lehmann's framework and specifically looked at how these two ways of learning and thinking operate in the lives of the girls themselves, and the way they live these two very different "discourses" in their personal practices and beliefs.

a *mitzvah*. But like, at the same time that was our punishment from Chava,[23] Adam and Chava, from their thing, like, we had to have birth-pains. So I don't think we can take that away, and just not have children, cause like we're not going to fill the world. We just learned in *Mishpacha*[24] that Hashem created a world so it could be filled, and if we don't have children, then we're not . . .

Bracha's use of the Chava story changes the lens through which the Talmudic story is read. Instead of looking at Yehudit's deception as acceptable or not, she uses the example of Chava to judge whether the goal of her deception (i.e. sterilization) is acceptable. Bracha's first construction is local and she tries to work through the rationale for the *mitzvah* of reproduction: since the man is the only one who is commanded to reproduce, why should women suffer? This objection is based on personal moral grounds—not one raised by the tradition as an objection to *halakha*. But like Leah, Bracha weighs this personal moral awareness of injustice against the lesson she learns from the biblical narrative of Adam and Eve, in which Eve's punishment is her birth pains. She moves from this point to a more abstract conceptual rationalization: that Jews are obligated to "fill the earth" (*peru u'revu*), and that this is an obligation on all people, even if they have no *halakhic* obligation.

Like her classmates, Bracha frames her analysis in personal terms when she says, "So now *I'm* wondering," and "So *I don't think* we can take that away"—where the first comment seems entirely personal and grounded in an autonomous morality and the second is framed by her understanding of the biblical story of Eve. However, she does move eventually to a more traditional, authoritative discursive stance. In her concluding phrase she says, "and if *we* don't have children, then *we're* not . . . " Here the "we" are Jews in general and their generalized set of obligations, rather than an individual or self-oriented language that reflects only the position of the individual speaking. As noted earlier, Lehmann[25] sees this distinction in language as a reflection of the "discourse of autonomy" versus the "discourse of authority." She found that the discourse of autonomy that is present in the English literature classroom she studied was characterized by students using "I" language, which reflected their individual opinions. The discourse of authority that is present in Judaic

23. Chava is the Hebrew name for Eve.

24. Literally: family. Here it refers to a class the girls have once a week about the family, marriage, relationships, etc.

25. See footnote 20; see also Lehmann, "Student and Teacher Responses to Prayer."

studies classrooms was characterized by students using "we" language, which reflected the opinions of tradition or communal norms. Neshama students rarely use "we" language when they interpret religious texts, so the example above is a significant exception.

Using A Rabbinic Reference to
Support the Moral Framework

In a later part of the discussion, a student named Devora also uses inter-textual references to determine the morality of Yehudit's actions, but she turns to a rabbinic story instead of a biblical one. Like the other girls, she personalizes the text, but in a different manner. The story she draws on is that of one of the Talmud's greatest sages, Rabbi Akiva.[26] Rabbi Akiva was a poor farmer, and yet Rachel, the daughter of a wealthy man, wanted to marry him despite her father's threats to cut her off financially if she did. Rachel married him nonetheless, living for many years in poverty while her husband spent years away studying and growing into a rabbinic leader. As Devora thinks about Yehudit, she makes an association about the willingness of Rabbi Akiva's wife to give up wealth for this man and live alone while he studied Torah. She then compares this woman's choices to those made by Yehudit. We enter this conversation after Devora has presented the Rabbinic text and has used Rachel as a foil for Yehudit. She sees Rachel as a success for having loved her husband and stood by him, in contrast to Yehudit, who, given her deceptive behaviors, did not properly love her husband as she should have and was not honest with him.

> Rivki: I kind of agree with Devora to an extent. Like what we said before, it was clearly a very dysfunctional relationship, and she [the wife] may have been scared to approach him [R. Hiyya], and that's why she went to him in that way. But I don't know if she thought it through because it really could have been just for herself and for her safety.
>
> Samantha: Maybe it's dysfunctional nowadays, but back then they didn't really marry for love.
>
> Rivki: You don't know that! You don't know whether they were in love or not.

26. A full translation of this text may be found at: https://www.sefaria.org/Nedarim.50a.

Devora: Ok, there's this story with Rabbi Akiva and he marries her for love and she stood up to her father and she went against him, so if you want power you can get it yourself.

Samantha: Ok, fine, there's the odd occasion where you marry for love and you get disowned. I'm saying nowadays they marry for love, but then they couldn't.

Devora: But I'm saying in those days they could have, there were instances where they did.

Samantha: I said there's rare instances, but most of the time you didn't.

Devora: So yes, I'm criticizing her because she had the potential to do something like Rabbi Akiva's wife did, and she didn't.

Devora uses the story of Rabbi Akiva's wife Rachel to do two things. The first is to make a point about the possibility of marrying for love in ancient times. For Devora, of course, this is a norm of contemporary relationships, and so can be taken for granted in the Talmud as well. Second, she uses this story to critique Yehudit's behavior and her lack of willingness to confront her husband, and frames it in very contemporary terms—as a lack of exertion of agency or, as she calls it, power. In both ways she personalizes her use of the text to support the correctness of her moral framework, both what is justifiable, as in the case of Rachel, and what is not, as in the case of Yehudit. What we observe here is the intersection between Devora's contemporary normative values and the text, and her ability to use the text seamlessly as her own.

Devora perceives in the story that "if you want power you can get it yourself." Like the other girls, she uses a different Torah text to make a moral claim in this story about correct, or in this case ideal, behavior. Devora uses the text to substantiate a contemporary claim about love and female power. Thus, an alternate rabbinic intertext forms the basis of her opinion but also leads her to make a comment about women's power, which she sees Yehudit as not having exercised. Her support text, in contrast to the one we were studying, substantiates a woman's right to act autonomously, no matter the historical circumstances. This notion of self-advocacy, which Devora uses the story to support, is a modern concept. While one may argue about whether Rachel acted for love or had some other motivation—since it is not clear from the text what her motivations were—she does stand up to her father in order to choose her husband, acting, in Devora's view, as women should act. Thus, her own personal expectation of relationships, combined with support from the Rabbi Akiva story, substantiates Devora's critique of Yehudit. She criticizes the lack of self-actualization and self-empowerment in the Yehudit story, qualities that are notably modern, and certainly so for a woman in a religious context.

Samantha, on the other hand, takes the opposite approach. For her, there is a big social and cultural gulf between how relationships operated in Talmudic times and today, so even if there is a story about Rachel and Rabbi Akiva and the love of one for the other, it is not generalizable. What makes this interaction fascinating is that, given the fact that Samantha and Devora both accept that relationships today need to be egalitarian and respectful, they differ in how they read those assumptions into traditional texts, and as such, how those texts operate to support or reject their critique of Yehudit as a Talmudic figure. This observation points not only to the way that texts can be understood so very differently by their readers, but also the way in which learners personally identify with some texts over others and, as a result, use those texts to explain or justify their own moral or cognitive frameworks.

Gender and Text Learning

I chose to study a Modern Orthodox girls' school because I believed the tensions between the values of modernity and those of traditional Judaism would be most obvious and explicit with girls, given the patriarchal elements of traditional Judaism and the strong valence of egalitarianism in modern life. While a full analysis of what emerged is beyond the scope of this paper, a few words on my findings will be helpful to contextualize my conclusions below.

One of the striking findings of my full study is the degree to which the girls of Neshama rarely described any tensions between egalitarianism and patriarchy (which is a version of the authority/autonomy binary) in ways I had assumed they would. For example, they were quite content about the lack of egalitarianism in practicing *halakha* (males are obligated in more *mitzvot* than women), since it meant far fewer demands on their time than it did for boys. Many also rejected the feminist label for themselves, since they reported feeling quite equal to boys in their social interactions, even if they recognized they were not treated the same way in the realm of ritual and *halakha*.

When asked about how their curriculum differed from that of the boys, they recognized that the boys spent more time on Talmud, the core text of the Oral Torah, and they understood that their studying Talmud counted in some measure as a decision meant to create equity between the girls' and boys' religious educations. However, they did not seem bothered by the difference in volume, nor did they consider that there were any significant implications of this difference.[27]

In light of this curricular difference and the girls' general lack of concern with feminist concerns, I would like to draw attention to the move to narrative texts (both rabbinic and biblical) amongst the girls in their analysis of the case of Yehudit, and the way that both gender and the hidden curriculum of a girls' school may be significant in understanding a narrative approach. The girls' use of intertextual biblical or rabbinic narratives to frame these discussions is notable, especially in contrast to the lack of reference to *halakhic* or more abstract conceptual Torah sources as a basis for critique.

To be sure, there is a powerful relationship between narrative and personal identity. Narrative provides the reader with an easy entry point to ideas. Some have argued that we relate much more readily to narratives than we do to abstract concepts.[28] For the girls of Neshama, narratives— whether biblical or rabbinic—provide moral guidance and religious coherence, and are owned more deeply. This is a good reminder that when we hope to make an impression, stories are a most powerful vehicle.

But something else is clearly going on here, beyond just the power of stories. It might be helpful to compare what we found in Neshama to what Sarah Benor[29] found in her comparative study of linguistic patterns in ultra-Orthodox girls and boys schools. Benor observed very different patterns in boys' and girls' learning, patterns that instantiated boys as "learners" and girls as "*tzedekeses*" or righteous, generous women. She describes an instance when she asked both classes to debate; the boys choose a legal topic, the girls a social (though religious) one, namely, the age of *bat mitzvah*. Boys brought textual proofs; girls did not. This seemed to happen because the girls lacked confidence in their knowledge of textual sources, as this knowledge is not emphasized in their religious education and environment in the same way as for boys.

At Neshama, the girls have no lack of confidence in their use of texts. This paints a stark contrast to Benor's ultra-Orthodox educational

27. Cashman, "Conflict and Creativity in Jewish Modern Orthodox Girls' Education."

28. Fasching, *Narrative Theology After Auschwitz.*

29. Benor, "Tamid Chachams and Tsedeykeses."

institution, which makes sense given that Neshama is a Modern Orthodox school where girls have a full Judaic studies education. However,
there is still a dramatic gender differentiation in which texts were used.
As I observed often in their classes, the girls of Neshama use the texts and
frameworks they are most familiar with from their curriculum: narrative,
and primarily biblical narrative, texts. Even though they, like the boys,
study the *halakhic* sections of the Talmud, which implies a formal equal-
ity of the sexes, they do so for much less time, and focus far more on the
biblical and Talmudic narratives. In general, the girls' environment gives
Talmudic learning far less status than in the boys' environment, and the
biblical narratives far more.

We might hypothesize that the girls do not have a broad array of
halakhic sources, or at least Talmudic legal sources, on which to draw
because of the biblical bent of their education. Or, it may be that the biblical sources are at the core of their religious hermeneutic, as Bible study
forms a larger part of their curriculum at Neshama than it does for the
boys, who focus more on Talmud. Either way, one can begin to see how
the materials and content chosen to be part of a curriculum, in this case a
"gendered" curriculum, can influence the way in which the students use
texts in new contexts.[30]

It is also noteworthy that, in making moral arguments, the Neshama
girls did not appeal to universal norms (a very modern notion) or even
universal religious/Torah principles (e.g. "love your neighbor as yourself" or "stay far away from lying/falsehood"), separate from specific *halakhic* expectations. For these girls, the Biblical and rabbinic narratives are
more salient than *halakhic* considerations or universal religious/Torah
principles as a guide in their analysis of the text. Even though abstract
theological concepts do arise, as with Devora, they are few and rarely
taken up as points of argument or reference in the conversations. Yet
even as the narrative texts are the first place they go to make sense of a

---

30. Of course, this was not a study of gender comparisons, so the implications of
my findings are limited, but the findings point in an intriguing direction about the
power of curriculum, and particularly a gendered curriculum, to impact a religious
outlook. My observation here has less to do with a gendered understanding of text
than with pointing out that even within the Modern Orthodox community that pur-
ports to value egalitarianism (at least as regards Torah learning), there are differences
in the lens each gender brings to a Torah text. This is especially thought-provoking
given the notable differences in the curricula of boys and girls in Modern Orthodox
schools. Where these differences may lead in terms of religious outlook and commitment are beyond the scope of this study, but would be fascinating to consider.

moral dilemma, almost all students end up making their decisions from a very personal place.

Concluding Thoughts

Texts, as one sees with the girls of Neshama, are not frozen. We might say, rather, that they are malleable in the hands of the learners, and (sometimes) actively used by them. In calling attention to the malleability of texts, we are not merely referring to the act of interpretation, although of course that is true as well. What is fascinating here is the way that texts are employed to make sense of normative moral problems. When Devora uses the story of Rabbi Akiva and his wife Rachel to challenge the notion that women in ancient times were subservient to the will of men, or when she refers to the case of Judah and Tamar to determine whether and when deception (even of a sexual partner) is morally acceptable, she is not so much deferring to the authority of the text as *thinking with the text*. She might have done otherwise. She and the other girls might have engaged in a principled, philosophical conversation about women as moral agents who are accountable for their actions, for example. Surely, at some level, Devora does hold this belief. But rather than engaging in that kind of conversation, she hangs the belief on the text.

This use of text reflects an act of personalization that points to the internalization of a modern, autonomous cultural framework. In the Rabbi Akiva case and in the other texts used throughout the girls' Talmud study, there is a close identification between the authoritative text used to support a particular moral position and the position of the girl herself. This observation is fascinating as a way to understand the complexity of living in modernity, disrupting our assumptions about a tension between authoritative patriarchal structures and the moral and intellectual autonomy of the (female) individual. In these cases, at least, the girls find creative ways to express their own autonomy, and yet live comfortably within the authorities of religion (God, Bible, *halakha*, etc.). To the outside observer, the girls are subservient to the demands of their culture, complying with the religious practices of the Modern Orthodox community. But when we pay close attention to what they say, and especially how they learn, we notice that the way they *understand* these religious practices differs from how they are conventionally understood.

Devora argues that, in the context of agency and responsibility, people have to "get power for themselves." While they might not use this phrase about themselves, these girls are doing exactly that—taking the power of authoritative texts and using them for their own autonomous moral purposes. It would be unfair and inaccurate to say that the texts were simply proxies for their opinions. Moreover, these young women were fully capable of expressing and exploring their own views on a variety of matters without reference to Torah texts, so it is not the case that they are only permitted to say something when they can find a text to back them up. In fact, they often move interchangeably between the text and their own opinions. But sometimes, as in the examples that I have been discussing, they do think with the text, borrowing the authority of the text to strengthen their arguments. In this sense, the girls of Neshama know how to operate within a patriarchal structure in a deeply modern way. They know how to get power for themselves.

Further Reflections About Jewish Learning

To use the traditional language of Torah learning, in the portrait shared here I see both a *klal* (a general principle) and a *prat* (a specific message). What strikes me most broadly is the notion of "thinking with the text" as a reflection of the openness and flexibility that is possible when learning traditional and authoritative Torah texts, an assumption that is not obvious when speaking about divine writings. This is a powerful and important message for those with a desire for relevant religious learning within our contemporary cultural milieu, and for Judaism's ability (or rather, the ability of a Jew learning text seriously) to respond to an ever-changing world from within our tradition.

My more specific observation is how an awareness of this openness points to the way female students are able to connect to, be empowered by, and become creative producers of Torah learning. That young women, conscious of their autonomy and the great opportunities in front of them, can find themselves—both as contributors and participants—within our learning tradition, is vital both for the sustenance of contemporary Jewish life, and as authors of Modern Orthodoxy's evolving practices and worldview.

Bibliography

Apple, Michael. "The Hidden Curriculum and the Nature of Conflict." *Interchange* 2 (1971) 27–40.

Benor, Sarah. "Talmid Chachams and Tsedeykeses: Language, Learnedness, and Masculinity Among Orthodox Jews." *Jewish Social Studies* 11 (2004) 147–70.

Berger, Peter. *The Heretical Imperative: Contemporary Possibilities of Religious Affirmation.* Garden City: Anchor, 1979.

Bieler, Jacob. "Vision of a Modern Orthodox Jewish Education." https://www.lookstein. org/resources/vision.pdf.

Cashman, Rafael Mark. "Conflict and Creativity in Jewish Modern Orthodox Girls' Education: Navigating Tradition and Modernity." PhD diss., University of Toronto, 2015.

Charmé, Stuart. "The Gender Question and the Study of Jewish Children." *Religious Education* 101 (2006) 21–39.

Dillabough, Jo-Ann. "Exploring Historicity and Temporality in Social Science Methodology: A Case for Methodological and Analytical Justice." In *The Methodological Dilemma: Creative, Critical and Collaborative Approaches to Qualitative Research*, edited by Kathleen Gallagher, 185–218. New York: Routledge, 2008.

El-Or, Tamar. *Next Year I Will Know More: Literacy and Identity Among Young Orthodox Women in Israel.* Detroit: Wayne State University Press, 2002.

Fabian, Johannes. *Moments of Freedom: Anthropology and Popular Culture.* Charlottesville: University of Virginia Press, 1998.

Fader, Ayala. *Mitzvah Girls: Bringing Up the Next Generation of Hasidic Jews in Brooklyn.* Princeton: Princeton University Press, 2009.

Fasching, Darrell. *Narrative Theology After Auschwitz: From Alienation to Ethics.* Tampa, FL: University of South Florida, 2002.

Jamal, Amina. "Feminist 'Selves' and Feminism's 'Others': Feminist Representations of Jamaat e-Islami Women in Pakistan." *Feminist Review* 81 (2005) 52–73.

———. "Gendered Islam and Modernity in the Nation-Space: Women's Modernism in the Jamaat-e-Islami of Pakistan." *Feminist Review* 91 (2009) 9–28.

Keane, Webb. "From Fetishism to Sincerity: On Agency, the Speaking Subject, and Their Historicity in the Context of Religious Conversion." *Comparative Studies in Society and History* 39 (1997) 674–93.

Krakowski, Moshe. "Dynamics of Isolation and Integration in Ultra-Orthodox Schools: The Epistemological Implications of Using Rabbeim as Secular Studies Teachers." *Journal of Jewish Education* 74 (2008) 317–42.

Lehmann, Devra Rose. "Literacies and Discourses in the Two Worlds of a Modern Orthodox Jewish High School." PhD diss., Columbia University, 2008.

———. "Student and Teacher Responses to Prayer at a Modern Orthodox Jewish High School." *Religious Education* 105 (2010) 299–316.

Levine, Stephanie Wellen. *Mystics, Mavericks and Merrymakers: A Journey Among Hasidic Girls.* New York: New York University Press, 2003.

Mahmood, Saba. *Politics of Piety: The Islamic Revival and the Feminist Subject.* Princeton: Princeton University Press, 2011.

Sacks, Jonathan. *Tradition in an Untraditional Age: Essays on Modern Jewish Thought.* Portland, OR: Vallentine Mitchell, 1990.

Safer, Lois Ballen. "The Construction of Identity Through Text: Sixth- and Seventh-Grade Girls in an Ultra-Orthodox Jewish Day School." PhD diss., University of Pennsylvania, 2003.

Schacter, Jacob J. "Torah U-Madda Revisited: The Editor's Introduction." *The Torah U-Madda Journal* 1 (1989) 1–22.

Seale-Collazo, James. "Charisma and Freedom: Religious Education and the Everyday Extraordinary in a Puerto Rican High School." EdD diss., Harvard University, 2006.

Tirosh-Samuelson, Hava, and Aaron W. Hughes, eds. *Tamar Ross: Constructing Faith.* Boston: Brill, 2016.

Weinberg, Noam Zvi. *Struggle From Within: The Complexity of Modern Orthodoxy, the Relationship Between Religious Actions and Beliefs and the Religious Development of Modern Orthodox Adolescents.* PhD diss., Yeshiva University, 2008.

7

GROWING MADRICHIM
Jewish Adolescents in a Relational Learning Community

Stefani E. Carlson

FOR THE EDUCATION DIRECTOR of a synagogue supplemental school, the first day back to school after winter break is almost always a busy one. Happy to see one another, teachers and students arrive eager to share stories of their vacation adventures and looking forward to beginning the work of the new semester. On a Sunday morning in January 2017, as I walked around Temple Beth Shalom, a small, exurban Reform Jewish congregation on the outskirts of Cleveland, I heard excited voices greeting each other all over the building. Parents clustered in the foyer, in the hallways, and even outside on the sidewalk on this unusually balmy winter day, catching up with each other's news. Students called out to their friends as they hung up coats and headed into classrooms. Several students and parents responded to my friendly calls of *"boker tov!"* ("good morning!") with tales of trips: to Florida, to visit grandparents, even to Thailand and other exotic locations. "Miss Stefani, I got to pet a tiger, and he wasn't even in a zoo!" exclaimed a first-grader. "Go find my mom, she has pictures!" Teachers, looking forward to that evening's community-wide *Erev Iyyun* (Evening of Learning), which would bring together religious school teachers from throughout our city for a speaker and workshops, stopped me to ask about logistics and carpool arrangements. Our congregation's board of directors and Brotherhood were also meeting that morning. The whole building was full, energized with the joyous sounds of this tightly-knit community reconnecting after a few weeks away.

With all this happy chaos in the building, it was no surprise that it was well into the morning before I had a moment to stop by the kitchen for a cup of coffee. While I was there, I overheard part of a conversation that made me take notice and gave me great pleasure:

> Jacob[1]: Hey, Mike, do you have David in your class?
>
> Mike: Yeah, why?
>
> Jacob: I was asked to pull him out for some extra Hebrew practice to-day. But the last time I worked with him, he really seemed to be strug-gling to remember anything at all. It was as if he didn't even know the letters. I wondered if you have any ideas about things that you think work well with him.
>
> Mike: Hmm . . . I think he knows the letters, he just gets frustrated and gives up really quickly if he doesn't recognize the words right away. It's hard when he's in class, because he gets embarrassed that the other kids are watching him, and sometimes they're not real nice about it, so he just quits. Maybe if you can get him to at least try when you're one-on-one with him, you can see if he actually knows anything and then kinda go from there.
>
> Jacob: OK, thanks. That helps. I'll come get him in a few minutes.

Had this conversation taken place between two veteran teachers I would have been pleased, but not particularly surprised. What was re-markable about it was that it occurred between two teenage boys, both high school sophomores, who were volunteering as *madrichim* (teaching assistants) in the religious school, and that until I walked into the room at the tail end of the conversation, there were no adults present at all. The discussion happened organically, without prompting by a teacher or other facilitator, and was entirely based in the teens' own desire to help the student learn, as well as their trust in each other as sounding boards and sources of potential help. No one told them to have this conversa-tion—they were both on break, just as I was. Nor did they engage me in the discussion, even after I entered the room: their own dialogue was sufficient to meet their purposes. While they greeted me warmly and we

---

1 All names of teachers, teens and students are pseudonyms. Some identifying characteristics have been changed to protect privacy. Conversations are reconstructed from notes and may not be verbatim.

visited for a few moments as we poured our coffee, the conversation did not turn back to the subject of the student. It was only much later, during a scheduled interview, that I debriefed the exchange with them and came to appreciate its potential significance in terms of the kind of growth and transformative learning that Temple Beth Shalom's teen engagement program had begun to foster.

Setting: The Madrichim Project

At the time of the break room conversation described above, the two boys involved had been participants in the pilot cohort of the congregation's innovative *Gesher* program (a three-pronged approach to post b'nai mitzvah engagement that includes classroom learning, youth group, and social action projects) for more than three years.[2] For the eighteen months leading up to that January morning, a key component of their participation in the *Gesher* program was their service as *madrichim* in the religious school and their inclusion in the intergenerational professional development program which I created to integrate the teens into the religious school faculty.

During the spring of 2015, the eighth-graders in Temple Beth Shalom's *Gesher* program met with me to co-create what would happen during their ninth-grade year. In this planning discussion the students indicated that they wanted to replace the social action component of their post b'nai mitzvah programming with work as *madrichim* in the religious school. Although individual students had volunteered in the religious school in previous years, there had never been a group of students serving together before, nor had there been any structured plan for the professional development of *madrichim*. During that spring meeting, we determined a structure for their involvement in the year ahead:

- class learning time would be reduced to one Sunday a month
- youth group meetings would be given a bit more structure and direction to encourage leadership development
- the teens would commit to attending four of the five scheduled faculty meetings for the year (including the orientation session before

---

2. For more information about the *Gesher* program, see: http://urj.org/blog/2017/05/04/how-we-bridged-gap-post-bnai-mitzvah-engagement.

the beginning of the school year and the wrap-up meeting at the end of the year), in order to learn alongside their mentor teachers

As I engaged with the teens in the negotiations around this agreement, I was struck by the mutually supportive nature of this group. While the majority was eager to work with younger students, one boy was hesitant. I was impressed by how the group talked their classmate through his resistance and found a way for him to participate that was more comfortable for him (by volunteering during weekday Hebrew school instead of on Sundays, and working with me on projects rather than in a classroom). Given the collaborative spirit of the group, I had reason to think about how to leverage this relational atmosphere to improve the teens' learning in the new *madrichim* program.

Teens in a Relational Learning Community

During the summer between my planning conversation with the teens and the official start of the new program, I did quite a bit of reading about the different models and theories of *madrichim* training that already existed, to see how they might guide the development of this endeavor. I found Patti Kroll's article, "Working with Teen Assistants," with its extensive references and portraits particularly helpful, especially around the idea of "growing" teen assistants;[3] this image resonated with my learning goals for the teens in this cohort. The work of Richard and Elaine Solomon[4] served as a bridge between the literature on teen engagement and the theories of learning and professional development that would ultimately form the foundations of the project. While I found useful information in curriculum-focused pieces such as Lisa Bob Howard's *Madrichim Manual*[5] fairly early in my planning process, I rejected the idea of a parallel learning track for the teens as not conducive to the inter-generational learning I wanted to have take place. I elected instead an approach in which the *madrichim* would learn alongside their mentor teachers in joint professional development sessions. Significantly, that summer I entered a professional development program as a learner

3. See Kroll, "Working with Teen Assistants."
4. Solomon and Solomon, *Toolbox for Teachers and Mentors.*
5. Howard, *The Madrichim Manual.*

myself, an experience that ultimately shaped the theoretical framework I brought to this project.[6]

Miriam Raider-Roth, director of the Mandel Teacher Educator Institute (MTEI), posits that for teachers, an optimal learning environment occurs when they can belong to a Relational Learning Community (RLC), a systematic "learning group" in which there is an intentional commitment to "the construction and nurturing of relationships between and among the participants, facilitators, texts/content, and context."[7] In my planning for the new *madrichim* program at Temple Beth Shalom, I began to wonder what it would look like for the teens' learning to take place within this type of structured and intentional environment, in which the relationships between the members of the cohort of *madrichim*, their mentor teachers, and the rest of the faculty and professional staff of the congregation would be seen as just as vital to the educational process as the content material being presented. As *madrichim*, the teens would need to learn important information, including Hebrew, Jewish texts, theories of teaching and learning, and practical classroom skills. I anticipated that their participation in a RLC could enable them to cultivate new types of relationships across the congregational community to support that learning.

The potential developmental benefits of a RLC to the *madrichim* might also extend well beyond the classroom. Not only would the teens be building peer relationships with each other, they would also be forging supportive bonds with their mentor teachers and other adults. By entering into mutually enriching mentoring relationships, and forming ties with clergy and administrators within the RLC, the *madrichim* would find role models from whom to shape their own sense of self. That this learning and development would all be taking place among a group of Jewish participants within the context of a Jewish school was also significant: the *madrichim* would be learning to be both Jewish teachers *and* competent and impactful Jewish adults.

---

6. This project is closely tied to my participation in Cohort 7 of the Mandel Teacher Educator Institute (MTEI) and the associated Certificate in Jewish Education program at the University of Cincinnati and reflects the theoretical framework of those programs. More information can be found at: www.mtei-learning.org.

7. Raider-Roth, *Professional Development in Relational Learning Communities*, 2.

Madrichim and Mentors in Egalitarian Learning

A distinctive (and possibly unique) feature of the RLC we developed at Temple Beth Shalom was that, by design, it was inter-generational and highly egalitarian. This group of students had been involved in the co-creation of their own learning experience since the *Gesher* program's inception in 2013, meeting each spring with administrators and teachers to set the priorities and schedule for the coming year. This process had afforded them an exceptional sense of ownership over and investment in their own Jewish learning and identity development. In turn, the teachers with whom they were working had been studying the "educative mentoring" model,[8] a democratizing and relational approach to teacher education in which the role of the more experienced partner is to help the novice think through the complexities of teaching and learning, rather than to dictate a particular course of action.

In the RLC, the *madrichim* worked alongside the teachers who served as their mentors and attended faculty meetings and trainings as equal partners. By learning together, the teachers and *madrichim* developed what education theorist David Hawkins describes as learning relationships built on "a shared concern."[9] Through collaborative discourse teachers and students "have a common theme for discussion, they are involved together in the world."[10] In the context of the RLC at Temple Beth Shalom, common themes included such diverse elements as Jewish texts, student work, classroom strategies, and the subject of teaching and learning itself. Because the teens and their mentor teachers learned side-by-side in professional development sessions, the power structure of the classroom was equalized, with teachers and *madrichim* relating to each other in a more egalitarian way than is typical of most classroom aides and their teacher supervisors. This shift in stance contributed to the formation of deep mentoring relationships that impacted the learning of the teens and teachers, as well as their younger students.

8. Feiman-Nemser, "Helping Novices Learn to Teach," 17.

9. Hawkins, "I, Thou, and It," 58.

10. Hawkins, "I, Thou, and It," 57.

From Project to Portrait: Focusing on Mike and Jacob

During the summer of 2015, I drafted an outline for the faculty meetings and leadership development sessions that would form the backbone of the RLC. Once the program was in place, however, it was clear that more than a curriculum would be necessary for me to fully assess the impact of this new structure. Even though there was already evidence of a high retention rate in the *Gesher* program, I wanted to probe in-depth the ways in which the *madrichim's* participation in an RLC alongside their mentor teachers impacted the teens' learning, development, and engagement in Jewish life.

To more carefully track the students' experience, during the 2015 and 2016 school years I collected qualitative data in the form of written and oral reflections from participants, notes and recordings from professional development sessions, classroom observations, and participant interviews. I also documented the teens' level of Jewish engagement by tracking their involvement in congregational and community-based programs. As I began to analyze the data, four episodes, each involving Mike and Jacob, stood out as representative of different stages in the process of maturation, transformative learning, and professional development that was taking place among all the teens in the *madrichim* program. Upon closer examination, I realized that the two boys had very different ways of engaging with the learning environment, and that these differences provided insight into how the RLC affects different people in different ways.

Episode 1: Mike and Jacob as Learners (Summer 2015)

If I had needed to choose the students to be the subject of this portrait based on the first RLC meeting of the 2015–16 school year, Mike and Jacob would have been far down the list. While they were eager to participate in the program from the beginning, their behavior at the RLC orientation session was less than exemplary. Their reaction to and level of participation in the session did, however, provide an excellent baseline by which to measure their learning over the subsequent two years of their participation in the program. Additionally, the differing patterns of engagement which characterized their individual learning approaches were clear, even from this first encounter.

To launch the *madrichim* program and to set the stage for the learning the teens and teachers would do together, I invited all of them to a

half-day orientation retreat, to be held at the temple on the Sunday before
the first day of religious school in August. While all of the teens in the
Gesher cohort had expressed interest in volunteering in the school when
we discussed it during the spring meeting, I was curious as to whether
giving the program more structure and requirements might turn them
off. In fact, the opposite turned out to be true: the teens responded to
my invitation by saying that they felt more comfortable about the idea of
working as *madrichim* knowing that there would be a structure in place
to support them in learning to work with students. Fourteen people,
evenly divided between adults and teens, attended this initial meeting.
This was the first time in the known history of the congregation that teens
had attended the faculty orientation meeting, so the change in tone for
the year was immediately established.

The session began with introductions (including the icebreaker
question, "What brings you here today?"), and a general welcome and
introduction of the year's theme: "Professionalizing our School." We then
transitioned into text study, using a text from Talmud which describes a
teacher's personal rituals for entering and exiting his classroom[11]:

> Rabbi Nehunya's Prayer
>
> Mishnah, Tractate *Berakhot* 4:2
>
> רַבִּי נְחוּנְיָא בֶּן הַקָּנָה הָיָה מִתְפַּלֵּל בִּכְנִיסָתוֹ לְבֵית הַמִּדְרָשׁ וּבִיצִיאָתוֹ תְּפִלָּה
> קְצָרָה. אָמְרוּ לוֹ: מַה מָקוֹם לִתְפִלָּה זוֹ? אָמַר לָהֶם: בִּכְנִיסָתִי אֲנִי מִתְפַּלֵּל
> שֶׁלֹּא תְאֱרַע תַּקָלָה עַל יָדִי, וּבִיצִיאָתִי אֲנִי נוֹתֵן הוֹדָיָה עַל חֶלְקִי
>
> Rabbi Nehunyah used to pray a short prayer on his entrance to
> the Beit Midrash. They [his students or colleagues] said to him,
> "What is the nature [literally, "the place"] of this prayer"? He
> said to them: "When I enter I pray that no mishap [or "offense,"
> literally it means "stumbling"] take place because of me, and
> when I leave I give thanks for my lot."

The inclusion of the text study exercise was directly related to the
theme of professionalization. I considered it critical for teachers and
madrichim alike to understand that to be a "professional" teacher, one
must also be a learner, and that reflection on one's own learning can (and
should) inform one's teaching practices. More specifically to the text, the
themes of creating sacred space in the classroom, and of marking the

---

11. This text study worksheet is from the materials developed by Professor Barry
W. Holtz for MTEI Cohort 7, Seminar 1, June 29, 2015.

division between that space and time and the "outside world" through the use of *kavannah* (prayer and intention), were also central to the discussion, which I guided using questions such as:

- Why do you think Rabbi Nehunya paused for prayer before entering the Beit Midrash?

- How do you set your intention before you enter your classroom?

- How do you feel at the end of each class? What factors impact your emotional state?

In terms of process, I asked the participants to divide themselves into *havruta* (learning pairs) but gave no direction as to the composition of the pairs. While the majority of the group formed pairs consisting of a *madrich(a)* and a teacher, two *madrichim*, Mike and Jacob, chose to study the text together.

Most of the attendees appeared very eager to participate in text study; several commented that they had not done an exercise like this one before, and several others said that they liked the idea of beginning a faculty meeting with a learning session. Mike and Jacob, on the other hand, had significant difficulty staying on task. Photos of the event show them deeply engaged not in text study but in opening and examining the contents of Kinder Surprise eggs.[12] Only with significant prodding and redirection were they able to get through the partner discussion assignment. Their participation in the larger group discussion was limited to replying when called upon. Their responses, although brief, were at least on topic. When asked what had changed between the two prayers quoted in the text, Mike responded, "What changed is that he [Rabbi Nehunyah] knew how the lesson went, so he wasn't worried about it any more, and could relax."

On the other hand, throughout the orientation meeting I observed that these boys seemed to be very much enjoying being in each other's company, talking and laughing together animatedly (they did not attend the same school, and their socialization with each other was generally limited to the context of the congregation and its activities), and staying

12. Kinder Surprise eggs are foil-wrapped hollow chocolate eggs, manufactured by the Italian company Ferrero, each of which contains a plastic capsule in which a small toy or other surprise is hidden. They are not available for sale in the US, but are a commonly-traded item among TBS students who attend events of the North East Lakes Region of the National Federation of Temple Youth (NFTY)—a region that includes teens from Canada as well the States.

together (including other students in their group as well) during breaks. And, while they might be described as having passively endured the text study activity rather than engaged in it, they did, in fact, complete the written assignment that followed the discussion, which was to write their own prayer for the beginning of the new school year.

> Mike's prayer: "To learn and be kind to others and be helpful to everyone and the Earth and to maybe even teach someone so that they learn and can help everyone and the Earth too."

> Jacob's prayer: "I want to make a positive educational impact on the students in the fields of both Jewish values and the fine arts relating to Judaism."

The boys' responses, even in this very first assignment, showed the different types of connections each of them made to the learning environment, which formed the pathways and motivations for their participation in the program. Mike, in his mention of "others," "everyone," and "someone," revealed the *relational* stance driving his involvement. This is a student who comes to temple because his friends are there. During the spring discussion leading to the formation of the *madrichim* program, his stated interest in working in the classroom was because he genuinely enjoys interacting with the teachers and the younger students: "I think it would be cool to hang out with [his future mentor teacher] and the kids, and help them learn," he said. At his public school, Mike is a well-rounded student, with good grades and high levels of involvement and achievement in sports and other extracurricular activities. He is, however, one of only a handful of Jews in his town (and has never attended Jewish summer camp), so he relies on the temple as the primary source of his Jewish community involvement and as the place where he can experiment with finding his own Jewish identity. He is popular with his peers, and at the time of the orientation meeting was serving as membership vice president of the temple youth group.

Jacob, in citing the content areas of "Jewish values" and "the fine arts" reflected a more *academic,* information-driven stance. He had said during the spring planning meeting that he wanted to participate because he is interested in the content matter to be taught and in the pedagogical processes of learning to be a teacher: "I think that if I work in our religious school, I can be prepared to be a Hebrew teacher when I am in college." He is an excellent, highly-motivated student in his public school as well, taking multiple AP and other advanced classes each year, and is also deeply involved in the performing arts. He is less dependent on the temple as the source of his Jewish community involvement, as he attends a school where a significant proportion of the students are Jewish (enough that the school is closed on the High Holy Days), has parents who are Jewish professionals, and has attended Jewish summer camp for many years. While relatively new to the congregation, and therefore lacking in some of the communal history with the other teens, he is also well-liked by his peers and at the time of the orientation meeting was serving as communications vice president of the temple youth group.

The orientation meeting, especially the text study activity, ultimately served a number of important purposes: it established the *madrichim* as members of the faculty and full partners with the teachers in learning; it set a precedent for teachers and *madrichim* to view themselves foremost as learners; it built community among the faculty; it introduced the idea of a Jewish classroom as a sacred place in space and time; it highlighted the importance of the role of teachers in ensuring the Jewish future; and it empowered the faculty to make changes in their classrooms. Most important, it established a precedent for communal study and professional development to form an integral part of what had previously been viewed as business meetings, and for text study as a basis for future *madrichim* workshops. The text itself made explicit the connection between learning, reflecting, and teaching. The learning was conducted in *havruta*, a traditionally Jewish form of study, which helps to reinforce the message of a text.[13] While Mike and Jacob's level of participation was limited, they did say they enjoyed the experience and were eager to begin their work with the students, providing a foundation for their learning in the RLC.

The participants' reflections and written prayers helped me to pair *madrichim* with mentor teachers for the year ahead. Since Jacob mentioned the arts in his prayer and is active in arts activities in his public school, I assigned him to the music teacher as his mentor. A college professor in addition to serving as music teacher and cantorial soloist of the congregation, this teacher was able to engage Jacob in the type of high-level idea-focused conversation that would keep him interested in the work of the school. And because Mike had mentioned the Earth, and had also spoken of the need to help people and to "relax" in the classroom, I assigned him to work with our sixth- and seventh-grade *Tanakh*

13. Holzer and Kent, *A Philosophy of Havruta.*

(Bible) teacher, who had an extensive background in Jewish mysticism and in martial arts and who held a deeply spiritual and relational view of learning.

Episode 2: Adolescent Rebellion (Fall 2015)

It is unrealistic to expect that any attempt at transformative change on an institutional level, such as implementing a complex *madrichim* program as part of an intergenerational RLC, will happen overnight or without complication. Indeed, organizational theorists warn educators that change will likely be fraught with resistance and transitions marked by moments of failure as well as success.[14] Likewise, just as the adolescent period of human development is often marked by turbulence as teens learn to navigate their new roles and frames of reference, as the *madrichim* program moved along it was rocked by turbulence—and even rebellion—as the teens and teachers settled, sometimes uneasily, into their new roles.

In the first year of implementing the intergenerational RLC, the intentional democratization of the learning process brought with it unexpected challenges. Throughout the year, the teens who were learning to serve as *madrichim* were being introduced to egalitarian dynamics in the faculty meetings and *madrichim* leadership development sessions. They were expected to serve as co-creators of learning with others in the RLC. By midyear, however, a shift occurred when the *madrichim* realized that the situation in their monthly *Gesher* classes was not as egalitarian as had been their experiences in faculty meetings and leadership development sessions. A catalyst for rebellion occurred in October, when the *Gesher* class teacher began to teach a lesson that (he later acknowledged) he had recycled from teaching at a Jewish day school that focused on a text study related to an upcoming holiday. Offended by what they perceived as a lesson that was "too babyish" and "not what we agreed to," the *madrichim* refused to participate in the activity. When the teacher pushed back and attempted to continue with his plan, Mike, Jacob, and a third classmate got up and left the classroom in a clear act of civil disobedience.

For me as the school's education director, this uncharacteristic behavior provided an unexpected "teachable moment" about *kavod* (respect/honor) to teachers, classroom management . . . and about speaking

14. Guskey, "Professional Development and Teacher Change," 381–91.

truth to power. A few minutes after the conflict with their teacher, I found the teens outside engaged in a heated venting session. They were outraged at having been overruled on the lesson content and initially refused my offer to mediate. They were not yet ready to re-engage with the teacher. Eventually, they did agree to come sit down with me for some more constructive discussion. Interestingly, in this conversation Jacob's and Mike's differing stances again came through. Jacob was angry because the topic of the lesson was not what he had agreed to study, reflecting his content-focused pathway of connection. Mike, on the other hand, was more upset that the teacher (his mentor teacher, albeit in a different class setting) had not listened to them when they complained and had continued to teach the lesson over their objections, reflecting his relational pathway of connection. Once the teens felt heard and had calmed down, I accompanied them back to class and sat in as an observer for the rest of the session. When the class reconvened, the students were able to complete the lesson and to express calmly to the teacher what they wanted in the future. Several highly productive conversations ensued—between the students and their teacher, the teacher and myself, and myself and the students—which informed planning for future lessons.

In the *madrichim* leadership development session that took place shortly after this incident, I encouraged the teens to apply their reflection on what they had learned as "learners" in this situation to what they might learn about themselves as "teachers." By asking questions requiring them to think about and discuss how the students with whom they work might feel in a similar situation, and how they might handle the scenario differently if they were the teacher, I sought to help them gain a deeper understanding of others' perspectives. The ability to look at the world through others' eyes, and to shift one's own actions accordingly, is frequently cited as one of the most significant developmental changes between adolescence and adulthood, and is also a characteristic of transformative learning.[15]

Episode 3: Acquiring Broader Perspective (Winter-Spring 2016)

During the second half of the year, Mike and Jacob began to demonstrate greater self-insight and a broader perspective about their roles as

---

15. Mezirow, "Transformative Learning," 5–12.

teachers. In a leadership development session in January, I invited them
to reflect on the prayers they had written at the fall orientation meeting,
asking:

- Looking back at your prayer for the year that you wrote in Meeting
  #1, do you feel like you are on track to fulfill it? What do you think
  you want/need to do to better actualize your prayer?

- Is there anything about your prayer which you would change? What
  is your prayer now, at the end of the first semester? What do you
  hope your prayer will be at the end of the year?

Their responses showed that both were starting to realize that some
of their previously held assumptions—their "truths"—might need to be
adjusted to accommodate others' realities:

> Jacob's responses:
>
> 1. I feel that I am succeeding in making my students enthusiastic
> and spirited in religious education, which in turn causes them
> to understand their educational materials/ lessons better. I may
> need to be even more enthusiastic, though, because specific
> children are more introverted and require extra motivation to
> willingly engage in learning about Judaism. I have trouble with
> being able to relate to those children.
>
> 2. In my prayer I do not mention anything about altering my
> own teaching approach to be more safe or make the experience
> more fun. I would add these motives to my prayer.
>
> Mike's Responses:
>
> 1. Yes. I think I need to maybe help a little more and try to have
> a happy aura that flows through others.
>
> 2. I like it the way it is. To keep on keepin' on and live life. I hope
> my prayer to help others will never change.

In these written reflections, Jacob's responses were considerably
longer than Mike's and were more explicit about his perceived impact on
his students' learning. He again mentioned content ("educational mate-
rials/lessons" and "learning about Judaism"), and was more detailed in
expressing his thinking about pedagogy ("causes them to understand,"
"require extra motivation," and "altering my own teaching"). He also
acknowledged his own difficulties and shortcomings, particularly in the

area of relating to children unlike himself. The solution he offered—"to be even more enthusiastic"—may or may not actually have helped to bridge that gap; however, his acknowledgment that he may need to change his "teaching approach" to accommodate others demonstrated a significant level of reflection on his developing practice as a teacher.

Mike's written responses were brief, but they were consistent with his outward-focused relational stance. For example, not just wanting to "have a happy aura" but for it to "flow through others." He, too, indicated that he was beginning to reflect on his practice and consider that he might need to make changes to "help a little more." Furthermore, in my notes of the teens' verbal responses during the discussion portion of the meeting (in which Mike and Jacob both participated voluntarily, in contrast to the fall orientation session), I recorded several comments Mike made about the responses of the students in his class to the Hebrew games he was designing to help them build their decoding skills (e.g., "They like it when I let them pop bubble wrap as a reward. It calms them down, and they actually will read more if I let them do it, so can we please get some more?").

Later in the first year of the program, Mike participated in a video investigation project in which a group of teachers and *madrichim* watched a video of a classroom and practiced observing the teacher. Responding to the question "What does the teacher do to help her students learn?" Mike wrote: "Kids remember old teachings, showing that they retain information previously taught." This response would appear to indicate a shift in his thinking: instead of simply recording what the teacher was doing, he was looking for evidence of student learning. Similarly, during the last faculty meeting of the year, as his final reflection/exit prayer Jacob wrote: "I pray that my contributions caused the students to engage in their studies later in Hebrew school and continue Jewish learning." Overall, Mike and Jacob's responses during this period of time suggest a shift in focus from the immediate to the future. Rather than focusing on their own actions and feelings in any given moment, both had begun looking for evidence of impact and to demonstrate understanding that their actions can have lasting effects on their students.

Episode 4: Transitioning to Jewish Adulthood
(Spring 2016-Spring 2017)

During the planning meeting at the end of the first year of the *madrichim* program (Spring 2016), the teens in the pilot cohort agreed that, since they were beginning to become more active with the Reform youth movement (NFTY) on a regional level, which would require more time, and since they were going to be starting more formal confirmation classes with the rabbi in the fall, they would not include service as *madrichim* as a mandatory cohort commitment for the following school year. Although it was no longer a requirement, five teens began the second year serving as *madrichim,* and attended the full-day faculty professional development retreat that summer. However, with the increased demands of school, extra-curricular activities, and NFTY, their attendance soon became spotty. By midyear, only Mike was attending regularly; Jacob participated when his schedule permitted. None of the other teens in the cohort volunteered more than a couple of times in the second semester of their sophomore year, although all completed the confirmation class and related requirements. In a year and a half, Mike and Jacob had developed from the disengaged teens playing with Kinder eggs during the initial orientation meeting into the leaders of their cohort in the *madrichim* program.

So what had changed? In the winter of 2017, I arranged with Mike and Jacob to interview them about their experiences as *madrichim,* what they had learned as members of the RLC, and their plans for the future. We decided to conduct the first interview informally, as a walk-and-talk during our congregational *shabbaton* (retreat) in February. As we walked the long boardwalk that skirted the partially-frozen lake at the state park lodge where the congregation was celebrating Tu B'Shevat, our conversation ranged all over the place, from what movies they were seeing, to what classes they were taking (and planning to take) at school, to Mike's new baby sister, to our beautiful and interesting natural surroundings. While for the most part I let the conversation go where they wanted to take it, I seized on this moment of openness to ask them what kept them coming to volunteer as *madrichim* after the rest of their peers had drifted away. While both mentioned some parental pressure to continue, they both acknowledged strong intrinsic motivation for participating—which corresponded to their initial feelings of connection to specific elements of the learning environment.

Mike spoke at length about his relationship with his mentor teacher, with whom he had continued to work for a second year. He said that he valued their partnership and felt that he had been given space and support to grow and to develop his skills in the classroom: "He lets me try new games and stuff with the kids, and if they work, great, and if they're not into it, he's there to help." Mike said that he enjoyed his work with the kids in the class, which included his younger brother, and felt that being together in this context had given them a valuable bonding experience: "It's different when we're at Sunday school. He's less annoying there." He indicated that he also appreciated the "down time" that coming to the religious school afforded him. "It's just nice to be able to go to TBS and hang out with [his mentor teacher], and learn, and be with the kids, and just relax and not have to worry about stuff."

Jacob, on the other hand, had chosen not to continue working with the music teacher for a second year. Instead, because his Hebrew skills were the most advanced of the teens in his cohort, he decided to train under my supervision to become a one-on-one Hebrew tutor for students who needed extra support. Sometimes he worked with students like David (the student mentioned in the dialogue at the beginning of this paper) who required remediation in their basic Hebrew decoding skills. Other times, he sat with students who were studying for their bar or bat mitzvah, to listen to them practice prayers or their Torah portions. Occasionally, he helped with behavioral issues, accompanying students who needed sensory breaks or giving one-on-one attention to those who were too shy to speak up in class regularly. Jacob said that he found that the variety of this type of work kept him more engaged ("It's just more interesting when every day is different, you know?"), and that he enjoyed the intellectual exercise of trying to understand each student's needs and respond to them accordingly. He and I had several other conversations over the course of the semester in which his most frequent questions were "Why do you want me to work with this kid?" and "What do you think s/he is going to get out of the one-on-one time?" Occasionally, if he did not, as he put it, "feel equipped to handle" the child's needs, he would push back on an assignment. He had begun to look ahead, to a time when he could potentially earn some income as a Hebrew teacher or tutor once he was in college, the prospect of which appealed to him. He emphasized the importance of having the religious school as a "safe space" where he could come and hang out and just be himself. He also shared that he valued having adults other than his parents with whom to talk about things like his interests in literature, film, and many other wide-ranging topics—people he could use as sounding boards for issues such as his desire to take more AP-level classes than his parents thought appropriate.

A further conversation with Mike and Jacob took place during their Confirmation class trip, an overnight journey to Cincinnati which included a "Jewish Life on Campus" tour led by an alumnus of our school who was then a student at the University of Cincinnati and very active in Hillel, a Jewish fraternity, and other Jewish organizations on campus. After the tour, I asked the boys for their impressions. While much of their response was limited to flippant remarks about how messy and smelly they had found the fraternity house, they also commented on several other things they had seen and people they had met, and said that they had found the experience valuable. They were particularly interested in the fact that someone from their small congregation could go on to hold so many leadership roles in the Jewish community on campus, and what that trajectory might look like for them when their time came. Later in the spring, when describing the trip in a speech he gave at their cohort's Confirmation service, Mike wrote:

> I saw that college can be a place where people can be themselves without having to worry about what other people think. As a young man in the Jewish community, a place where everyone is accepted sounds pretty good to me . . . I can imagine college as a place where everyone is accepted and everyone has a place in the community.

Again, Mike's strong relational awareness provided him a lens through which to see his Jewish future in a positive light, even if it was still unclear what that future would be.

In May 2017, on the last day Jacob volunteered in the school, I had an interaction with him that reflected this transitional state through his more academic lens. He asked me if he could sit in my office and study instead of working with students that morning, as he was worried about needing to prepare more for an AP test he was taking the next day. I asked him why, if he had so much schoolwork, he had come to the temple at all. His reply was honest and reflected an extrinsic motivation: "My parents made me." Yet a couple of hours later, when I declared a study break and sent him to the nearby park to assist a teacher who was taking her class for some outdoor Hebrew games as a reward for good behavior, he took the initiative to take photographs of the event and text them to me with the message "because I know you like to *document* things like this." I found his choice of words significant because documenting classroom activities with photographs, video, and audio recordings for the purpose of later study was a concept we had discussed frequently in professional development sessions. In the end-of-the-year reflection he subsequently wrote, he mentioned his appreciation of the extra study time that day and also my having helped him "gain tutoring abilities I can forevermore use in my future." Like Mike, Jacob's words showed that he was beginning to look at his Jewish future and to see how his participation in the *madrichim* program might help him achieve his goals.

Jewish Adolescents Learning in a Relational Context

In our modern world, where practically unlimited information is available at the touch of a screen, it is not enough to define the goal of education solely as the acquisition of knowledge. Educational leaders must pay attention to how students, particularly teens and adults, use learning experiences to shape and reframe their senses of self. If we return to the break room conversation with which this portrait opened, we see evidence of the type of *shift in frame of reference* that defines what educational theorist Jack Mezirow labels "transformative learning."[16] It is not just the acquisition of information that is important for learning to occur, Mezirow says, but also the development of interpersonal relationships and communication skills which ultimately will help the learner to process and apply this information in various contexts, particularly in situations which challenge the learner's previously-held assumptions.[17]

The break room conversation was an example of the teens using their peer relationships as a pathway of support when faced with a challenge in the learning environment. As teacher development expert Thomas Guskey points out, for teachers (of any age) to become proficient, they have to learn new ways of doing things; although change brings a measure of anxiety and uncertainty, with support from others they gradually

16. Mezirow, "Transformative Learning," 5.

17. While there has recently emerged some controversy around the use of the language of transformative learning to describe Jewish education programs (See Levisohn, "Theories of Transformative Learning," 209–38), these developmental theories are central to the theoretical framework of MTEI, as described above, and were therefore integral to the framework of this project.

acquire an increased sense of their own authority.[18] Jacob's solution to his concerns—both about how to handle a student's difficulties *and* his own difficulties as a novice tutor in working with the student—was to seek out a friend who had experience with the same student in a different classroom context. In so doing he found the support he needed and he created a mutual learning situation.

Transformative learning, with its emphasis on examining one's own assumptions and working in dialogue with peers to reshape them, has been recognized by many scholars as essential to both personal and professional development for adults and adolescents. Developmental psychologist Robert Kegan argues that because adolescence is a transitional time when teens' "meaning-making" about the world and their place in it undergoes profound change, transformative learning experiences are not only desirable, but necessary.[19] Like Mezirow, Kegan places the locus of transformative learning within meaningful interpersonal relationships, suggesting that during this time of transition adolescents need to engage in a new type of peer interaction in which shared experiences, and dialogue about those experiences, can help them to construct their understanding of the world and their behavioral choices.

The break room conversation between Mike and Jacob seems to be evidence of these teens' emergent transformative learning. It occurred spontaneously, driven not by a facilitator but by the needs of the participants. Mike and Jacob solved their problem in dialogue, helping each other to examine their assumptions about the situation at hand. This brief interchange also suggests the beginnings of a shift in frame of reference in how these teens had begun to think of themselves—as teachers. It reflects the teens' concern with themselves and the quality of their own interactions with the student, and with the substance of the student's learning. Furthermore, they did not consider how the student's behavior affected them—which might be expected in a casual venting session—but how their behavior affected the student's learning experience. The student-centered nature of this exchange attests to Mike and Jacob having begun to become less egocentric[20] and able to take into account the points of view of their peers and students along with their own. This, Kegan would

18. Guskey, "Professional Development and Teacher Change," 381–91.
19. Kegan, *In Over Our Heads*, 32.
20. Elkind, "Egocentrism in Adolescence," 1025–34.

suggest, exemplifies the type of psychological growth necessary for adolescents who are making their way toward adult life and responsibility.

Transformative learning does not happen in a vacuum. By its very definition, it depends on relationships with others. Kegan, Guskey, and Mezirow, as well as many other educational theorists, pay close attention to the types of learning environments that are conducive to this type of growth. Relational Learning Communities, as described by Raider-Roth and others, are one response to the need for transformative learning in the professional development of teachers. The experience of Mike and Jacob in the RLC at Temple Beth Shalom suggests that the benefits of this type of professional development are not limited to adults, nor are they limited to the classroom setting. These teens' participation in an intergenerational, relationship-driven learning environment provided them with a profound Jewish learning experience and the opportunity to explore pathways toward their futures as Jewish adults. For Mike, this was an interpersonal connection, and for Jacob, an academic one. For another student it might be something different. By including teens in meaningful intergenerational relational learning experiences such as these, we can help them to build and strengthen these connections, leading to transformative learning and emotional growth.

The overall experiences of the two teens in this study resonate strongly with the findings of current research in the area of teen engagement, which conclude that the types of programs which are most impactful are "mission-driven and aspirational programs that allow teens to be challenged and inspired," and which seek to answer these "important 'teen centered' questions":

How . . .

- will this engage me intellectually, physically, and socially?
- can I share this with my friends? (Jewish and other)
- will this help me feel more connected to the many communities in which I exist?
- can I apply this to my life?
- will this help me develop skills that will benefit my life?
- will this help me feel proud of being Jewish?
- will this help me be a better citizen of the world?

- will this help me make the world a better place?"[21]

As illustrated in the portraits of Mike and Jacob above, the *madrichim* program at Temple Beth Shalom offered its participants the opportunity to uncover their own answers to many of these essential questions. By creating space for relational learning, and paying attention to the pathways through which individual teens connect to the learning environment, educational leaders can strengthen teens' engagement in Jewish life and help them to shape their visions of their Jewish futures.

Further Reflections About Jewish Learning

A question I hear often in conversations with Jewish professionals is "how do we get them to . . . ?" Much of the time, the question arises because we have an idea of what we want to do, or a program that already exists, and we want the magic formula that will make more people attend. After all, they can't engage in Jewish learning if they don't come to class, right?

What I discovered in the process of developing and studying the *madrichim* program is the power of flipping that question on its head. Instead of thinking about how to get people to a program we've already designed, what if we explore the various pathways of connection people have with our institutions, and create learning opportunities that capitalize on and enrich those connections? In asking that question, and revisiting it through the four years of the *Gesher* project, I ended up with a program that looked very different from what it might have been had I created it in a vacuum. The transformative learning experiences described in this profile, where teens grew from laggards to leaders, depended heavily on their sense of ownership in that process.

I also learned that participation in Jewish learning is not a choice a student makes once. It must be renewed at every step of the way. Here again, awareness of the various pathways through which individuals engage with the learning environment is critical. Fortunately, as I also learned during this project, different pathways of connection don't need to come from separate programs. Even a small congregation, like the one profiled here, can engage its learners in multiple ways with a small number of programs, if its leadership pays attention to the various lenses through which participants view their involvement. When teens ask "Who else is going to be there?" or "What exactly is the point of this

21. Bryfman, *Generation Now*, 25.

program?" or "Will we get service credit for this?" what they're really asking is "Is this going to be worth my time?" As we help them to answer these questions, we not only involve them in our programs, but begin to help them shape their own vision of their Jewish futures.

Bibliography

Bryfman, David. *Generation Now: Understanding and Engaging Jewish Teens Today.* New York: The Jewish Education Project, 2016.

Elkind, David. "Egocentrism in Adolescence." *Child Development* 38 (1967) 1025–34.

Feiman-Nemser, Sharon. "Helping Novices Learn to Teach: Lessons from an Exemplary Support Teacher." *Journal of Teacher Education* 52 (2001) 17–30.

Guskey, Thomas. "Professional Development and Teacher Change." *Teachers and Teaching: Theory and Practice* 8 (2002) 381–91.

Hawkins, David. "I, Thou, and It." In *The Informed Vision and Other Essays*, 49–62. New York: Agathon, 1974.

Holzer, Elie, and Orit Kent. *A Philosophy of Havruta: Understanding and Teaching the Art of Text Study in Pairs.* Brighton, MA: Academic Studies, 2013.

Howard, Lisa Bob. *The Madrichim Manual: Six Steps to Becoming a Jewish Role Model.* Springfield, MA: Behrman House, 2003.

Kegan, Robert. *In Over Our Heads: The Mental Demands of Modern Life.* Cambridge, MA: Harvard University Press, 1994.

Kroll, Patti. "Working With Teen Assistants." In *The Ultimate Jewish Teacher's Handbook*, edited by Nachama Skolnik Moskowitz, 675–88. New York: Behrman House, 2003.

Levisohn, Jon A. "Theories of Transformative Learning in Jewish Education: Three Cases." *Journal of Jewish Education* 83 (2017) 209–38.

Mezirow, Jack. "Transformative Learning: Theory to Practice." *New Directions for Adult and Continuing Education* 74 (1997) 5–12.

Raider-Roth, Miriam B. *Professional Development in Relational Learning Communities: Teachers in Connection.* New York: Teachers College Press, 2017.

Solomon, Richard, and Solomon, Elaine. *Toolbox for Teachers and Mentors: Moving Madrichim to Mentor Teachers and Beyond.* Tucson: Wheatmark, 2013.

8

NOT THE ISRAEL OF MY ELEMENTARY SCHOOL

High School Students Encountering Moral Complexity[1]

Matt Reingold

IT WAS NOT UNTIL my fifth year of teaching at Tanenbaum Community Hebrew Academy of Toronto (TanenbaumCHAT),[2] a coeducational non-denominational Jewish day school in Toronto, Canada, that I was asked to teach the grade 12 Jewish history course on the Arab-Israeli conflict. My first two years of teaching it were a whirlwind of learning content, considering pedagogical approaches, and ensuring that I finished the material on time. I don't recall pausing to question how the students were understanding, interpreting, and integrating the material into their cognitive frameworks about Israel.

It was during my third year that I began to wonder how learning about controversial events in Israel's history might be influencing the way these teenage learners related to Israel, and how the course content aligned with the school's Zionist orientation. Specifically, I began to ask

---

1. A different version of this paper was published in *The Social Studies* 108 (2017) 87–98 and can be found at: https://www.tandfonline.com/doi/full/10.1080/00377996 .2017.1324392

2. See: http://www.tanenbaumchat.org

myself some questions about my students' learning and my own responsibilities as their teacher. These questions included:

- How do my students navigate their way through controversial topics in Israel's history?

- How do they synthesize potentially disruptive narratives into their larger understanding of Israel?

- Does learning about controversial events, some of which do not reflect well on Israel, weaken or even rupture the relationship that my students have been building with Israel since they were very young children?

- In the long run, do my students want to learn about these events or would they prefer to keep their relationship with Israel less morally complex?

With the support of the TanenbaumCHAT administration, I decided to initiate a small research study to document the students' responses over an academic year. I planned to use surveys, class writing assignments, and interviews to get a better idea of their learning process and how the study of controversial material about Israel's history might be influencing the students' views of Israel overall.

As a high school teacher teaching a course about Israel, I wanted to paint a rich and complex picture of Israeli history for my students. This would be a history organized to instill Jewish pride and to show that Israeli history has instances in which Israel has made controversial and upsetting decisions. As an educator and researcher, I wanted to understand how learning about these upsetting narratives affected the students' pride and love for Israel. In short, given the morally complex nature of some of the history, I wanted to assess whether my twin goals—to teach a full history and to instill a love for Israel—could be achieved simultaneously. I also wanted to gain insight into how the students' learning about these disturbing narratives shaped their relationship with Israel.

The Setting

TanenbaumCHAT was founded in 1960, and as of 2016 enrolled 960 students. The school is religiously diverse and draws from a number of feeder schools that represent different Jewish denominations. Most students were born in Canada, but some students are American or Israeli. The school's mission statement establishes that the school is committed to helping students to deepen their intellectual curiosity and their connection to their Jewish roots. Students are encouraged to confront the diversity of the Jewish people, both locally and globally, and to search out meaningful ways to contribute to the community. All students are required to take four years of Jewish history, beginning with study of the Babylonian exile in 586 BCE and culminating in their final year with a semester of learning about the Arab-Israeli conflict and a semester-long elective where they choose from such options as the Holocaust and contemporary Israeli society. As part of my research, I asked Lee Buckman, then TanenbaumCHAT's head of school, about the rationale for the required course in "Israel studies." He explained,

> It's to connect students to Israel in a way that they see that Israel adds an important dimension to their Jewish identity. That is, Israel somehow completes or rounds out their identity as a Diaspora Jew. By the time they graduate, I would hope they can explain how Israel "completes" them and what Israel contributes to their identity.

Buckman's view extended the school's stated mission about Israel education:

> Recognizing the significance of the State and its national institutions, we seek to instill in our students an attachment to the State of Israel and its people as well as a sense of responsibility for their welfare.

In describing what he hoped the students would gain in their studies, Buckman continued:

> I would want students to see Israel in terms other than a safe haven and refuge, an insurance plan, for Jews in trouble or for themselves when they need to flee anti-Semitism. I would want their relationship with Israel to be one based not on fears, but hopes and aspirations, that they find meaning in their relationship with Israel even when they, as Canadian Jews, don't feel threatened and even when they are not called upon to defend the State of Israel on campus.

Learning "Complex" History

As I grappled with how to structure my course,[3] I also spoke with a colleague in TanenbaumCHAT's Jewish history department who described how important it is for students who are learning about Israel to understand that there are diverse ways of getting at the topic. She noted:

> Students should realize that Israel and its history are very complex. There is not one side to the story and if we don't understand different narratives we won't ever be able to have dialogue with others who have different opinions. It's important for students to realize that Israel is not a dreamland. It is a country like every other that has its own internal difficulties that it needs to deal with, as well as past events that it might not be proud of.

She went on to speculate that students needed to become better equipped intellectually about Israel:

> It is important for students to know about these things so that they are not naive about the situation. Also, when students are on university campuses, they will be faced with these types of arguments that will make them feel uncomfortable. Unless they have some background about it already, they will either not know how to counter these arguments (while realizing that there are truths to what they say) or they could be blindly convinced by them.

With these views in mind, I developed a curriculum to introduce aspects of Israel's history that would challenge the students to question various historical decisions and actions and that would complicate their image of Israel. Ultimately, course topics included how Arabs were treated under the Tochnit Dalet plan,[4] the massacres of Arabs by Jewish fighters at Deir Yassin in 1948 and the Israeli military at Sabra and Shatila

---

3. A yearlong sequence for grade 12 students in which the first semester was entitled "Arab-Israeli Conflict" and focused on the history of Zionism and the Arab-Israeli conflict; the second semester was labeled "Israeli Culture and Society" and addressed issues involving ethnic and religious communities in Israel.

4. Tochnit Dalet was a plan in which Jewish groups attempted to take control of land allocated by the United Nations to the Palestinians, to be incorporated into Israel in order to create contiguous borders and to ensure that the future Jewish state would have defendable borders. During the course of the fighting, many Jews and Arabs were killed and there is evidence that Jews forcefully removed Palestinians from their homes (and did not permit them to return) and, in limited instances, non-combatants were killed.

in 1982, the absorption of Jews from Arab lands between 1948 and 1980, and the negative treatment of Jewish Ethiopian immigrants after their relocation to Israel in the 1980s and 1990s. These topics all involved disruptive counter-narratives that might conflict with students' prior understanding of Israel's history, social order, and political decision-making.

As an educator, I believe that learning about morally complex material is a crucial component of preparing students for real life and its messiness. This approach is supported by the scholarship of Barton and Levstick[5] and Wineburg,[6] who all found that learning about upsetting or difficult narratives connected to historical events pushes learners to develop greater moral awareness. My pedagogy is informed by Lawrence Kohlberg's theory of moral development which posits that as children mature, they proceed through a series of cognitive stages that lead them to consider the world, and their position in it, in gradually more complex ways.[7] Prior to adolescence, children view morality as a set of binary positions—right and wrong, do and don't. Later, as they encounter life situations that are not so black and white, teens and adults likely will face moral dilemmas that will require them to think in more abstract, analytical, and flexible ways. Kohlberg pointed out that when confronted with complex moral situations, some young people—but not all—have the cognitive capacity to perceive and be sensitive to "shades of gray." These individuals recognize that morality is an abstract concept and that a person's (or a country's) moral stance is not always absolute. Individuals develop an awareness of how people and groups behave and how circumstances can change actions and choices.

Carol Ingall's stance on the importance of moral education in Jewish education is also relevant to my research; in 2002, she asserted "If moral education in Jewish schools is to be taken seriously, it must grow organically from the curriculum of the Jewish school, informing all three domains of educational life: intellect, affect, and experience."[8] Given my interest in understanding how students reacted to learning about morally-challenging narratives in Israeli history, Ingall's points about moral education and the importance of tying it to complexity and personal connection strongly resonated with the goals of my inquiry.

5. Barton and Levstick, "It Wasn't a Good Part of History."
6. Wineburg, "On the Reading of Historical Texts."
7. Kohlberg, "Moral Stages and Moralization."
8. Ingall, "Pendulum Politics," 19.

Finally, my study was heavily inspired by the words of Israeli scholar Danny Jacoby:

> Only an open and liberal approach to the national history will be accepted by the youngsters and bring them closer to the national ethos. Anyone who wishes to present students with a nationalism that is cloistering from the global world, who argues that nationalism means blurring and hiding the truth, and who argues that nationalism means opposing intellectual pluralism will eventually lead the youngsters in the public schools to steer clear of everything that is connected to the national cause.[9]

Jacoby's position towards truth-telling in Israel education and its relationship with strong and positive associations with Israel aligns with my pedagogic position. I believe that students need to be introduced to age-appropriate events in their Israeli history classes, and through this will develop more sophisticated understandings of Israel and build a more nuanced relationship with the country.

In gathering data about my students' responses, I was particularly interested in how, when encountering inherently upsetting material, my students did or did not develop greater moral awareness, utilize higher (more abstract) levels of moral reasoning, benefit from moral education that was "messy," and demonstrate a more sophisticated understanding of the moral complexities that are part of Israel's history.

Tracking My Students' Learning Experiences

In my classes, I emphasize discussion and debate. When I present new texts and ideas, students have an opportunity to discuss in groups what their impressions of the texts are and how they connect to or complicate what they already know. The range of student knowledge and experience in the Arab-Israeli conflict course is diverse, which can present a challenge. Unlike a Jewish history course on ancient Persia or medieval Germany where very few, if any, students have preexisting knowledge and opinions, every TanenbaumCHAT student begins the course on Israeli history with pre-formed perspectives. This is because most have learned about Israel throughout their elementary studies and have visited Israel at least once. They also learn from interactions with Israeli

9. Jacoby as quoted in Al-Haj, ""National Ethos, Multicultural Education, and the New History Textbooks in Israel," 56.

students in some of their Jewish Studies classes. By providing students an opportunity at the beginning of a course to express their opinions and by slowly integrating texts that challenge these assumptions, I strive to build a classroom culture in which a range of ideas is not only acceptable, but encouraged. At times students find my tolerance of diversity difficult to understand. In response, I meet regularly with students who appear to be struggling to discuss their evolving understanding of Israeli history and their personal relationship with Israel.

For the 2015–16 school year, I planned to track systematically the ways in which students navigated through controversial topics in Israel's history and to explore how these topics affected their feelings and associations with Israel. I focused on the experiences of forty students from two course sections. At the outset of the fall semester, I invited the students to rate their emotional connection to Israel on a ten-point scale and to indicate on a checklist how familiar they were with various events in Israel's history (including some that would be presented in the course). I also asked them to submit a short written reflection detailing their feelings, connections, and personal relationship with Israel.

Throughout the year I introduced narratives that both reflected and challenged the students' prior learning and assumptions. While my goal was not to teach "good" or "bad" things about Israel, I certainly was committed to teaching simultaneously contrasting narratives, narratives that included voices that might criticize Israel—from the Jewish Israeli left and the right, as well as from non-Jewish Israelis. As we completed each unit of study, the students composed journal entries responding to a series of questions including "How, if at all, has studying [X] impacted the way you think about Israel?" From time to time I conducted brief follow-up interviews in order to have more in-depth conversations about what they had written. The students rated themselves again at the end of the year and also composed one-page reflections about how learning about these events had formed their thinking about the State.

Introducing Tochnit Dalet/Deir Yassin

The unit about Tochnit Dalet and Deir Yassin took place at the start of the school year in October. Early on, it became clear that the students' reactions to the material about these events were especially intense. This material constitutes a morally complex dimension of Israel's history because it directly addresses Israel's relationship with non-Jews and violence perpetrated by Jews against non-Jews. It is an important aspect of Israeli history, and I anticipated that learning about it would challenge students' assumptions about and expectations of the country. Additionally, I expected that even when learned in a historical context, studying this material could potentially cause a disruption in how the students related to Israel and their relationship-building with the country.

The students were introduced to creation of the Tochnit Dalet in the course text, *The Arab-Israeli Conflict: A Timeless Struggle*. The "plan" was designed to defeat the Palestinian militias in the area that the United Nations had allocated for Jewish statehood; it was timed to "prepare for invasion by regular Arab armies"[10] before the mandate expired. Piggott identified the key objectives of the plan: (1) to control strategic points vacated by Britain, (2) to regain control of roads, main towns, and lines of communication, and (3) to secure the Jewish state's borders. Because these objectives meant it would be necessary for the Israelis to evacuate Arab villages on main roads "so they could not be used to attack from the rear once the Arab invasion began," Israel commanders were given permission to "empty and/or raze" hostile villages.[11]

In addition to the textbook, the students probed a series of sources from historians that presented a range of explanations for why Tochnit Dalet happened. These included:

1. A narrative by Israeli historian Ilan Pappé who argued that the Tochnit Dalet "blueprint spelled it out clearly and unambiguously: the Palestinians had to go . . . The aim of the plan was in fact the destruction of both rural and urban areas of Palestine."[12]

2. An opposing view from historian David Tal: "The plan did provide the conditions for the destruction of Palestinian villages and the deportation of the dwellers; this was not the reason for the plan's composition."[13] Tal went on to explain that the aim of the plan was to "ensure full control over the territory" so that the Haganah (pre-independence Zionist military groups) would be "strategically positioned to face an Arab invasion."[14]

10. Piggott, *The Arab-Israeli Conflict*, 97.

11. Piggott, *The Arab-Israeli Conflict*, 97.

12. Pappé, *Ethnic Cleansing of Palestine*, 86 and 126.

13. Tal, *War in Palestine 1948*, 87.

14. Tal, *War in Palestine 1948*, 87.

3. The practical perspective of Benny Morris, who claimed in an interview in the Israeli newspaper *Ha'Aretz*: "Under David Ben-Gurion a consensus of transfer was created. He understood that there could be no Jewish state with a large and hostile Arab minority in its midst. There would be no such state. It would not be able to exist. If he had not done what he did, a state would not have come into being. That has to be clear. It is impossible to evade it. Without the uprooting of the Palestinians, a Jewish state would not have arisen."[15]

4. A perspective on the intended outcomes by Israeli historian Yoav Gelber: "The [Tochnit Dalet] text clarified unequivocally that expulsion concerned only those villages that would fight against the Haganah and resist occupation, and not all Arab hamlets."[16] Moreover, Gelber argued, decisions about treatment of the Arabs were left to field commanders and local advisors, while the Tochnit Dalet plan was focused on preparing for the Arab invasion—not expelling the Palestinians.

The students also watched a short news segment in which a Palestinian woman told her family's story and shared the trauma that she felt over not being able to return to her home village for over sixty years.

In addition, the students studied the events that took place in the village of Deir Yassin on April 9, 1948. As Piggott summarizes:

> Members of the Irgun and Stern Gang attacked the Arab village of Deir Yassin, located on the road between Jerusalem and Tel Aviv. After a fierce battle, the Jewish fighters carried out brutal acts of revenge for their losses, killing Arab fighters who had surrendered and some civilians. Arab and Jewish eyewitnesses reported that 20–25 villagers were shot in a nearby quarry."[17]

Other accounts gave details of rape and murder in Arab villages, which led to historical debates about the perpetration of war crimes (such as rape) and how these might differ from the kind of mass expulsion of Palestinians from their villages that Tochnit Dalet authorized.

15. Shavit, "Survival of the Fittest."

16. Gelber, *Palestine 1948*, 306.

17. Piggott, *The Arab-Israeli Conflict*, 98.

How the Students Responded

Before taking this course, none of the students recalled having had any familiarity with Tochnit Dalet, and only a handful indicated that they had heard about Deir Yassin. Their written reflections shed light on how they grappled with issues of moral complexity and how they negotiated their ongoing relationship with Israel. These responses, gathered at various times during the year, suggested four distinct perspectives on how the students understood or explained Tochnit Dalet and Deir Yassin in relation to their continued relationship with Israel.

Group 1: Students who integrated moral complexities about Israel's actions.

Some of the students indicated that learning about Tochnit Dalet and Deir Yassin gave them a fuller and more complete view of their country— one that strengthened their relationship with Israel. They explained that even though this was the first time they had learned that Israel had done "bad things" and that they deplored the acts, they felt that grappling with the complexities of Israel's history increased their regard for the country. Several written comments exemplify these reactions:

> Noam[18]: Tochnit Dalet and Deir Yassin strengthened my connection with Israel. This is because I no longer look at Israel as a utopia. I look at Israel as a country that sometimes needs to make tough, imperfect decisions in order to protect its people.

> Raizel: Deir Yassin and Tochnit Dalet have caused me to realize that the Arab-Israeli Conflict is not black and white, but rather lies in the grey area ... the events have not caused me to see Israel as an instigator nor a country in the wrong because I think one could justify even both of these controversial acts.

> Dov: For me to understand these actions goes back to my idea about "normalcy." I've said in class many times that all countries have history that they would like to forget, and I think that Israel is also one of those countries. In a way, I am somewhat relieved, because knowing this allows me to see the beauty of Israel, despite its faults, instead of a curriculum that has attempted

18. All names have been changed to protect the identity of the students.

to guard Israel's negatives for my 11 years of Jewish education. My love for Israel remains just as strong as it was before I knew about TD and DY.

Taken together, these students' voices present a nuanced portrait of how learning about morally complex events led the teens to recognize that Israel's history is not linear and has messy parts. Their responses demonstrate their ability to move beyond simple right and wrong attitudes about Israel and towards a more sophisticated understanding of the country as having both admirable and reprehensible aspects of its history. These students showed their capacity to integrate conflicting perspectives into their understanding of the world and that they were able to acknowledge the realities of Israel's negative history while simultaneously celebrating in its many accomplishments.

Group 2: Students who adhered exclusively to their previously held (positive) assumptions about Israel.

A second type of student response was one of unwavering pride. For these teens, knowing what pre-state soldiers did to Palestinians only reinforced their positive identification with the State, and, for some, identification with the type of politics they wished that current Israeli leaders would exhibit towards the Palestinian people. In their words:

> Jaclyn: Tochnit Dalet and Deir Yassin have only made me think that Israel is even smarter than I previously thought. It showed how good their intelligence-gathering capabilities are and how good they are at stopping problems before they even happen.

> Sonya: I still stand by them and understand why Israel had to do so. If anything, I am more surprised that Israel today does not do anything similar. If the Israelis were to take more action today like they used to, Israel would be a safer place with less terrorists. Initially I was a little bit surprised after hearing the story of Deir Yassin, but after, I understand why the Israelis did what I think they did: it was best for their existence.

> Alex: Tochnit Dalet and Deir Yassin have not impacted the way I think about Israel because Israel used appropriate tactics in order to secure a Jewish state.

Combined, these voices paint a portrait of students who did not have a problem integrating Israeli aggression with their pervasively positive view of the State. Rather, these students identified with how Israel behaved and found moral clarity in how its military had treated the Palestinians. Unlike Group 1 students who could acknowledge that something terrible had occurred without that consciousness ruining their greater love and reverence towards Israel, Group 2 students adamantly denied *any* wrongdoing on Israel's part. They tended to completely reject the negative implications of the counter-narratives they read for the course and did not seem to grasp that they could love Israel despite its flaws. This group did not question Israel's decisions and did not allow any of the messiness to disturb their perception of the country as having an unblemished history.

Group 3: Students who struggled with integrating alternative views about Israel.

For a few students, learning about Tochnit Dalet and Deir Yassin disrupted their previously held Israel narratives and caused them to question their overall relationship with the country. Two students wrote that they saw Israel's founding as part of a process that used terror, and that now, given the Palestinian people's interest in self-determination, they found it difficult to be critical of the Palestinians' use of terror:

> Robin: By learning about this, while it does not dignify Palestinian terrorism today, it makes us understand a darker side of Israel and make us sympathize with Palestinians.

> Aubrey: I realize that I can no longer think of Israel as a perfect country that earned all their rights to the land justifiably. These occurrences opened up my eyes to the negatives in the history of the Jews. We learned about a part of their history where they are no longer seen as the sufferers, but rather causing the suffering. I love Israel and will always view it as my second homeland, but with my newfound knowledge, I may have a tougher time defending them against terrorism. Terrorism is definitely an awful way to get what you want, but if Israel uses it to achieve their goal, what prevents us from criticizing the Palestinians from using this exact same method in order to receive what they believe they deserve?

Others wrote about feelings of doubt or insecurity with their relationship towards Israel:

> Abe: I always believed that Israel is far from perfect . . . although I am a strong believer in Zionism, some of the things Israel does can make me unhappy and disappointed.

> Chaim: We know today that Israel may not have been what it is today without these events and it concerns me that this "wonderful" place that all Jews can call home was founded on these terrible acts of murder.

One student expressed distress that the story he and his classmates had always been taught was, at best, incomplete and, at worst, wrong:

> Lyla: I had always assumed that Israel had always been the victim of Arab and Palestinian attacks, and only ever retaliated when it was necessary for their own survival. Tochnit Dalet and Deir Yassin make me realize that this is not the case and that sometimes Israel can be wrong. I had never before expected there to be an instance in which Jews attacked and massacred Arab civilians.

These students' statements suggest that learning about the complexities in Israel's history was challenging. They indicated that engaging the counter-narrative material had left them unresolved about their relationship with the State. These teens typically had entered into the course with fixed assumptions about how Israelis had behaved and how the State came into being. Their encounter with this material caused disruptions in their moral reasoning process, by which they were unable to fully synthesize their new perspectives with their loyalty to Israel. Whereas Group 2 students chose to dismiss completely criticism of Israel in favor of maintaining their relationship with the State, Group 3 students expressed ongoing uncertainty and ambivalence about how to maintain a positive relationship with Israel in light of their newfound knowledge.

Group 4: Students who justified Israeli actions.

The most common form of response—and this explains how students could simultaneously (a) be unaware about the violence prior to the course, (b) view it as aggressive action against the Palestinian people and Arab armies, and (c) be unaffected by it—came in the form of a justification of Israeli aggression. Their comments suggested six distinct justifications for why Israel planned and participated in the April 1948 events:

Unethical but necessary.

This response saw the decisions made by pre-state Jewish leaders and soldiers as morally reprehensible yet necessary to ensure that the future of the country was secure.

> Jimmy: It was unethical, but it had to be done and I am sure that along the way many Israeli leaders felt terrible about it as well.

Disappointed and shocked but they had good motives.

Similar responses from two students reflected more flexible thinking:

> Dianne: I have always recognized that Israel's actions are not perfect . . . I am still comfortable supporting the State because they're usually right and the motives behind their transgressions are, usually, noble.

> Eli: I now see that Israel has been aggressive and offensive, con-tributing to the war rather than stopping it. I still believe that what Israel is doing is right.

While similar to the first type of justification, what distinguishes the two is that whereas the former is absolute in its orientation and position on morality, the latter is more fluid in its understanding and judging of the choices made by pre-state soldiers.

Israel has improved.

Directly linked to the idea that no country is perfect was the students' most common justification: Israel today is not the same as pre-state Israel in 1948. These students independently arrived at some type of under-standing that not only is today's Israeli government different, but that (in their view) Israel as a whole has improved from what took place under Tochnit Dalet and at Deir Yassin.

> Sara: It disappoints me to know that the Jewish people did something so horrific, especially at the time that Jews were being murdered the same way in Europe. I feel, though, that this generation has taken responsibility for the maltreatment of Arabs.

> Carol: I believe that Israel has grown and strives to be in the light.

The Palestinians and Arabs are to blame.

This type of response recognized that what Israel did was objectively bad, but it shifted the focus and blame away from Israel's actions and towards the Palestinian and Arab people.

> Jordyn: Despite these horrific events, my love of Israel has not changed. If the Palestinian population had been willing to compromise with the Jewish population, the violence would not have occurred to the extent that it did.

> Jonathan: I would have never expected something like [Deir Yassin] from [Israelis]. However, it does not change my perception of Israel's history, Israel's current affairs, or my lack of sympathy for the Palestinians.

Discrediting the Palestinian narrative.

One student directly challenged the legitimacy of the Palestinian narrative and questioned the way that it has been transmitted.

> Rob: If Deir Yassin occurred exactly like the Arabs described, I would be appalled . . . however, I do not believe the Arabs' depiction of the events are completely truthful.

These students' responses showed that, for a variety of reasons, they didn't (or wouldn't) fully engage with the moral complexities of Israel's history. They tended to dismiss the history or to find ways to gloss over or ignore it without accepting its legitimacy. This group was made up of a range of black-and-white thinkers who were not willing or able to think critically about Israel's behavior or to come to terms with narratives that disrupted their old views.

Interview Comments

After the teens submitted their course journals for my review, I conducted interviews with ten of them to have more in-depth conversation
about their takeaways as learners. These students were selected because
they were representative of the four groups. A consistent refrain in their
comments was that despite the difficulty in hearing about what Israel had
done, they appreciated learning about this history and deeply valued getting a more complete and authentic picture of Israel. In discussing the
impact of learning about Tochnit Dalet and Yair Dassin, they indicated
that they now felt more prepared for university and college in relation
to Israel and anti-Israel activism. Specifically they mentioned that it was
better to learn about the events now, as opposed to hearing about them
from anti-Israel groups and feeling unprepared to defend their pro-Israel
position. For example,

> Sandy: I think that it's really important to learn about it. I think
> that it helps when you're talking to someone who's maybe anti-
> Israel, about Israel, to know all of the facts, because you don't
> want them to be bringing these things up and not really talking
> about. It helps if you have the information.

> Ari: Because going to university and being exposed to all these
> different opinions outside the [Jewish] bubble, it's important
> that we know both sides so we can defend the Israeli side.

> Daniel: I think it's good just to make people aware of what actu-
> ally happened, because when we go into university and if we
> haven't heard about these events, then let's say I'm discussing
> the issue with someone, just on a personal level. If I don't know
> about these things that have happened, I don't want to hear
> about them for the first time in university when I'm trying to
> discuss the issue on an intellectual level, on a high level with
> someone else. That shouldn't be the place where I learn about it.

The interviews also yielded a critique about the timing and nature
of the Israel education they had previously received. Several students described feeling disillusioned and disappointed in their earlier schooling;
they challenged the validity of their earlier education, asserting either
that it had been designed to shield them from truths that their schools
felt they could not handle or that their teachers had purposely chosen

to show them only one side of the Israel narrative. Two students were especially outspoken about their concerns:

> Adam: I think that they shielded a little bit too much of the negatives of Israel. I think that if they would have explained this at an earlier age, it would have been better because then people would have been more understanding. I think that this is more of a shock that I found out about this later on.

> Adeena: Whenever I studied the establishment of Israel there would always be that video in November 1947 when everyone was partying on the streets. And that's just the kind of image I had in my mind. It was more a celebration. And there wasn't the sense of violence towards other groups. So, it was just very, very surprising for me because it was an act of violence against a certain people . . . and I wasn't given the whole picture. I think they didn't teach it to us because they wanted us to see Israel as a beautiful place and no problems with it . . .

Both Adam and Adeena indicated that they understood the pedagogical difficulty with introducing Tochnit Dalet and Deir Yassin with younger students. Nonetheless, they remained resolute in their conviction that their elementary schools should have done more to help them grapple with moral issues inherent in understanding Israel.

> Adeena: I don't think I was even necessarily ready before when you taught it. But, once you go through something a little bit difficult, then you grow from it. And fourteen-year-old Adeena maybe would have been better because then [she] would have started understanding Israel at an early age. And although you can say that some kids, including myself, may not have been mature, but maybe it's because we're censoring all the education. So, maybe if we want them to be more mature, we have to really tell children what's going on.

> Adam [Defending his position]: I still think that there's a way to kind of hint that Israel wasn't as moral and as ethical as everyone thinks without actually getting into the details of it. Just so that kids aren't as surprised when they hear about this in grade 12. You know what I mean. Because then they almost feel that they've been lied to. Even though they haven't been. Because there's a lot of things about Israel that's amazing about how they deal with other situations. So, I think that just hinting at it at a younger age would have been a little more beneficial.

Year-End Survey

As the year drew to a close, I asked the students to complete a survey that once again asked them to place themselves on a continuum that would measure how strong a connection they felt towards Israel. The survey also asked them to think about the year's course content and to identify the topics that for them were (1) the most meaningful and (2) the most challenging. Although over the year the curriculum had introduced the students to a broad range of counter-narratives about Israel's history, seven months later it was the material about Tochnit Dalet and Deir Yassin that stood out in their survey comments. The survey responses showed that some students vividly remembered their learning about Tochnit Dalet and Deir Yassin and felt anger at Israel for committing crimes while simultaneously defending Israel in how it treated the Palestinian people:

> Zachary: As a kid, we are taught to put Israel on a pedestal and that although we are living well in Canada, it is MUCH BETTER to live in Israel. Learning about these really threw me a curve ball, although it was important to know. I believe that learning about these situations only reaffirmed my love for Israel because I had to reevaluate and battle with myself to see that past isn't sparkly clean. This strengthened my relationship because, while it was a shocking discovery, it shows how hard Israel worked to survive and it made me take Israel off that pedestal and really evaluate the right and wrongdoings of the Jewish homeland. It doesn't mean that I have to accept what Israel has done in the past; it just means that Israel isn't perfect and I learned to accept the good and the bad. This course now allows me to look objectively at Israel and not just blindly love the country, as some of my friends do, and I am appreciative of that.

> Raoul: It was a tough time for me in the sense that I had to rethink my previous notion that Israel had not acted in the same way as the other side. After learning about these events, it's fair to conclude that both sides have their faults, and the conflict is not a simple one.

In terms of emotional attachment to Israel, at year's end the students' self-ratings showed that their positive feelings had held firm. In September the students' average self-rating about this issue on a 10-point scale averaged 7.48; in June the average was 7.57. These findings are based on a small sample and are not statistically significant. Nonetheless, it is noteworthy that despite the serious emotional challenges of learning about morally complex events and the students' own perception of this learning as difficult and challenging, their reported relationship with Israel slightly *strengthened* over the course of the year.

Concluding Thoughts

TanenbaumCHAT's educational orientation requires teachers to navigate tricky pedagogical terrain. As described by members of the school's administration, this is because there are clear and explicit goals to strengthen students' emotional and social connections to Israel through formal instruction. At the same time, there is also a commitment to presenting Israel in a morally complex way that introduces students to narratives that run counter to what they had previously learned, in order to provide them with a more complete picture of the country. There is also a commitment to helping adolescents negotiate moral tensions, become responsible citizens, and prepare for their future as members of the Jewish community.

Through their participation in my class on the Arab-Israeli conflict, the students I studied clearly and consistently gained new knowledge about topics that they had not previously known about. On its own, the fact that these teens now had a better familiarity with these historical events is not surprising given the course curriculum. However, their writings and self-assessments suggest that not only did they learn the material, their engagement with course content significantly influenced how some—though not all—conceptualized and related to Israel and its history.

The range of responses shows that the students did not all learn the material in the same way. In fact, some emerged from the course with contrasting perspectives about Israel. Some students fully justified and defended Israel's actions, while others denied that anything wrong had even occurred. Others were able to synthesize their new learning into their broader understanding of Israeli history while others remained fixed in their previous spot.

The students' explanations of what transpired in 1948 show that not all of them displayed the same capacities for Kohlberg's stages of moral reasoning. Some were better able to synthesize and accept complexity while others were quick to reject and dismiss new information that conflicted with pre-formed knowledge. However, as evidenced in their written journals and interviews, all students affirmed Ingall's assertion that Jewish education needs to make use of moral education[19]—even those who dismissed the information made strong claims about the value of their understanding of morality in relation to Israel's actions.

As a teacher in a school committed to positive connections with Israel, I was pleased to find that none of the students described feeling that because of their disappointment with Israeli actions, they no longer had a relationship with Israel. All of the students remained committed in their Zionist beliefs. My experience made me aware of how the introduction of controversial narratives requires teacher sensitivity to the difficulty some students will have when asked to examine critically preexisting attitudes and knowledge and to incorporate new and complex ideas into their thinking.

Of all the results of the study, the one that pleasantly surprised me the most was how consistent the students were about wanting to learn about the Tochnit Dalet and Deir Yassin narratives (as well as other "disruptive" material introduced throughout the year). As an educator, I appreciated the intellectual honesty that students brought to this experience and was happy that their learning reflected the school's position on Israel as well. Not only did they want to gain a more complete understanding of Israel, most showed an increasing capacity to see that they could love Israel even more if they learned more about it.

Further Reflections About Jewish Learning

Studying the ways that students learned about morally-complex narratives in Israeli history has reinforced for me how messy and non-linear Jewish education can be. Jewish education cannot work like mathematics, which proceeds by building upon pre-learned skills to learn new skills, or literature study, which introduces stories with content that reflects the maturity and age of the learners. Because of the sophistication of Jewish texts and the Jewish experience as a whole, the content that students learn needs to be scaffolded so that students learn in an age-appropriate way that encourages them to return again and again to the material in a cyclical pattern. This model allows them to discover new aspects of the material and, it is hoped, their own connections to it. My study has

19. Ingall, "Pendulum Politics."

reminded me of this important value when I observed how students reacted to learning about Tochnit Dalet and Deir Yassin and began to fill in the gaps from their previous Jewish learning.

Prior to this research activity, I had thought of this cyclical model of learning as something positive that fostered continued learning and growth and encouraged students to reflect on what they had previously learned. Developing this portrait showed me a new aspect to cyclical learning: the necessity of a specific type of framing so that students will remain invested in the learning and not view their previous learning as having failed them by omitting certain details. As the students indicated, when carefully scaffolded content is provided, they can progressively acquire a full picture of Israel and discover how important it is for them to receive this picture. Repeatedly, these high school students indicated that they craved a more complete understanding of Israel's successes and failures and recognized that only through seeing both sides can they develop a real relationship with the country.

Bibliography

Al-Haj, Majid. "National Ethos, Multicultural Education, and the New History Textbooks in Israel." *Curriculum Inquiry* 35 (2005) 47–71.

Barton, Keith C., and Linda S. Levstik. "'It Wasn't a Good Part of History': National Identity and Students' Explanations of Historical Significance." In *Researching History Education: Theory, Method and Context,* edited by Linda S. Levstik and Keith C. Barton, 240–72. New York, NY: Routledge, 2008.

Gelber, Yoav. *Palestine 1948: War, Escape and the Emergence of the Palestinian Refugee Problem.* Brighton, UK: Sussex, 2006.

Ingall, Carol K. "Pendulum Politics: The Changing Contexts of Jewish Moral Education." *Journal of Jewish Education* 68 (2002) 13–20.

Kohlberg, Lawrence. "Moral Stages and Moralization: The Cognitive-Developmental Approach." In *Development and Behavior: Theory, Research and Social Issues,* edited by Tom Lickona, 31–53. New York: Holt, Rinehart and Winston, 1976.

Pappé, Ilan. *The Ethnic Cleansing of Palestine.* Oxford: Oneworld, 2006.

Piggott, Leanne. *The Arab-Israeli Conflict: A Timeless Struggle.* Marrickville, New South Wales: Science, 2008.

Shavit, Ari. "Survival of the Fittest: Interview with Benny Morris." *Ha'Aretz* (January 8, 2004). http://www.haaretz.com/hasen/spages/380986.html

Tal, David. *War in Palestine 1948: Strategy and Diplomacy.* London: Routledge, 2004.

Wineburg, Samuel S. "On the Reading of Historical Texts: Notes on the Breach Between School and Academy." *American Educational Research Journal* 28 (1991) 495–519.

9

Learning to Take Ownership, Learning Equanimity

Two Portraits of Encountering Biblical Criticism in College

Jon A. Levisohn

Introduction

About ten years ago,[1] eight students at Brandeis University enrolled in my undergraduate course, "Studying Sacred Texts." They were familiar with the course description, which posed the following questions:

- What does it mean to study a sacred text?
- What are the problems with doing so?
- What is sacred about a sacred text?
- How is studying a sacred text similar to and different from studying other texts?
- How do different religious traditions study texts differently?

The students also knew that there were no official prerequisites for the course. In our first session, I told them that the only requirement for

---

1. I am leaving the exact year ambiguous to protect the privacy of the students. I will use pseudonyms for the same purpose.

the course is that the students should have had some experience studying sacred texts in some setting—religious or academic—and an interest in the variety of ways that people encounter them. In other words, they did not need to know anything, in particular, about sacred texts. But I wanted students who cared about the topic.

The students had also seen the syllabus in advance. So, they could anticipate that they would undertake an observation of some location where sacred texts were being studied, and would report on that observation to the group; that they would learn about the sacred texts of Islam and Christianity, in addition to Judaism; that they would consider the various genres of sacred texts; that they would learn about why and how commentaries on texts are generated, and how those commentaries sometimes themselves acquire a special status; and so on.

However, by mid-way through the course, the topic of what is known as the "historical-critical" study of the Hebrew Bible—the academic study that assumes that human authors, rather than a divine author, wrote and edited the text, and that investigates (among other things) exactly how that process took place—became a central focus of student presentations, discussion, and writing. At the heart of an historical-critical approach to the text is the Documentary Hypothesis, which argues on the basis of textual evidence that the Hebrew Bible as we have received it is actually a compilation of four discrete sources.[2] As the semester progressed, I responded to the students' interest in this topic by adjusting the syllabus to accommodate further exploration. I knew, from the experience of colleagues as well as my own experience in teaching similar material in the past, that students from religiously traditional backgrounds are

---

2. The sources are known by their initial letters J, E, P, and D. While there is healthy debate in the scholarly community about the specifics of these sources and the process of their integration or "redaction" into the text that we have today—and in particular, there is a significant school of thought that argues for a fifth discrete source, known as H—the basic contours of the Documentary Hypothesis remain the accepted understanding within the academic field. Contemporary Bible scholar Joel Baden writes, for example, "When the Pentateuch is read with a careful eye toward the narrative inconsistencies and continuities alike, the individual fragments coalesce into four strands or sources, each of which is internally consistent, and markedly distinct" (Baden, *Composition of the Pentateuch*, 20). It is also important to note that the investigation of the pre-existing sources of the biblical text, known as "source criticism," is only one aspect of the broader historical-critical approach to the text. In other words, many academic scholars of the Bible pursue questions unrelated to how the text came to be the way it is. But they all proceed on the assumption that the text was composed and redacted by human hands.

sometimes destabilized when they encounter critical perspectives about religion in general and about their sacred texts in particular. But what I was observing in my classroom seemed more nuanced than this. The students seemed to be deeply engaged. While there were some indications of discomfort, they did not seem opposed to the inquiry—quite the contrary. I became curious about what the students were actually thinking and feeling.

I began to document the course dynamics, taking more detailed teaching notes than I typically do, keeping records of the students' work (online discussions, reading responses, in-class writing, and assigned papers), and even audio-recording some sessions of class discussion. About two years later, I asked a colleague to interview a subset of the students about their recollections of the course. Finally, ten years later, having already spent a good deal of time reading and reviewing the students' words and work, and sharing some of my analyses with others,[3] I reached out by email to two students whose reactions had piqued my interest in order to ask them some follow-up questions. The twin portraits of learning in this chapter of the two students whom I call "Ruth" and "Ellie" are based on this data.

By way of introduction to Ruth and her story, consider the following reflection, two years after her experience in "Studying Sacred Texts":

> All of a sudden it was like someone handed me a key and said, okay, choose which door you want to go through . . . This was the first time where I took ownership of my religious identity, and my faith in however I choose to define it . . .

For Ruth, the central quality of the encounter was not disruption or destabilization, but rather a sense of "ownership," of agency. Ruth was in control of her religious path in ways that she previously had not been.

Now meet Ellie, from her final reflection at the end of the semester:

> I was first introduced to the "JEPD" theory in my junior year [in a Jewish day school] . . . I rejected the ideas and really never learned much about them . . . This course forced me to confront these struggles . . . For me, this was the perfect environment to approach the topic. I feel that I am now old enough, and

3. I presented these analyses on three occasions: at the Network for Research in Jewish Education in 2007, at the Association for Jewish Studies in 2014, and at the Brandeis Seminar in Contemporary Jewish Life in 2017. I am grateful to the audiences at those presentations for their interest and critical feedback.

advanced enough in both my religious and academic self, to really analyze biblical criticism honestly.

For Ellie, the course was not her first encounter with biblical
criticism.[4] But she reported that, by the time of her participation in our
course, she was now mature enough to revisit the topic and that the environment in the course was the right place for her to do the work that
(she felt) she needed to do. Ironically, her Jewish day school had not been
the right place, or perhaps not the right time. But an academic course in
a secular university was the right place, and three years after high school
was the right time.

In telling the stories of Ellie and Ruth, I mostly use their words, as
expressed in their written coursework, transcripts of their contributions
to class discussion, the interviews that were conducted two years later,
and finally their emailed responses to the questions that I posed to them
ten years later. I present these stories as case studies of what can happen
when Jewish college students encounter biblical criticism—not what always happens, not what generally does happen, but what *can* happen, for
certain students, under certain conditions.

Are Ellie and Ruth outliers? Do they represent others, and if so,
how many? We have no way to know. We can simply pay close attention
to their words, and learn from them, deepening our appreciation of the
nuances of their experiences. As we learn from them, we will begin to
broaden our thinking about what kinds of learning college students actually experience at this formative moment in their lives, as they are reflecting on what matters most to them and who they want to be in the world.

Setting the Stage

My course focuses on the ways that we encounter and think about sacred
texts in various times and places and in various traditions. Together, the
students and I ask questions about what constitutes a sacred text, what
makes it sacred, and what that sacredness indicates about how to approach it. We do some comparative work, learning about how different

4. As discussed above, her phrase "the 'JEPD' theory" is a reference to the Documentary Hypothesis, which is the accepted understanding of the development of the
Hebrew Bible within the field of source criticism, itself a sub-field of biblical criticism.
All these terms—"JEPD," "Documentary Hypothesis," "source criticism" and "biblical
criticism"—are often (though imprecisely) used interchangeably to refer to the approach to the biblical text that assumes human rather than divine authorship.

traditions approach their sacred texts. We do some direct ethnographic observation of the study of sacred texts in various settings. We study a variety of texts ourselves and try to reflect on those experiences. And, while it is not a course on Bible, we also study some biblical criticism. We are also critical with regard to biblical criticism—not in the sense of offering a critique (although we sometimes do read critics) but rather in the sense of holding it at arm's length and inspecting it with a bit of critical distance. We ask: How does it work? What are its assumptions and commitments? What are its criteria and what are its outcomes?

"Studying Sacred Texts" is an upper-level undergraduate course in the Near Eastern and Judaic Studies Department at Brandeis; when they enrolled in the class, Ruth was a junior and Ellie was a senior. That year the course was a bit smaller than usual, with only eight students. All of them identified as Jewish.[5] Moreover, that cohort of students created an unusually tight-knit community, engaging with ideas and with each other with a great deal of openness and honesty. "Our class was truly an ideal laboratory for spiritual experimentation," according to Ruth. She elaborated by noting that, even though many of the students were observant Jews, and thus presumably committed to a set of beliefs, they "were nevertheless incredibly open-minded . . . I was continually surprised by my peers' honesty, vulnerability, and intellect."

Before moving on to the portraits of Ruth and Ellie, however, there are three important elements of the context that are worth noting—three ways that we need to set the stage. First, the eight students who enrolled in "Studying Sacred Texts" are instances of an important and complicated sociological question: What happens to college students' religious beliefs and practices when they (leave home and) go to college?

College can be a challenging place for religious practice and belief in various ways. College faculty tend to be more liberal than most Americans. In the case of residential colleges, simply leaving home can be disruptive. College coincides with the developmental stage of "emerging adulthood" (about which more later), which is marked by greater autonomy and disaffiliation from established structures. But scholars who

5. While Brandeis University was founded with sponsorship by the Jewish community, the undergraduate population is only around 40 percent Jewish. The Jewish enrollment in Jewish studies courses tends to be higher than that, to be sure. Still, in my experience, it is unusual for classes to be exclusively Jewish. Depending on the pedagogies employed, instructors in higher education may or may not know about the background of the students; in this course, in their responses to various assignments and questions, the students were all open about their own identification.

have studied these issues empirically have concluded that the idea that "college is bad for religion" is overly simplistic.[6] Some religious practice does seem to decline, but other measures of religiosity do not. In fact, in certain respects, those who go to college seem to be more religious than those who do not.

Moreover, whatever may be the case in the larger population may not quite match the experience of American Jewish college students in particular. Jews tend to be far more liberal than the national norm. They tend to be far less conventionally religious. Finally, they tend to identify as members of their religion regardless of whether they are religiously active. Someone who was raised Christian but is no longer observant might well report that she is no longer a Christian. In the parallel case, a Jew is likely to (continue to) call herself a Jew. As a result, the story about the relationship between college attendance and Jewish practice and commitments is complex—some indicators go down, others go up, and some stay right where they were.[7]

All this is relevant as background to understand the broader experience of my students. But this paper is more narrowly focused on what happens when students encounter new and potentially disruptive ideas: not just about religion in general, but about Judaism or Jewish texts in particular. This particular phenomenon is challenging to Jewish students from more liberal backgrounds as well as more traditional backgrounds. Even liberal Jews, in other words, may possess unexamined traditionalist beliefs about Jewish history, despite the "official" tenets of the liberal denominations to which they supposedly adhere.[8]

6. Bryant et al., "Understanding Religious and Spiritual Dimensions," 723–45; Uecker et al., "Losing My Religion," 1667–92.

7. Kotler-Berkowitz, "College Doesn't Turn Jews Away From Judaism."

8. This is why, for example, a Reform Jewish educator (studying for a master's degree) declared to me a number of years ago that she would never teach the Documentary Hypothesis in her Hebrew school, despite the fact that Reform Judaism has accepted source-criticism since the origins of Reform Judaism 200 years ago. This is why Susan Tanchel, in teaching the Documentary Hypothesis to high school seniors (as described and analyzed in Tanchel, "Judaism that Does Not Hide"), encountered resistance not only from traditionalist students (who identified as Orthodox) but from Conservative, Reform, and even some self-declared "secular" students as well. And this is why a colleague reports that, in his years as a Residence Director for undergraduate students at the Jewish Theological Seminary, he learned to expect a stream of students disrupted and upset after the first meeting of their Bible class, at which the instructor explained that God did not write the Bible and, moreover, that Conservative Jews (which is how the students identified) do not generally believe that God wrote

This is the first element of the context, the first way that we can set the stage: This portrait takes place against a background of questions about the relationship between college and religion, or more specifically, the encounter in college with challenging ideas about religion.

The second important element of the context is that, as briefly noted above, college students are in the developmental stage now known as "emerging adulthood." What does it mean to be an emerging adult? Jeffrey Arnett introduced the term into the literature on psychological development because it captures the way in which human beings in the modern West between 18 and 25 are exploring who and how they want to be in the world, in a way which is qualitatively different both from that of adolescents and from that of adults who are older than they are, who have achieved markers of settled adulthood such as launching careers, finding partners, and even starting families.[9] Sharon Daloz Parks writes that the "promise and vulnerability of [emerging adulthood] lie in the experience of the birth of critical awareness and the dissolution and recomposition of the meaning of self, other, world, and God."[10] She believes that this is where college students tend to be developmentally, and her observation is confirmed by Braskamp and Barry et al.[11] Thus, we should keep in mind questions such as the following: When and where did my students display the characteristics of emerging adults? How did those characteristics affect their experience, if they did?

Finally, the third element of the context worth noting is that, in this course, my learning goals have very little to do with knowledge of facts or dates, or even knowledge of ideas. Nor am I trying to teach a particular skill or set of skills. When we read texts together, pursue conceptual questions about what constitutes a sacred text, or critically examine a particular setting where sacred texts are studied, my goal is for students to practice and develop a stance towards this material marked by a capacity for critique and for appreciation. I want them to be as curious about these phenomena as I am, and to learn to see patterns and connections within them. When I assess their midterms or finals, I am not looking for

the Bible.

9. See Arnett, *Emerging Adulthood*.

10. Parks, *Big Questions, Worthy Dreams*, 6. Parks actually uses the term "young adulthood," since Arnett had not yet established the term "emerging adulthood" in the literature when she was writing. But she is referring to the same age group.

11. Braskamp, "The Religious and Spiritual Journeys of College Students," 117–34; Barry et al., "Religiosity and Spirituality During the Transition to Adulthood," 311–24.

accuracy but rather for insight and thoughtfulness. I care very little about their ability to remember, but I care a lot about their ability to notice, to understand, and to analyze.

This suggests that, when we look for learning in these stories, we should be looking not for content knowledge and not for the skills that they might have developed. Instead, we should be looking at the kinds of people that they have become, or are in the process of becoming. We can call this their dispositions. I do not mean to focus on their moral or interpersonal dispositions, how they treat each other. Instead, I mean their "subject-specific" dispositions, their stance towards this specific subject—the subject of the study of sacred texts. Knowledge is of course important; one cannot be a competent analyst of a phenomenon without knowing about that phenomenon, its central characteristics, its patterns, and its historical precedents. But simply having that knowledge in your head is not enough. The question is what you do with the knowledge that you have.

My point about subject-specific dispositional goals is informed by the work of Sam Wineburg, who has spent his academic career studying how students understand history.[12] His research on this topic has led him to skepticism about the existence of generic (subject-neutral) capacities. What does this mean? Here is how Wineburg talks about the generic capacity of "critical thinking":

> I really don't believe that these are generic, domain-general, free-floating cognitive capacities that hover above a person's ability to read a poem, to solve a physics problem, to interpret historical documents, or to figure out infelicities of grammar in an essay.[13]

Wineburg's argument is that we learn to think critically about poetry, physics, history, and grammar—but each case is different. Just because we learn to think critically about poetry does not mean that we have any capacity to do so in physics or the other domains. We can use the analogy of language: We do not learn to speak language (in general), we learn to speak a particular language. Learning takes places within particular domains or subject areas.

---

12. For example, see Wineburg, *Historical Thinking and Other Unnatural Acts*.

13. Wineburg, "Online faculty seminar conversations: A conversation with Sam Wineburg."

In this case, the domain or subject is the study of sacred texts. I therefore wonder: Who are these students becoming, as analysts of the study of sacred texts? What kind of people did Ruth and Ellie become through their experience?

Ruth: A Story of Finding the Key and Taking Ownership

Ruth grew up in a traditional Mizrahi family, i.e., a Jewish family with its roots in the Middle East. Like many Mizrahi families, hers was traditional but not religious. Typically, this pattern is manifest in a kind of relaxed observance of certain aspects of Judaism—perhaps gathering together for a traditional Shabbat dinner before going out on the town—combined with an embrace of traditional faith positions and an aversion to change. Her own articulation of this upbringing highlighted the nuances. "I say not religious," she clarified, "even though we do all the religious observances." In what sense, then, was it not religious? "I say that because we didn't engage in, say, text study at home. We didn't do that." In her conception, then, what might look to some outsiders as a deeply traditional and, yes, religious upbringing, was actually not as it appears.

But Ruth was not just describing a more flexible kind of traditionalism. There was also the matter of text study (or its absence), as she notes. So she was differentiating between a realm of practice on the one hand, and a cognitive or intellectual realm on the other. This carried over into an amusing description of her father and his beliefs.

> Even though my father is not a believer, he doesn't believe in tampering at all with religious institutions, with religious tradition. He's like, "You don't mess with religious texts." That's just the way it is. You don't do it. So, he's a very funny character in that he doesn't believe in God, but if you . . . but he always quotes the Torah, all the time. He says, "The rabbis say this," and, "The Torah says this," and if you ever say, "But I'll bet you don't believe in that," he says, "Don't tell me what I believe in or don't believe in."

It is not clear to me how Ruth was so confident that her father is "not a believer," given the exchange at the end of this delightful, loving description. Perhaps she was thinking about other conversations that they have had. Regardless, the setting in which Ruth was raised was one

of deep Jewish involvement but also what she experienced as an attenu-
ated cognitive or intellectual Jewish framework. Her family belonged to
a Conservative synagogue, and she went to Hebrew school once a week.
She was active in her Conservative youth group (known as USY). She was
very clear, however, that her Jewish education was minimal.

At Brandeis, Ruth was drawn to Islamic and Middle Eastern Studies
(IMES) because of her interest in politics, but she developed new interests in religion itself. She wrote:

> In coming to Brandeis, I decided to pursue a degree in IMES
> as a way of bridging gaps between nationalities and peoples of
> the Middle East. However, what I found was that the religion of
> Islam itself became most fascinating. I loved learning about the
> various interpretations of Islam . . . I took a course exclusively
> on the Qur'an last year and [discovered] my interest in exegesis
> [text interpretation] . . . This semester, I am also enrolled in a
> course on the New Testament.

Surprisingly, then, her decision to enroll in "Studying Sacred Texts"
did not flow from her Jewish upbringing or her feelings about what was
missing in her home. Instead, she depicted that decision as a logical next
step in her intellectual trajectory; having discovered an interest in qur'anic
exegesis and in the New Testament, she was now interested in thinking
more broadly about the phenomenon of the encounter with sacred texts.

Fairly quickly, however, she began to make the connections to her
own tradition. In an early assignment, a response paper after reading
some of Wilfred Cantwell Smith's *What is Scripture?*, she began as follows:

> Having studied both the Qur'an and the New Testament, I think
> Smith is very convincing in arguing the differences between
> each text's role in its respective religious community . . . How-
> ever, he fails to note that the Qur'an itself was not codified for
> some time after Muhammad's death.

This comment provides a flavor of Ruth's confidence, her own self-
perception as someone who has studied both the Qur'an and the New
Testament in college and who feels some ownership in those domains.
She then concluded her response paper as follows:

> Additionally, as Jews, do we have a revelation comparable to ei-
> ther the Qur'an or to Christ? Obviously, the Torah is the best ex-
> ample one can proffer; however, one must ask, "Does the Torah

serve as the one and only transmission of God's word and does
it serve as God's word itself or just the recording of it?"

The question itself that "one must ask" (a curious phrase that ab-
stracts from any actual person, to the anonymous "one," while simultaneously asserting an imperative that this is what someone "must" do) is
actually confusing. What, for example, is the difference between "God's
word" and a "recording" of God's word? What is clear, however, is that,
for Ruth, the dam had begun to crack; she had moved from thinking
about the sacred texts of other traditions to thinking about her own.

And in fact, in the interview two years later, that was exactly how
she described her experience:

> I knew that the idea of God giving the Torah at Sinai was not
> something I was totally on board with, but . . . I mean, I think at
> different points in my life I may have been more on board or less
> on board, but it wasn't until it came to an academic approach to
> it, I thought, well, this makes sense. If I can approach any other
> religious text this way, why can't I approach my own religious
> text? And it really put things in a new perspective for me, be-
> cause as much as I value my tradition and my religion, it made
> me realize I don't really think that Judaism has a monopoly on
> the word of God. And there's no reason inherently why I should
> treat this text any differently than any other faith community
> treats their own text.

The perspective that she presented here has two elements. One element has to do with the question of "monopoly," i.e., whether only Jewish
sacred texts have value or whether the sacred texts of other traditions do
too. The second element is even more fundamental: If she can treat other
texts critically, why shouldn't she treat her own texts critically? Both
of these insights were driven by Ruth's experience studying Islam and
Christianity seriously and then coming home, as it were, to think about
Judaism. For this student, the process of engaging the academic subject
of studying sacred texts enabled her to bring her critical gaze from other
traditions to her own.[14]

---

14. Interestingly, this part of the story—coming from the experience of studying
Qur'an and New Testament—is entirely absent from Ruth's reflections ten years later.
Does this mean that it was not actually as important? It is hard to say. After all, I
reached out to her regarding the course, and asked her questions designed to elicit her
thinking about it. A different set of questions, perhaps questions about her intellectual
trajectory more generally, might have generated different reflections.

But it was not quite that simple or that easy. As I look back on Ruth's written work, I detect hints of struggle, such as repeated references to what a Jew is supposed to believe, what qualifies someone as a heretic, and the role of questioning in Jewish faith. For example, in a class email discussion, she responded to another student who asked, "Can a person be Jewish without believing in God and the Torah?" as follows:

> I would instinctively say, "yes, of course one can be a non-be-lieving Jew," yet the issue is obviously more complicated. Juda-ism encompasses more than just faith; it is a term that includes ethnic identity, community, culture, and even a particular worldview. For many of my Jewish friends and relatives (and for probably some of yours, too), being "Jewish" encompasses cultural identity and tradition more than belief in God or reli-gious law. Growing up in a non-observant Jewish community, I never even questioned the idea that one could be Jewish without adhering to Jewish law; however, I only recently started think-ing about whether or not one could be Jewish without adhering to belief in God or Torah.

When she wrote that she "never even questioned the idea that one could be Jewish without adhering to Jewish law," she seemed to be say-ing that of course one's personal status is not dependent on ritual per-formance—because she grew up in a non-observant Jewish community, i.e., a community of people who did not adhere to Jewish law but who nevertheless saw themselves as Jews and were seen that way by others. But she recognized that there is a deeper question here than just whether a person keeps Shabbat or *kashrut* (Jewish dietary laws), a question that she was starting to think more about.

Interestingly, she did not spell out precisely why the question of be-lief is actually "more complicated." For many people, it is not actually that complicated. There is a strong tradition of thought in Judaism about the priority of deed over creed, according to which what is important is *not* what you believe (about God or Torah) but what you do.[15] Ruth, however, was apparently wondering what happens if one does not believe in God or in the authority of Torah. Perhaps she was wondering whether, with-out some shared underlying belief, there is anything that holds the Jew-ish community together. Perhaps, too, she was wondering what would

---

15. See, for example, Kellner, *Must a Jew Believe Anything?*, but also the classic articles by Solomon Schechter: Schechter, "Dogmas of Judaism," and Schechter, "Dog-mas of Judaism (continued)."

remain of her own Jewish commitments if she were to abandon a "belief in God or Torah," whatever exactly that means.

Before the last session of the course, I assigned a final reflection paper in which students were asked to compose a "brief but thoughtful reflection on the course and the issues that it has raised." I added that the students ought to review the response papers that they had written during the course, to help ground their reflection.

Ruth's final reflection paper made it explicit that, for her, the status and authority of the Torah was not just an academic question:

> Discussing Bible criticism on the one hand was incredibly ex-
> citing and intellectually engaging . . . Yet, on the other hand, it
> presented me with a religious crisis: I had already disqualified
> the oral law because of my belief in its human origins, so where
> would the Torah be left if it, too, were based in human creation?
> What authority could the Torah hold if it were just another hu-
> man creation and not God's word?

I was unaware, while teaching the course, that Ruth was undergoing a "religious crisis;" certainly her thoughtful reflections and substantive engagement with the material did not betray any sense of crisis during the semester. Note that in this reflection she indicated that the crisis preceded the course. Ten years later, she similarly recalled that time in her life: "I was having a bit of a spiritual crisis during the time I was enrolled in your class, and the coursework challenged me to think critically about my beliefs." Even more pointedly, in retrospect she characterized the experience in the course not as changing her beliefs but as giving her permission to own them: "I don't really think it was a choice to believe or not believe, but rather a choice to accept the (dis)belief that was already there."[16]

In Ruth's final reflection paper, she also explained the position at which she had arrived:

16. The focus of this portrait is Ruth, not me or my pedagogy. So the main point that I want to emphasize here is that Ruth's "crisis" was apparently not precipitated by the course, but rather, that the course served as an opportunity for her to work out her thinking. Still, the fact that I as her teacher was unaware of what she was experiencing—even with all the class conversation and opportunities for reflection—is sobering. This raises larger questions: What else is going on with my students just below the surface of which I am unaware? And what are my responsibilities regarding those emotions?

I adopted [the position that] the Torah's holiness, in my mind, lies not [in] its divine origins but in its significance to the Jewish people and to their lives. Thus, I resolved to accept and appreciate Biblical criticism without having to throw out Torah or compromise my Judaism.

Strikingly, even ten years later, she articulates a similar position: "I believe it is the Jews who made the Torah holy, not the other way around."

I should make it clear that my goal in teaching the course was neither to convince the students of the truth of the Documentary Hypothesis nor to provoke a religious crisis. This was not a course that promoted religious belief or behavior or their opposites, and I had and have no desired outcomes around either. Clearly, I made space for the intense personalization of the material, but I also maintained boundaries. I am pleased, for example, that the students reported that they wondered about my own religious views, which indicates that I was successfully able to conceal them.[17]

What, then, did Ruth learn through her experience in "Studying Sacred Texts" and her encounter with biblical criticism? How can we characterize her learning? To be sure, there are various facts and theories that she learned about, but the real impact on Ruth has little to do with facts and theories. In the follow-up interview two years after the course, she talked about her beliefs about the Bible, but more importantly, about her own self-understanding:

If I don't think that this text has its origins in a divinely written way, then that's okay for me to choose how I interpret and it's okay for me to choose how I interact with it, and how that affects my religious life.

And so, all of a sudden it was up to me. It wasn't up to anybody else. It was not up to my rabbi; it was not up to a guilt complex, which I'd had for a long time. It was just me. And again, I don't think Professor Levisohn ever taught us that. I don't think it was a matter of anyone teaching that to me, but I think through my own study that was the conclusion that I came to.

And that was a very powerful conclusion for me to say, well, I'm not alone in this. There are decades of other people that have

17. Concealing my own religious views is not the same as denying that these questions are relevant to me just as they are to the students. On the contrary, I try to frame my teaching as a shared inquiry, a quest for understanding in which the students and I are equally invested (see Levisohn, "Eros and (Religious) Education.")

come to this conclusion, and do you know what? I kind of agree
with what they have to say. This is great. Someone— it was as if
somebody had vocalized everything that I had felt for years. All
of a sudden I found someone else that could vocalize it in an
academic way, and then it was a very powerful discovery for me
in that way.

In this reflection, Ruth articulated a powerful and compelling trajectory towards ownership, agency, and empowerment. It was a trajectory of
increasing independence, although at the same time, one that was fueled
by an understanding that she was not alone. It was a trajectory, also, of
self-acceptance; as she wrote ten years later, "Where I had previously felt
like a hypocrite for not accepting Torah MiSinai,[18] the class allowed me
to feel intellectually honest with myself." To return to the phrases from
her interview that I quoted earlier in this chapter, Ruth felt that "someone
handed me a key," and that "this was the first time where I took ownership of my religious identity."

Lee Shulman, a scholar of education who has done a great deal of
work on the use of cases in teaching, often reminds us to ask about any
particular case, "What is this a case of?"[19] So what is Ruth a case of? Ruth
seems to be a case of a student who, through an encounter with biblical
criticism, achieves a level of both maturity and autonomy in unexpected
ways. It is not accurate to say that the material was comfortable for her,
exactly; she testified that it was challenging. But it was also "exciting"
and "engaging" because she brought to the encounter a set of questions
with which she was already grappling. Ruth developed, through the
course, a set of subject-specific beliefs—about Bible and its authorship,
as well as other aspects of the subject of the study of sacred texts—but
also and more importantly, a set of beliefs about her beliefs. These latter,
second-order beliefs were not just beliefs in the sense of propositions to
which she assented, but rather something more like a stance, a disposition towards her subject-specific beliefs, a stance of intellectual honesty
and empowerment that flowed out into her religious self-conception
more generally. Earlier, we quoted Sharon Daloz Parks: the "promise
and vulnerability of [emerging adulthood] lie in the experience of the
birth of critical awareness and the dissolution and recomposition of the

18. Literally, "Torah from Sinai," a traditional Hebrew shorthand for a belief in the
divine authorship of the biblical text.

19. For example, see Shulman, "Foreword."

meaning of self, other, world, and 'God.'"[20] For Ruth, the "dissolution" was happening even before the course; that was her "crisis." Her work in the course, however, seems to represent exactly the kind of "recomposition" that Parks is writing about.

Ellie: A Story of Emotional Growth
From Anger to Equanimity

Ellie grew up in a traditional Conservative home and went to Jewish day schools through high school. At Brandeis, she was very involved with the Conservative Jewish community. By the fall of her senior year when she took my class, she was already exploring the possibility of going to rabbinical school, which she eventually did. Like Ruth, Ellie also brought a range of experiences with our subject into the course. But rather than a quiet crisis like Ruth's, Ellie's stance before walking into "Studying Sacred Texts" might be characterized as one of "conscious avoidance" that she deliberately cultivated in order to stave off any religious conflict.

I first met Ellie via email before class began, because she was petitioning to have my course count for a requirement for majors in the Department of Near Eastern and Judaic Studies, of one course in the Biblical period. To that point, Ellie had not yet met the requirement. That itself made me a little suspicious, and as we saw earlier in the brief quote from her final reflection paper, my suspicions were well-founded: Ellie reported that she had learned about biblical criticism in high school but had rejected it out of hand, which is why she had avoided taking a Bible class at Brandeis. While I did not understand this at the outset, in retrospect it is clear that Ellie was avoiding a critical encounter with the texts of her tradition and hoped that my class would help her get around the department's expectation that students would do so as part of their major.

The first assignment for the course—before any discussion of biblical criticism—was for each student to write a "Studying Sacred Texts Autobiography." I asked them to tell the story of their experiences studying sacred texts (in whatever setting), and in particular, like any good story, to pay attention to any key turning points or moments of tension. Ellie introduced the topic of biblical criticism herself, even without a specific prompt to do so, and her hostility was clear:

---

20. Parks, *Big Questions, Worthy Dreams,* 6.

> I cannot tell you when—I don't remember learning it—but I remember believing that "every word in the Bible is there for a reason" . . . [In high school,] I was confronted for the first time with biblical criticism. I can remember being thoroughly irritated my freshman year with a rabbi who explained all problems in Kohelet as "corrupt text." I really hated that explanation . . . I had a similarly negative reaction to JEPD when that was first explained to me. I desperately wanted (still want?) to believe that God wrote the Torah . . .

Alongside her hostility towards an approach that did not treat the words of the biblical text with the generosity that she believed that they deserve, as well as towards the larger theory of source criticism in general, Ellie also demonstrated in this initial assignment an impressive ability to reflect on her own position. Far from lashing out blindly, she seized the opportunity to describe her own emotions.

Her autobiography then took an unexpected turn:

> Honestly, I was happy to believe [that God wrote the Torah] until last semester in Israel when I attended a lecture . . . about homosexuality in the Tanach. It hit me hard—a strong realization that in this one case, the Torah is wrong. I have still not worked this out for myself . . .

Thus, even though Ellie had resisted the idea of biblical source criticism, she did not entirely reject a critical approach to the text, in the sense of establishing some critical distance from the text's stance on a particular issue. In articulating her provisional conclusion that, "in this one case, the Torah is wrong," Ellie was also engaging in serious reflection about what it meant for her (or for anyone) to stand in judgment of the text.

Another early indication of Ellie's openness came in her short written response to Wilfred Cantwell Smith's argument about scripturalization, that is, that texts become transformed into something that we call "scripture" by virtue of how they are read or the function that they play.[21]

> Another point that moved me [in the Smith reading] is the instruction not to look at the text, but rather to look at how the people interact with it. This is similar to a comment I made in class that scripture is a "human doing." I said, "Sacredness has to be in relation to something, it can't just be sacred alone, it must be sacred to someone."

21. Smith, *What is Scripture?*

Now, on the one hand, I am not that impressed when a student writes that she likes the reading because it agrees with something she already believed! But on the other hand, I have found that Smith's point about scripturalization can sometimes generate defensiveness among traditionalist students. Smith says, explicitly, that his argument is agnostic on the question of where the texts actually come from; he is saying, rather, that regardless of where the text comes from, a group of people have to come to *believe* something about the text in order for them to treat it as scripture, and it is only when they do treat it that way that, in fact, it comes to *be* scripture. Traditionalists tend to assume that Smith is simply debunking their traditional beliefs and therefore undermining the sacredness of their sacred texts. Ellie, however, had already arrived at a fairly sophisticated understanding of the complicated relationship between a text and a community. As opposed to the defensiveness that she reported in her experiences in high school, here she was open to exploring religious phenomena, even ones that hit close to home.

In a subsequent exercise, in which the students read and responded to sections of James Kugel's *Early Biblical Interpretation*,[22] Ellie was up front about the personal meaning that she derived from Kugel's arguments:

> Commentary is inherently a part of Jewish sacred texts—there is no escaping it . . . There is something about this idea of commentary being essential to sacred texts that I find intriguing. It potentially leads to the idea that commentary is an essential part of Judaism. I think this speaks volumes about the values of our religion—and I like what it implies.

Note the first person plural—"our religion"—which is a formulation that I try never to use in my undergraduate teaching, even when the students and I all happen to share a particular religious tradition, and that I generally discourage students from using as well. Note, as well, the forthright personalization of the argument: "I like what it implies." Ellie did not mean that she finds the argument intellectually compelling as an analysis of a phenomenon into which we were inquiring. She meant that, as a Jew, she found the idea powerful and useful in her own spiritual life.

As the semester progressed, Ellie's openness and equanimity seemed to disappear when the class turned to a heated discussion of the question of whether students ought to study biblical criticism—whether there is

22. Kugel and Greer, *Early Biblical Interpretation*.

some ethical or epistemological imperative to do so. Following that class discussion, I asked them to write about this issue for homework. Ellie responded:

> I object to the question. I disagree that there is a responsible and irresponsible way to relate to your religion that is based on the kind of theological questions you ask of the text. In short, my answer is NO. Biblical criticism is not an imperative.

Her response was unequivocal. She wanted to protect the rights of individuals, including presumably herself, from the suggestion that avoiding biblical criticism represented any kind of failure, especially ethical or epistemological. Religious beliefs, she said, should not be challenged in this way. Even to raise the question was objectionable.

However, a rather more complicated picture emerged as the course continued. The following week, the students read Susan Tanchel's article about the teaching of source criticism in Jewish high schools.[23] In response, Ellie wrote:

> My thoughts on the documentary hypothesis are not clear, and as a result, my thoughts on teaching of the Documentary Hypothesis in high school are not clear . . . I greatly object to [Tanchel's] implication that a student with traditional beliefs and not [traditional] practice has a "disconnect" in their Judaism. I resent the idea that students without exposure to these beliefs maintain, a "childlike attitude" toward their Judaism. On the other hand, I found the last few pages very compelling. I agree with the idea that if a transdenominational education claims to teach every view, there is no excuse to leave this out.

As in the previous passage, here too she used the verb "object." She was explicitly resentful. She seemed to be taking these issues very personally. In fact, at times she seemed to have no critical distance from the subject whatsoever. Yet, in the last two sentences, she admitted that she found an aspect of Tanchel's argument to be compelling.

Then, in a class discussion, Ellie produced the following multi-layered formulation about this topic:

> I very much object to the idea that a student that didn't learn this must have a child-like understanding of Bible. I think that, maybe as *teachers* they have a responsibility to teach it, but I

---

23. Tanchel, "A Judaism That Does Not Hide."

don't think that students necessarily have a responsibility to be
learning it, inherently.

Once again, for a third time, she used the verb "object." She was
clearly committed to a defense of religious traditionalism from those
who would represent it as immature or irresponsible. She then suggested,
surprisingly, that teachers have some kind of professional responsibility
to teach biblical criticism to their students. It should be part of the curriculum, presumably because it is important for students' understanding
and perhaps even their intellectual or religious development. But as for
the students themselves, they have no moral, intellectual, or religious responsibility to learn about biblical criticism if they do not want to.

Ellie's comments point to a position that is both remarkably ele-
gant—splitting the difference between teachers' intellectual responsibility
to teach and students' intellectual responsibility to learn—and also utterly
illogical. If there is some responsibility (in whatever sense of "responsibility") that teachers have to teach biblical criticism to students, then how
could it possibly be the case that students do not have a responsibility
to learn what the teachers have a responsibility to teach? But as I have
discovered, sometimes we learn more about students from their failed
efforts to work out their ideas than we do from articulations of familiar
or rehearsed positions. Setting aside the logicality of the position, when
I read Ellie's reflection I was impressed that, despite her resentment, this
student was actively grappling with serious ideas.

Ellie's final reflection paper continued the theme of ambivalence:

> This class has helped me to think about sacred texts in ways that
> I have either not been exposed to, or have been avoiding . . . For
> me, this was the perfect environment to approach the topic. I
> feel that I am now old enough, and advanced enough in both my
> religious and academic self to really analyze biblical criticism
> honestly . . . I have no "final reflection" on what I have learned
> about biblical criticism. What I have are initial thoughts, and
> the desire to continue learning, asking questions, and struggling
> with the true meaning and implications of biblical scholarship.

In these reflections, Ellie acknowledged that the time had come for
her to stop avoiding the topic of biblical criticism and that the course had
been an opportunity for her to do that.

We might still wonder: Was Ellie describing an experience of actual
learning or was she merely reporting the kind of ambivalence that she

imagined that a professor (or at least, a certain kind of professor) would appreciate? At the same time, I am intrigued by a further sentence in Ellie's final reflection paper:

> While this is an academic class, it has helped me to work through my personal theological questions without the stress of a religious atmosphere.

As we saw above, questions about biblical authorship and authority were not foreign to Ellie. But this sentence suggests that, until this class, she had lacked the right place to do the exploratory work, a place without the "stress of a religious atmosphere." Within that religious atmosphere, for all the warmth and meaning that it can provide, Ellie felt that she was unable to emerge as an adult ("I am now old enough . . . "). For this student, such a setting had a certain kind of "stress," perhaps due to the expectations of conformity to traditionalist norms. In the academic classroom, on the other hand, her emerging adulthood had room to flourish.

The interview with Ellie two years later provided additional evidence of an increasing flexibility about learning alternative perspectives:

> If I was looking at courses at Brandeis that [included biblical criticism], I would specifically not want to take that course, not really for any sort of religious reason. I just rejected it. So then when I got into this class and he was like, "Okay, now we are going to learn this about the documentary hypothesis," I was very irritated at the beginning . . . I was like, "Oh, I have been trying so hard to avoid this and here you are going to make me talk about it." But I definitely left with less animosity towards that, which clearly is good because that came totally from an emotional place and not an intellectual place . . .

> [I was thinking,] here I am a college senior. I have got to suck it up . . . I have to admit that at some point you are not too young and this is probably it and I probably need to get over that . . .

> I said something the other day [to my mother about biblical criticism] and [she] was like, "Wow. You really used to be really angry when I would talk about that, and now you are not so angry anymore," which again, I don't know if it is so much that I learned something in particular but that it forced me into saying okay, it is solid, it is worthwhile.

What Ellie seemed to report in this interview is a movement away from reactivity and defensiveness. She displayed some of the same impressive self-reflection that we noticed in her first assignment in recognizing her own emotional reactions. Ten years later, she told a similar story (although interestingly she did not reference the "Studying Sacred Texts" experience in particular): "I do know that I made this shift [from emotional reactivity to a more "intellectual place"] at some point between high school and rabbinical school." Unlike Ruth, Ellie's learning was not an "opening up" of religious possibilities. Hers was not about the click that Ruth described, when things all of a sudden started to make sense. If anything, Ellie was more troubled by what she had learned about studying sacred texts, because her new insights made it harder for her to reflexively reject the academic study of Bible.

At the same time, Ellie also seemed genuinely grateful for the opportunity to have the dedicated space within an academic environment to consider her own stance towards the biblical text. She was not lacking in critical distance before the class; recall her observation about the biblical texts on homosexuality. Nor was she unaware of biblical criticism, which she had learned about already in high school. What she seemed to have developed is greater capacity to critique her own reactions and greater emotional stability.

She used to be angry, as her mother noted. She showed flashes of the same hostility in the class itself (never, it should be clear, towards the class or towards the instructor, but towards positions with which she disagreed or that she found threatening). But through the course, she developed a greater maturity and a diminished defensiveness.[24] Ten years later, she reported: "I don't reject biblical criticism, which was my response in high school, but I also don't usually find it particularly rewarding." The disposition that she has developed, perhaps, is a kind of equanimity or composure. But just as Wineburg is skeptical about the existence of a generic, cross-domain capacity called "critical thinking,"[25] so too we might

24. In referring to Ellie's "maturity," I do not mean that acceptance of biblical criticism is the mature position and that traditionalism with regard to biblical authorship is immature. I am referring to Ellie's self-described immature emotionality in discussing the issues and her more mature equanimity, not her conclusions. To put the point another way, there may be both mature and immature versions of a rejection of biblical criticism, and equally, both mature and immature versions of an *acceptance* of biblical criticism. I appreciate my colleague Ariel Pardo's encouragement to clarify this point, following my presentation at the Brandeis Seminar on Contemporary Jewish Life in early 2017.

25. Wineburg, "Online faculty seminar conversations: A conversation with Sam Wineburg."

be skeptical that Ellie has developed a generic, cross-domain capacity of equanimity. Is Ellie reactive and defensive in her life in general? Or is she composed and even-keeled? We have no way of knowing. Instead, what we can affirm is that she has developed a *subject-specific* equanimity, a stance of composure specifically with regard to the study of Bible and biblical criticism.

Conclusion

In the final session of the course, the class undertook a discussion of Ben Sommer's article, "The Source Critic and the Religious Interpreter."[26] After some exploration of Sommer's specific arguments for how source criticism opens up new avenues for religiously meaningful readings of the biblical text, I asked the class whether and how his arguments changed their views about studying sacred texts. One student shared a view about the experience of reading sacred texts in community, and then Ruth chimed in:

> A different part of my brain . . . has sort of been turned on and it's . . . very fulfilling intellectually and personally as well to have that . . . It doesn't feel as removed for me in some ways . . . It is rooted in something that is easier for me to put my head around at least at this point in my life.

Echoing positions that we heard from her earlier, Ruth embraced source criticism both "intellectually" (she refers to both her "brain" and her "head") and "personally" (the text "doesn't feel as removed from me" as it did before her exposure to source criticism). We even hear echoes of increased ownership.

Immediately, Ellie followed Ruth with a quite different response.

> I just, in no intellectual way, but in a purely emotional, gut way, respond exactly the opposite way. For me, it's very easy to feel close to a text if it's God's text . . . It's very hard for me to relate to the text through biblical criticism in a religious way. I can relate to it in an academic way. But just sort of the gut reaction is exactly the opposite. Biblical criticism makes it much harder for me to relate to the text than easier.

---

26. Sommer, "The Source Critic and the Religious Interpreter," 9–20.

Here, too, we can see themes that are familiar to us from other things that Ellie has said. We see her emotionality, but also her awareness of her emotionality. We do not see the hostility and resentment that she displayed at earlier stages of the course; she "can relate to it in an academic way." We see her displaying subject-specific equanimity, even though her fundamental religious position seems like it has not changed.

Two students, two reactions, two stories. Obviously, neither one represents the entire truth of how Jewish students respond to the study of biblical criticism in college, nor what they learn from that experience. Instead, Ruth and Ellie provide us with two windows through which we can view the complexity of the learning process, and the complexity too of the kinds of intellectual, emotional and spiritual development that students undergo—sometimes—from the meaningful learning opportunities that we struggle to create.

Further Reflections About Jewish Learning

As a teacher, I have "lived" with these two students, Ruth and Ellie, for a decade now. Of course many students, who are memorable for a variety of reasons, live on in my mind even if I am no longer in contact with them. But Ruth and Ellie are different. Ever since I identified them in my early analyses of my data, ever since these portraits began to emerge, their ideas and experiences have a vivid quality for me, grounded in their spoken and written expressions.

What do I learn from the cases of Ruth and Ellie? What have they taught me? These two cases do not prove that Jewish college students should learn about biblical source criticism. Nor do they prove the opposite, that Jewish college students should not learn about biblical source criticism. There are too many significant variables: Ruth's and Ellie's respective educational backgrounds, their interactions with their parents, their prior experiences studying sacred texts of various traditions, and more. I cannot generalize responsibly from these stories. However, these two portraits do illuminate for me aspects of learning that typically go unnoticed, certainly unassessed, and likewise unvalued.

First, the portraits of Ruth and Ellie remind me of how much is going on for our students. Any stage of life has its characteristic challenges. Students—whether "emerging adults" or otherwise—come into our classes (and other educational environments) with ideas, assumptions, and emotions, not just about stuff going on at home or with their friends but about the world and the subjects that we are studying. Sometimes I get a brief window into those ideas, assumptions, and emotions. Rarely do I get the opportunity to gather the kind of data explored here, or to follow up with students intensively two and ten years later. What else would I learn if I did?

Second, Ruth and Ellie have taught me something about the nature of the "Jewish" in "Jewish learning." In this case, regarding the specific subject of biblical criticism, some readers will assume that students in Jewish educational settings ought to be exposed to and explore the best and most current academic research on aspects of Jewish intellectual and cultural history (including the best and most current academic research on the Hebrew Bible and other texts of the Jewish tradition). Other readers will argue that dispassionate academic scholarship is not what Jewish education is all about, that Jewish education ought to foster loyalty, allegiance, and love, not critical distance. But the situation is much more complicated than that; in some circumstances, biblical criticism may support the development of autonomy and maturity. The conclusion to be drawn, then, is not about whether biblical criticism itself is or is not an important element in the Jewish educational curriculum. Instead, the portrait highlights the conditional and circumstantial nature of that curriculum. As a teacher, my foremost concern is to contribute to the growth of my students—but the question of what contributes to the growth of the students, as Jews and as human beings, is always context-dependent.

Third, Ruth and Ellie have helped me to see what it looks like when a student develops a certain disposition with regard to a specific subject, and thus have helped me to imagine what it can look like to teach towards those objectives. The notion of a subject-specific disposition as the desired educational objective does not eliminate or exclude the objective of developing the students' knowledge. As we saw, Ruth and Ellie learned a lot of content. So the point here is not about skills versus content (which is generally a false dichotomy). Instead, as noted at the outset, the knowledge that they gained was, for me, instrumental towards the development of certain kind of stance towards the subject. When I tried to give language to that stance, I wrote about students' "capacity for critique and for appreciation," about their curiosity regarding these particular phenomena (the study of sacred texts), and about their attentiveness to and ability to analyze the patterns and connections within them. What I had not yet seen, until Ruth and Ellie taught me, is that there is also a subject-specific disposition of equanimity (in Ellie's case) and of ownership (in Ruth's). I now know that these dispositions, too, are what I aspire for my students to learn, when we explore the study of sacred texts together: a subject-specific equanimity and a subject-specific sense of ownership. A question that these stories generate for me, then, is how we might encourage dispositional goals, in other settings and perhaps also other subjects.

Bibliography

Arnett, Jeffrey Jensen. *Emerging Adulthood: The Winding Road from the Late Teens through the Twenties.* New York: Oxford University Press, 2004.

Baden, Joel S. *The Composition of the Pentateuch: Renewing the Documentary Hypothesis.* New Haven: Yale University Press, 2012.

Barry, Carolyn McNamara, et al. "Religiosity and Spirituality During the Transition to Adulthood." *International Journal of Behavioral Development* 34 (2010) 311–24.

Braskamp, Larry A. "The Religious and Spiritual Journeys of College Students." In *The American University in a Postsecular Age,* edited by Douglas Jacobsen et al., 117–34. New York: Oxford University Press, 2008.

Bryant, Alyssa N., et al. "Understanding the Religious and Spiritual Dimensions of Students' Lives in the First Year of College." *Journal of College Student Development* 44 (2003) 723–45.

Kellner, Menachem. *Must a Jew Believe Anything?* Oxford: Littman Library of Jewish Civilization, 1999.

Kotler-Berkowitz, Laurence. "College doesn't turn Jews away from Judaism." https://www.jta.org/2017/05/08/news-opinion/opinion/college-doesnt-turn-jews-away-from-judaism.

Kugel, James L., and Rowan A. Greer. *Early Biblical Interpretation.* Philadelphia: Westminster John Knox, 1986.

Levisohn, Jon A. "Eros and (Religious) Education." http://www.hillelofficeofinnovation.org/sites/default/files/ooi_salons_eros_and_religious_education_jon_a_1.pdf.

Parks, Sharon Daloz. *Big Questions, Worthy Dreams: Mentoring Emerging Adults in Their Search for Meaning, Purpose, and Faith.* San Francisco: Jossey-Bass, 2002.

Schechter, Solomon. "The Dogmas of Judaism." *The Jewish Quarterly Review* 1 (1888) 48–61.

———. "The Dogmas of Judaism (continued)." *The Jewish Quarterly Review* 1 (1889) 115–27.

Shulman, Lee. "Foreword." In *Ethics of Inquiry: Issues in the Scholarship of Teaching and Learning,* edited by Pat Hutchings. Menlo Park, CA: The Carnegie Foundation for the Advancement of Teaching, 2002.

Sommer, Benjamin D. "The Source Critic and the Religious Interpreter." *Interpretation* 60 (2006) 9–20.

Smith, Wilfred Cantwell. *What is Scripture?* Minneapolis: Fortress, 1993.

Tanchel, Susan E. "A Judaism that Does Not Hide: Teaching the Documentary Hypothesis in a Pluralistic Jewish High School." *Journal of Jewish Education* 74 (2008) 29–52.

Uecker, Jeremy E., et al. "Losing my Religion: The Social Sources of Religious Decline in Early Adulthood." *Social Forces* 85 (2007) 1667–92.

Wineburg, Sam. *Historical Thinking and Other Unnatural Acts: Charting the Future of Teaching the Past.* Philadelphia: Temple University Press, 2001.

————. "Online faculty seminar conversations: A conversation with Sam Wineburg." Virtual Knowledge Project (2001). (website discontinued)

10

LEARNING ABOUT JEWISH LEARNING

Sharon Feiman-Nemser

THE PORTRAITS OF JEWISH learning that make up this unique collection offer fascinating and inspiring reading. They invite us into a variety of Jewish educational settings where they provide close-in descriptions of serious, engaged learning. The authors are, in Diane Tickton Schuster's words, "witnesses to the learning," some as insiders to the action and others as observers. Besides giving us powerful "images of the possible" in Jewish education, they help frame a conversation about what high-quality Jewish learning entails and what it can do for individual learners and for the Jewish community.

Both David Bryfman in his preface and Schuster in her introductory chapter refer to the commonplaces of education (students, teachers, subject matter and milieu), the active ingredients or building blocks of any educational experience. This framework reminded me of a compatible but more dynamic model often referred to as "the instructional triangle" which emphasizes the interaction among the four educational commonplaces.

I first encountered the idea of the instructional triangle in an essay by David Hawkins, philosopher of science and education, called "I, Thou, It" in which Hawkins characterizes the educational encounter as an interaction between the teacher (I), the student (thou) and some compelling piece of the world (it). For Hawkins, what distinguishes the relationship of teacher and student is their purposeful engagement with some content or subject to be learned, an external "it."[1]

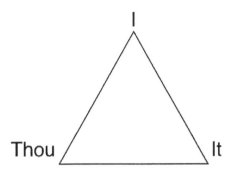

Other scholars of teaching and learning have created a more elaborate diagram of the instructional triangle.[2] In this version, two-way arrows connect the points of the triangle to highlight the dynamic nature of the relationships between and among teacher, students, and subject matter. Intersecting student arrows signal the centrality of peer relationships and interaction in the learning process. Two concentric circles labeled "environments" surround the instructional triangle with arrows connecting them to the other elements. This addition reminds us that students, teachers, and subject matter both influence and are influenced by the environments in which they are situated.

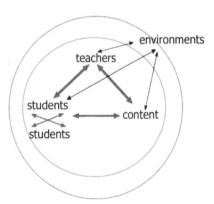

Most recently, in her presidential address at the 2018 annual meeting of the American Educational Research Association, Deborah Ball

---

1. Hawkins, "I, Thou, It," 48–62.
2. Cohen et al., "Resources, Instruction and Research."

introduced further changes to the instructional triangle.[3] First, Ball positioned students at the apex to indicate their centrality in the teaching/learning process. Second, she renamed what was formerly called "subject matter" as "stuff" to broaden our thinking about the myriad things that students learn and teachers teach, both intentionally and unintentionally, when they interact in educational settings. Third, she represented the multiple environments of teaching and learning in a more fluid, less defined manner, to remind us that classrooms and schools, families and communities, and policies and cultures both shape and are shaped by the participants and activities of teaching and learning. Finally, she enlarged the arrow connecting students and teachers to underscore the importance of that relationship; she also enlarged and bolded the arrow connecting teachers and environments to highlight the myriad expectations and outside influences that press on teachers today.

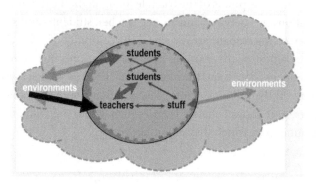

Ball's rendering of the instructional triangle represents schematically what the *Portraits of Jewish Learning* (PoJL) authors capture through their detailed descriptions of individual learners and educators in actual Jewish educational settings engaged in learning and teaching all manner of Jewish stuff. Reading the portraits through this lens led me to probe their internal dynamics and ask certain questions: What kind of relationships do learners form with each other and how does this influence their learning? How do the curricula reflect institutional missions, parental expectations, and student interests? What assumptions about learners and content do Jewish educators hold and how does this influence their purposes and pedagogy? How do the educators build meaningful bridges between students and subject matter?

3. Ball, "Just Dreams and Imperatives."

My reading of the portraits was also influenced by John Dewey's experiential philosophy of education.[4] Dewey, leading twentieth-century philosopher, reformer, and theorist of progressive education, argued that all learning takes place through experience but not all experiences are educative. For Dewey, an experience comes about through the interaction of two factors: the individual with his needs, desires, purposes and capacities, and the physical and social conditions that surround him. The educative value of that interaction depends on its effects in opening up or closing off subsequent worthwhile learning or growth. As Dewey puts it, "if an experience arouses curiosity, strengthens initiative, and sets up desires and purposes that are sufficiently intense to carry a person over dead places in the future,"[5] we may judge it an educative experience.

Looking at the portraits through the lens of Dewey's theory led me to consider who the learners are and what they bring to their learning in terms of background, interests, and capacities. It focused my attention on salient features of the learning situation including the physical set-up, the social structures, and the human and material resources. It led me to consider how the learners were interacting with their learning environment and what effects that had on their understanding, skills, and ways of being in the world. From the start, I wanted to know whether these were examples of educative Jewish learning and what made them so.

This chapter is organized around a set of questions and ideas stimulated by my reading of the portraits in light of the instructional triangle and Dewey's theory. First I unpack the concept of "learning" and consider what the portraits have to say about learning as a process and learning as an outcome. Next I explore the question of what's Jewish about the learning depicted in the portraits. Finally I highlight the indispensable role of the educator in enabling educative learning. I conclude with some reflections on how to strengthen the quality of Jewish learning by focusing more attention on the learning agenda represented by these portraits.

Unpacking "Learning"

Learning is one of those words that carry two meanings. Analytic philosophers differentiate the "task" sense and the "achievement" sense of

4. Dewey, *Experience and Education.*
5. Dewey, *Experience and Education,* 38.

the word.[6] On the one hand, we say that "students are learning to decode Hebrew, to understand Biblical criticism, and to take responsibility for their own and each other's learning." In these examples, learning refers to processes of acquiring new skills, gaining new knowledge and understanding, and developing new habits and appreciations. On the other hand, we say that "students have acquired a basic Jewish life vocabulary, can support their interpretations with textual evidence, understand that the history of Arab-Israeli relations is filled with moral complexities, and feel at home in their synagogue." In these examples, learning is an accomplishment or achievement, and students have been changed in some way through their learning experiences.

I thought of this distinction—between learning as a process of growth and change and learning as an outcome of that process—as I reflected on the portraits of Jewish learning. How do the PoJL authors conceptualize and illuminate the processes of Jewish learning? What examples and evidence do they provide of learning outcomes?

The Learning Process

In most of the portraits, learning is depicted as an active process of sense-making and problem-solving in the company of others. Learning does not happen in the heads of individual learners alone. Rather it happens as learners solve problems and engage in authentic tasks and activities with their peers and with the guidance and support of more experienced, knowledgeable others. This characterization resonates with Dewey and with contemporary theories of learning, like social constructivism and activity theory, which emphasize the importance of learning environments that are intensely social and feature novices and experts working with each other.[7]

More than half the portraits explicitly reference the social or relational nature of learning, not just as a source of motivation and fun but as a resource in personal growth and learning. The authors call on various theories of learning and development to conceptualize and explain the learning processes they portray. The use of similar frameworks across so-called formal and informal settings problematizes this distinction and

6. Ryle, *The Concept of Mind*, 149.

7. See especially Lave and Wenger, *Situated Learning*; Rogoff, *Apprenticeship in Thinking*; and Vygotsky, *Mind in Society*.

reminds us, as Dewey put it, that "all genuine education comes about through experience."[8] I will return to Dewey's distinction between "educative" and "miseducative" experiences when I consider the outcomes or effects of the learning experiences described in the portraits. But first, some observations about the learning process as the authors describe and conceptualize it.

In chapter one, Ziva Hassenfeld uses social constructivist theories of learning to frame her portrait of second-graders learning to interpret Biblical narratives. She explains how, over many months, she observed with surprise and delight as a class of seven-year-olds learned to engage in "sophisticated textual interpretation" by doing the interpreting themselves. Paraphrasing social constructivist Gordon Wells, she points out that young children learn through authentic activity, in this case the activity of discussion and inquiry, with the help of adults like their teacher Kobi.

"Depth of relationships" and "depth of learning" are core principles in the design of Mayim Tamid, the Jewish after-school program described by Jordana Schuster Battis and Rachel Happel in chapter two. Children come to relax, do homework, engage in projects, participate in daily prayer, and play in this home-like environment designed to give them the experience of living Jewishly. Relationships develop through the building of content knowledge and content knowledge develops through the building of relationships. The authors compare the learning process in Mayim Tamid to the organic learning that children would experience growing up in a home where Judaism is woven into everyday life, where parents have the time and background to engage children in holiday preparation and to incorporate Hebrew into their conversations.

In chapter five, Nicole Greninger highlights the social nature of the innovative Hebrew program in JQuest, a synagogue-based religious school, as key to its success. In the fifth-grade Hebrew Through Movement lesson she describes, we see students "laugh at one another, help one another and cheer for each other" as they act out the silly Hebrew commands issued by their teacher. Invoking socio-cultural theorist Lev Vygotsky, Greninger suggests that students are not only having a good time, they are helping one another do with assistance what they are not

---

8. Dewey, *Experience and Education*, 25.

yet ready to do on their own.[9] Social learning also contributes to the building of community around a shared Jewish life vocabulary.

Relational learning is key to the partnership model that undergirds the Seventh Grade Beit Midrash developed and described by Orit Kent and Allison Cook in chapter four. They understand *havruta* learning as a partnership of three—two people and the text—which they also represent as a triangle. To actualize this ideal, "students must work on both the skills and attitudes which enable them to build and take responsibility for the relationships among self, others and texts." We see how this plays out for two students, Jim and Nate, as they identify habitual modes of learning with others, practice new ways of talking and listening, and "learn to learn in partnership."

Relational learning shapes the intergenerational professional development program created and described by Stefani Carlson in chapter seven. Like the leaders of Mayim Tamid, Carlson believes that relationships are just as critical to the educational process as the content being presented. She draws on Jack Mezirow's theory of transformational learning and Robert Kegan's theory of adult and professional development to account for a process of "maturation, transformative learning, and professional development" which she observes in two teen volunteers serving as classroom assistants in the religious school. As we follow Mike and Jacob across the school year, we see how serious and sometimes difficult interactions with peers and mentors lead to shifts in how they see themselves as teachers and leaders.

Not all of this learning happens smoothly. In several portraits, disruptions or bumps in the road occur as learners encounter challenges to their previously-held beliefs and understandings and try to figure out what to do with new knowledge and information. Examples of this process occur in Matt Reingold's portrait of high school seniors in a Jewish day school learning about troubling events in Israel's history in chapter eight, and in Jon Levisohn's portrait of two learners in his undergraduate class at Brandeis University, "Studying Sacred Texts," in chapter nine. Both portraits also remind us that different learners experience the same learning opportunity in different ways.

---

9. In *Mind in Society,* L. S. Vygotsky refers to this cutting edge of learning as the "zone of proximal development"—that place where a learner can perform with assistance what he is unable to do on his own. His prototype is the way a mother scaffolds the efforts of babies and young children learning to talk.

Informed by Lawrence Kohlberg's theory of moral development, Reingold wondered how his twelfth-grade students would react to learning "potentially disruptive narratives" about Israel. Not surprisingly, he discovered that students' learning experiences differ, revealing variations in their capacity for moral reasoning. Some were able to integrate new information into a broader, more complex understanding of Israel; others struggled to integrate alternative views of Israel or quickly rejected new information that conflicted with their previously-held positive assumptions about Israel.

We also see disruptions in the learning trajectories of Ruth and Ellie, as described by Jon Levisohn. Knowing something about their backgrounds, including their prior encounters with biblical criticism, helps explain their responses to course discussions, readings, and written assignments. For Ruth, who grew up in a traditional but not religious family, the course provoked a quiet "spiritual crisis," challenging her to think critically about her religious beliefs. Ultimately the academic encounter with biblical criticism helped her own her personal belief that "the Torah's holiness lies not in its divine origins but in its significance to the Jewish people and to their lives." For Ellie, a day school graduate from a Conservative home who had strenuously avoided biblical source criticism, the course provided "the perfect environment" to rethink her previous negative reactions and to re-consider her stance. By the semester's end, she exhibited greater awareness of her emotional reactions and greater openness to the implications of biblical scholarship.

Both Matt's and John's portraits highlight another Deweyan insight about learning—that no two learners experience the same learning environment in exactly the same way. What learners make of their experiences and what they ultimately learn depends not only on what they encounter physically, socially, and intellectually, but also on who they are and what they bring in terms of prior experiences and beliefs.

Learning Outcomes

So what are students learning in these portraits of Jewish learning and what kind of evidence supports this? Since learning in the achievement sense involves some kind of change in the learner, we can scan the portraits for descriptions (or speculations) about how students are changed by their learning experiences. Even though the portraits were not written as academic studies of learning, almost all of them have something to say about the outcomes or effects of the learning experiences and some provide evidence to support or illustrate their claims.

Of course, most claims about learning outcomes are inevitably tentative. What did students know before they entered a particular learning environment? How reliable are self reports? How do we know whether an apparent indicator of growth is attributable to a given aspect of the learning environment? Assessing learning always raises these kinds of questions. Still, we are better served when we look deeply at learning outcomes rather than superficially, as so often happens when we rely on such measures as standardized texts.

We generally think about learning outcomes in terms of the broad categories of knowledge and skills and, indeed, the portraits describe students gaining new knowledge and developing new skills. Greninger's students learn more Hebrew. Reingold's students broaden their knowledge of Israel's complex history. Kobi's students get better at close reading. Students of Kent and Cook learn to use new talk moves (what they call "Torah study speech prompts"). Levisohn's students learn how other religions study sacred texts.

But these outcomes hardly capture the full story of what students are learning in these rich Jewish learning environments. What seems equally or perhaps more important is how changes in knowledge and skill are accompanied by or lead to shifts in learners' attitudes, mindsets, and perspectives. The holistic nature of the learning opportunities results in a combination of learning outcomes that connect head, hand, and heart. Attitudes toward learning Hebrew change as JQuest students gain mastery while having fun. Shifts in frames of reference take place as Carlson's teen *madrichim* learn with and from their mentor teachers and students. Curiosity, open-mindedness, and equanimity develop as Levisohn's students gain a deeper appreciation for biblical criticism. A sense of belonging emerges as Mayim Tamid students contribute to their synagogue community. New self-awareness emerges as *havruta* students assess their typical patterns of learning and work on changing them. These dispositional changes illustrate what Dewey means by "collateral learning" and meet his criteria for "educative" experiences.

As Dewey explains, people do not learn only what they are studying. They also form enduring attitudes, including likes and dislikes, which may be more important than the particular subject matter being learned. Those attitudes, by which he means habits or dispositions, are what count in the future. For Dewey, the most important attitude that can be formed is "the desire to go on learning":

> What avail is it to win prescribed amounts of information about geography and history, to win the ability to read and write, if in the process the individual loses his own soul; loses his appreciation of things worthwhile, of the values to which these things are relative; if he loses desire to apply what he has learned and, above all, loses the ability to extract meaning from future experiences?[10]

If, in the passage, we substitute the geography of Israel, Jewish history, and the ability to read and write Hebrew, we have a powerful cautionary note about the miseducative effects of boring, superficial, aimless, didactic Jewish education.

The portraits make persuasive claims about the educative effects of the learning experiences depicted. Sometimes the effects are presented explicitly; other times the authors offer their speculations about how learners are affected by their experiences. In either case, we can accept the evidence as compelling but partial.

Greninger's portrait of learners in JQuest illustrates how developing positive attitudes accompanies the increase in skill. As she explains, one of the main goals in rethinking the Hebrew and prayer curriculum was "to improve the affective component of students' learning experiences." Without giving up on competence in decoding Hebrew and reciting prayers, the educational leaders sought "meaningful improvement in students' attitudes toward learning Hebrew as well as their confidence in the language." Results from a survey of 103 students in grades 3–6 provide some evidence of success: 75 percent indicated that they liked learning Hebrew and were enjoying Hebrew Through Movement activities. A survey of parents confirmed this attitudinal shift.

Quantitative data are not the only source of evidence regarding learning. Student interviews, samples of student work, transcripts of classroom discourse, and teacher observations also carry evidentiary weight in trying to understand and assess the effects or outcomes of learning. When Nate says, "I definitely got better at attentive silence ... and by the end, I was letting my partner talk," and these changes are evidenced in transcripts of his interactions with Jim and the biblical text, I

---

10. Dewey, *Experience and Education*, 49.

am persuaded that powerful learning took place for this individual. When Ellie writes in her final paper that she now has "the desire to continue learning, asking questions and struggling with the true meaning and implication of biblical scholarship," I accept Levisohn's interpretation that her outlook on biblical criticism has been transformed. When Mayim Tamid students choose to bake muffins, distribute them to people who work at the temple and explain when asked, "We just wanted to make you something, just to be kind," we can infer that they are developing a sense of responsibility and agency for their own Jewish community. Because many of the portraits incorporate samples of actual discourse between teachers and students and among the students, readers can form their own judgments about whether these data provide compelling evidence that powerful learning is taking place.

What Makes the Learning Jewish?

What makes these portraits of *Jewish* learning? The question has two meanings. We can direct our attention to the character of the learning opportunities and try to discern if there is something inherently Jewish about the learning activities themselves. We can also consider how learners are influenced or changed by their learning and ask whether there is anything distinctively Jewish about those learning outcomes or effects.

In thinking about the Jewish character of the learning opportunities, the educational commonplaces are a good place to start. This includes the purposes, needs, and interests of the learners, the goals and subject matter of the curriculum, the purposes and pedagogy of the teachers, and the mission and aims of the institutions and communities in which the learning is situated. How do these aspects individually and in combination contribute to the Jewish character of the learning opportunity? But perhaps the ultimate criterion for what makes these portraits of Jewish learning stems from the personal meanings that learners construct and the ways in which their understanding of Judaism, their relationship to the Jewish experience, and the sense of who they are as Jews are affected.

All portraits but one are set in a Jewish educating environment. In these day schools and synagogues, institutional missions orient the educational programs around goals related to Jewish literacy and values, knowledge of and attachment to Israel, and a sense of Jewish belonging and citizenship. There is nothing inherently Jewish about learning

Hebrew Through Movement or using games to enliven the learning of middle school students. What gives JQuest and "All In!" their Jewish character are the goals of the programs, the content of the learning, and the mission of the sponsoring institutions. What makes the learning outcomes "Jewish" is the sense of Jewish meaning, mastery, and connection which students develop.

Three chapters portray learners engaged in "studying sacred texts," a quintessentially Jewish learning activity. This set of portraits offers a developmental perspective on the close reading and interpretation of classical Jewish texts in the company of others. The sophistication of the learners varies by age and background, and the form of the study reflects normative practices in each context. Still, in all three portraits, we see students engage in an empowering form of text study; over time they develop a sense of mastery, ownership, and accountability to the texts and their peers.

In the second-grade day school classroom that Hassenfeld studied, Kobi, the teacher, gives the seven-year-olds a wide berth to probe the biblical narratives on their own terms. Students follow their own interpretative interests, asking questions that speak to them and offering interpretations they find compelling. The teacher wants the students to "play in the text," and along the way he helps them learn to notice patterns, ambiguities, symbols, and perspectives.

In a Beit Midrash designed for seventh-graders in a congregational school, Kent and Cook teach students how to learn in partnership by helping them develop a particular set of attitudes and skills. As they parse the Jacob and Esau narratives, the students practice "attentive silence" and try out specific talk moves such as "Tell me more about what you mean," "What's your evidence?" and "I don't think you understand me. Let me explain." The result is an increased ability to listen to themselves, their peers, and the text, and to co-construct rich interpretations based in evidence.

Finally, we get to Rafael Cashman's portrait of twelfth-graders in an all-female Orthodox school who are studying a Talmudic text about egalitarian issues in marriage. Reading excerpts of the discussion, we see how the students' broad Torah education allows them to use biblical and rabbinic narratives to generate autonomous moral positions. For Cashman, this ability to "think with the text" signals the learners' developing capacity to synthesize the values of modernity with traditional Judaism.

It struck me that Cashman's characterization of the young women as "contributors and participants in our learning tradition" could also apply to the second- and seventh-grade students described by Hassenfeld and by Kent and Cook. In their portraits, students are participating in and contributing to a distinctively Jewish way of studying Torah. It seems plausible that these learning opportunities not only develop students' interpretive skills and positive stance toward such text study, but also foster a sense of membership in a broader interpretive community.

Other portraits feature text study as part of a larger set of learning activities. Jewish texts supply the "big ideas" in the mystery containers that make up Nachama Skolnik Moskowitz's "All In!" curriculum and some of the clues. Jewish text study adds a Jewish learning dimension to Carlson's intergenerational professional learning community. The inclusion of text study in these programs reflects the educators' appreciation for the centrality of text study as a Jewish learning activity.

Jon Levisohn's portrait of two emerging adults in his Brandeis University course, "Studying Sacred Texts," is an interesting counterpoint. This is an academic course taught in a secular university, albeit one with close ties to the Jewish community. It does not deal exclusively with Jewish sacred texts, but includes the sacred texts of Christianity and Islam. Here again, what makes this a portrait of *Jewish* learning is neither the curriculum, nor the setting, nor the religious background of the students who all happened to be Jewish that semester. Rather it is the personal Jewish meanings which Ellie and Ruth derive from their learning.

As Ellie writes in her final paper, the course "helped me work through my personal theological questions." Ruth notes "this is the first time where I took ownership of my religious identity and my faith in however I choose to define it." For both young women, the course fostered new understandings and directions in their religious or spiritual development. Coming at the right time and place, it was an ideal setting to work on what kind of Jewish person these emerging adults wanted to become.

Matt Reingold's course on the Arab-Israeli conflict also provides an opportunity for personal meaning-making provoked by exposure to new and disturbing historical information. In contrast to Levisohn's course, however, the goals of the teacher and mission of the school reflect an explicit Jewish learning agenda: to present Israel in a morally complex way while instilling a love of Israel and a strong sense of Jewish and Zionist pride. Reingold identifies four ways that students negotiated their ongoing relationship with Israel in light of their learning about Tochnit Dalet and Deir Yassin. A year-end survey revealed that students' positive feelings for Israel still held firm. As Reingold puts it, most saw that "they could love Israel if they learned everything there is to know about it."

Perhaps the most organic Jewish learning environment is represented in Mayim Tamid, the after-school program that offers a home-like atmosphere where Judaism is woven into everyday life. As Battis and Happel explain, "The idea is to make Jewish rhythms, awareness of Israel and use of Hebrew part of the daily fabric of the children's experience." Israel and Hebrew are taught one-on-one or around the snack table in what might seem like incidental conversations. There are no explicit lessons about Jewish holidays. Rather, children learn what they need to know through holiday-related cooking and art projects. The same goes for learning to care for others and contribute to the larger community. It happens by doing for others in age-appropriate, student-initiated ways. In this "education for citizenship in Jewish life now," the means and ends converge in the present moment.

The Indispensable Role of the Jewish Educator

Until now I have examined learning in the portraits from the perspectives of process and outcome and in relation to the Jewish character of both. But none of the Jewish learning would have occurred without the contributions of the educators. In my view, one of the most important "lessons" we can glean from these portraits of Jewish learning relates to the indispensable role of the Jewish educator.

Many people assume that in progressive or learner-centered education, students' needs, interests, and activities take center stage and the educator plays a peripheral or supporting role. A popular expression of this idea casts the teacher as "a guide on the side rather than a sage on the stage." While this saying contains a kernel of truth, it communicates a misleading picture of the progressive educator's role. The portraits of learning help us understand that content-rich, learner-centered Jewish education requires more than a "concierge" who provides a menu of options. It requires knowledgeable and skillful educators who know how to create learning environments that support and challenge, build meaningful bridges between students and Jewish "stuff," and intervene in ways that promote desirable learning.

In laying out his theory of experiential learning, Dewey highlights two aspects of the educator's role. First, the educator is responsible for creating the physical and social conditions that are conducive to worthwhile learning. Second, the educator is responsible for seeing that each learner is growing in productive ways. This means paying attention to what is happening with individual learners and intervening in ways that promote their continued growth. Dewey expresses some of this in the following passages (emphasis added):

> A primary responsibility of educators is that they not only be aware of the general principle of the shaping of actual experience by environing conditions, but that they also *recognize in the concrete what surroundings are conducive to having experiences that lead to growth*. Above all, they should know how to utilize the surroundings, physical and social, that exist so as to extract from them all that they have to contribute to building up experiences that are worthwhile.[11]

> It is then the business of the educator to see in what direction an experience is heading . . . to be on the alert *to see what attitudes and habitual tendencies are being created . . . to judge what attitudes are actually conducive to continued growth and what are detrimental*. He must, in addition, have that *sympathetic understanding of individuals as individuals which gives him an idea of what is actually going on in the minds of those who are learning*.[12]

Some of the portraits help us see in the concrete how accomplished educators promote worthwhile learning in large and small ways, both directly and indirectly. They do this by creating a safe and stimulating learning environment, planning and implementing an engaging curriculum, forming genuine relationships with students, and enacting a pedagogy that respects students' thinking and promotes their learning. Different portraits highlight different ways that educators make (Jewish) learning possible. Even in the most non-directive, student-centered environments, we see the indispensable role of the educator at work.

The portrait of Mayim Tamid shows how Jewish educators influence learning by arranging the physical and social conditions for learning and by teaching indirectly. The authors explain how the classroom has been furnished like a living room with couches, books, a play area, and slippers, and how the children form sibling-like relationships with one

11. Dewey, *Experience and Education*, 40.

12. Dewey, *Experience and Education*, 38–39.

another. They also show us how teacher Liron directs learning indirectly by the way she handles the "kerfuffle in the block corner," weaves Hebrew into a cooking activity, and seizes students' interest in an optional "Shanah Tovah" activity to create a year-long project aimed at "giving back to the community."

I noticed another example of consequential, indirect teaching leading to valuable life lessons in the way Stefani Carlson, religious school director and portrait writer, handled the "adolescent rebellion" of three teenage *madrichim*. We read how she used this "teachable moment" to convey some lessons about classroom management, *kavod* (respect) to teachers, and speaking truth to power. Through several highly productive conversations, Carlson helped the teen volunteers gain a deeper understanding of the perspectives of others—their teacher, their mentor, their students—and the implications for future actions.

We might have expected to see indirect teaching in the exploratory, game-like "All In!" curriculum where, as Nachama Skolnik Moskowitz puts it, "all the learning is in the containers." In her portrait, Moskowitz shows how hard she, the teacher, and the *madrich* have to work to help a small group of sixth-graders decipher the coded messages and figure out the overarching theme of their mystery box, "Don't separate yourself from the community." Assisting in and observing the group's inquiry leads Moskowitz to the Deweyan insight that deep learning on the part of each student depends on "a concerted effort by teachers to probe and shape student thinking as it develops." In the end, she concludes that

> the open-ended, exploratory features of "All In!" genuinely engaged and empowered these learners, but when asked to apply their thinking to 'big ideas,' they still needed considerable guidance and support from their teachers.

While the teachers of the "All In!" curriculum directly lead students to particular Jewish ideas, Kobi, the teacher in Hassenfeld's portrait of second-graders studying Torah, takes a different approach. Kobi believes that his young students are capable of text study, and he encourages students to "dive into text study and probe the text on their own terms." He does not worry that they will walk away with the wrong ideas. Rather he trusts that, through discussion and debate, students will help each other move toward new understandings.

The other part of Kobi's agenda involves building students' interpretive skills. He does this not by teaching skills ahead of time, but by

introducing them "at the right moment" in response to students' interest
in some textual matter. Hassenfeld shows us Kobi's "pedagogical brilliance" at work in several extended examples of student-teacher dialogue
drawn from two years of observing his teaching and his students' learning.

I see a further example of masterful pedagogy in the partnership
curriculum which Kent and Cook design and enact in their Seventh
Grade Beit Midrash project. While the portrait mainly focuses on the
interactions and learning of Jim and Nate, what contributes to the learning is "a systematic and explicit curriculum" designed to develop a set
of partnership attitudes and skills and operationalized through specific
"Torah study speech prompts" and regular reflection on the process of
learning in relationship. This is not your typical *havruta* learning experience in which learners are invited to find a partner, read and discuss the
text, and then regroup to share ideas and hear what the teacher thinks
about the text.

I was particularly taken with a self-assessment exercise that took
place midway through the Beit Midrash project. The instructors drew a
continuum on the floor with one end representing "needs work," the other end representing "doing well," and the middle position representing
"working on it." Students placed themselves along the continuum in relation to particular skills such as "asking for clarification when you don't
understand" and "supporting your partner's understanding by finding
additional evidence in the text." Students shared why they took particular
positions and, in the end, each student identified one skill to work on.

In an interview conducted three weeks after the Beit Midrash ended,
Nate acknowledged that his biggest learning was seeing himself as someone who has trouble listening to his partner and then becoming a better
listener. He attributed his "turnaround" to this reflective exercise which
helped him realize that "I was most of the time in the not good at all area
and it came to me like I need to turn this around and get on the other
side." In the same interview Nate also explained that he was also doing
a better job of listening in other relationships outside class, compelling
testimony to the educative effects of this Jewish learning opportunity.

A final example of the indispensable role of the educator comes
from a description of a fifth-grade Hebrew specialist teaching a Hebrew
Through Movement lesson. Greninger describes how the warm and
cheerful sixty-year-old teacher issues a series of rapid commands, some
clearly intended to surprise and amuse the students, and how the students respond by running around the room, touching various places on a

map of Israel, dancing over to a table, putting a piece of matzah on their head, and singing the blessings over the wine. Seeing how skillfully the teacher encourages playfulness without losing control, we understand why the students report that learning Hebrew is fun.

Concluding Thoughts

All too often Jewish education is justified on the grounds that it prepares people for some future Jewish experience. We teach Hebrew and prayers as preparation for b'nai mitzvah. We teach Jewish values as preparation for future Jewish living. We teach Israel history or biblical criticism so that when high school students get to college they won't be thrown by anti-Zionist arguments or encounters with source criticism. For decades, Jewish continuity has provided the main rationale for Jewish education, the whole enterprise resting on the hope that whatever is learned in the present will pay off in the future.

What feels so compelling about these portraits of Jewish learning is the intention to make Jewish learning matter *in the present*. In accomplishing this goal, as several authors point out, there is no need to choose between substance or enjoyment, skills or content, deep knowledge or personal meaning. Whether the students are young children, adolescents, or emerging adults, knowledgeable and creative Jewish educators can capture the minds and hearts of Jewish learners in ways that make Jewish learning compelling and meaningful. Surely this is our best hope for motivating continued Jewish learning and cultivating an appreciation that such learning connects one to enriching personal, social, and intellectual resources.

I have already highlighted the indispensable role of the Jewish educator in promoting worthwhile Jewish learning. This reality has implications for the preparation and ongoing development of Jewish educators. The practice of teaching, like other complex human improvement practices, must be learned and can be taught. Although many people fall into the field of Jewish education, excellent teaching does not automatically follow. Some learning to teach occurs before teachers take charge of others' learning, and the Jewish community should see that anyone who wants to become a Jewish educator has access to appropriate professional preparation. But most learning to teach happens in the doing—as teachers get to know their students and try to figure out the best ways to help them learn worthwhile Jewish "stuff." Seeing that Jewish educators learn well from their on-the-job experience requires a different strategy.

Stefani Carlson's portrait gives us a glimpse of how one Jewish educational leader has made professional learning a regular part of the work of part-time teachers by transforming administrative meetings into professional learning opportunities and implementing a mentoring program. We need other models of how to promote the ongoing professional development of Jewish educators so that Jewish learners will have access to the kind of ambitious teaching and learning portrayed in this collection.

Finally, I want to comment on the study of Jewish learning as a strategy for improving the quality of Jewish education. Parents and teachers, funders and researchers all have a vested interest in understanding more about the experiences of Jewish learners and the outcomes of Jewish learning. Promoting such a coordinated research agenda would yield multiple benefits for all those concerned about the character, quality, and effects of Jewish learning.

The study of learners and learning raises a host of fascinating and important questions. What is actually being learned in different Jewish educational contexts? What features of those contexts contribute to that learning? How can the different outcomes of Jewish education be documented and assessed? What kinds of Jewish learning opportunities do different stakeholders seek? How do Jewish learners think and feel about their learning experiences?

Questions like these can be explored in large- and small-scale studies by practitioners and academic researchers using a variety of research methods. They cut across Jewish educational programs and settings and apply to learners of all ages. Directing resources toward such a research agenda would greatly benefit the field of Jewish education by framing and grounding a much-needed conversation about the insides of Jewish education and its effects on learners and learning. The portraits are a strong start on this agenda but they mainly focus on learning in day schools and religious schools. We also need portraits of Jewish learning in the range of settings where it occurs (e.g., early childhood programs, camps, travel programs, text study groups, leadership development initiatives, introduction to Judaism classes, online learning platforms, spirituality retreats, etc.)

Besides providing a taste of what can be learned from close-in descriptive studies of Jewish learning, the portraits suggest who can contribute to that agenda. Seven of the nine portraits were written by practitioners studying their own programs or classrooms which may reflect growing interest in and acceptance of practitioner research in Jewish education. Certainly, practicing Jewish educators are well-positioned to investigate questions about what and how their students are learning. Encouraging and supporting such inquiries by thoughtful practitioner-researchers across the many contexts of Jewish education could yield a unique body of research that illuminates Jewish learning from the inside.

This does not replace the need for studies by well-trained academic researchers. Imagine the multiple benefits of having systematic descriptions of Jewish learning opportunities across a range of settings linked to systematic assessments of participants' learning. Such research would not only reveal whether particular programs are succeeding in fostering desirable Jewish learning but also what features or aspects of the programs or settings contribute to the learning outcomes. It could also yield useful and reliable instruments and strategies for assessing meaningful Jewish learning, something we lack in Jewish education.

Developing support for such research will require a broad conversation on the part of all those concerned about Jewish education. What should be learned? What is being learned? How do we know? What makes the learning possible? Reflective Jewish educators ask themselves such questions about their local practice on a regular basis. Some talented researchers are pursuing such questions in small-scale studies of Jewish learning. Both groups would benefit from opportunities to learn from and collaborate with one another.

But we also need to include others in the conversation if we want to focus communal attention on what it means and what it takes to support meaningful Jewish learning in a range of settings serving diverse learners. Here I'm thinking about education committees in synagogues, boards of Jewish day schools, policy makers at federations and bureaus, and national providers of professional development. Perhaps the portraits of Jewish learning could be used in such contexts to expand thinking about new possibilities and pique curiosity to know more about the experiences of Jewish learners and the outcomes of Jewish learning.

Bibliography

Ball, Deborah. "Just Dreams and Imperatives: The Power of Teaching in the Struggle for Public Education." Presidential Address. 2018 American Educational Research Association Annual Meeting: New York, April 15, 2018. https://www.youtube.com/watch?v=JGzQ7O_SIYY

Cohen, David K., et al. "Resources, Instruction and Research." *Educational Evaluation and Policy Analysis* 25 (2003) 119–42.

Dewey, John. *Experience and Education.* New York: Touchstone, 1997.

Hawkins, David. "I, Thou, and It." In *The Informed Vision: Essays on Learning and Human Nature*, 48–62. New York: Agathon, 2002.

Lave, Jean, and Etienne Wenger. *Situated Learning: Legitimate Peripheral Participation.* Cambridge, UK: Cambridge University Press, 1991.

Rogoff, Barbara. *Apprenticeship in Thinking.* New York: Oxford University Press, 1990.

Ryle, Gilbert. *The Concept of Mind.* Chicago: University of Chicago Press, 1949.

Vygotsky, L. S. *Mind in Society: The Development of Higher Psychological Processes.* Cambridge, MA: Harvard University Press, 1978.

GLOSSARY[1]

bar/bat mitzvah (pl: *b'nai/b'not mitzvah*)	coming of age, when a Jewish boy/girl becomes responsible for taking on Jewish obligatory responsibilities, usually marked by the child leading the synagogue service and reading from and offering blessings over the Torah scroll
beit midrash	house of study, used to indicate a setting in which people come together to study Jewish text
chesed	acts of lovingkindness
halakha (noun); *halakhic* (adj.)	traditional Jewish law, behaviors associated with it, and texts codifying it
havruta (pl.: *havrutot*)	learning partner(s)
kibud	snack
kiddush	blessing over wine
madrich/madricha (pl: *madrichim/madrichot*)	teaching assistant
midrash (lower case)	a rabbinic story
mishnah (lower case)	a short passage from the Mishnah, a classic rabbinic text that is also quoted in the Talmud
mitzvah (pl:mitzvot)	an obligatory responsibility; or, colloquially, any good deed
Sh'ma	passages from Deuteronomy that are the centerpiece of Jewish morning and evening prayer services
siddur	Jewish prayer book
Tanakh	the Hebrew Bible
tefillah	Jewish prayer, or prayer services
V'ahavta	a phrase used to refer to the bulk of the Sh'ma prayer

1. Many of the transliterations used here and throughout the book were used by the authors in their chapters and have not been modified to follow a consistent transliteration system of the original Hebrew.

Made in United States
North Haven, CT
07 June 2023

37466464R00143